Do the Crime, Do the Time

Do the Crime, Do the Time

Juvenile Criminals and Adult Justice in the American Court System

G. Larry Mays and Rick Ruddell

 PRAEGER

AN IMPRINT OF ABC-CLIO, LLC
Santa Barbara, California • Denver, Colorado • Oxford, England

Library of Congress Cataloging-in-Publication Data

Mays, G. Larry.
  Do the crime, do the time : juvenile criminals and adult justice in the American court system / G. Larry Mays and Rick Ruddell.
    p. cm.
  Includes bibliographical references and index.
    ISBN 978–0–313–39242–9 (hardback) — ISBN 978–0–313–39243–6 (ebook)
1. Juvenile justice, Administration of—United States. 2. Juvenile delinquents—Legal status, laws, etc.—United States. 3. Justice, Administration of—United States. I. Ruddell, Rick, 1961– II. Title.
KF9794.M395   2012
364.360973—dc23   2011045318

ISBN: 978–0–313–39242–9
EISBN: 978–0–313–39243–6

16 15 14 13 12   2 3 4 5

This book is also available on the World Wide Web as an eBook.
Visit www.abc-clio.com for details.

Praeger
An Imprint of ABC-CLIO, LLC

ABC-CLIO, LLC
130 Cremona Drive, P.O. Box 1911
Santa Barbara, California 93116-1911

This book is printed on acid-free paper ∞

Manufactured in the United States of America

Contents

Acknowledgments

Transferring Juveniles to Criminal Courts (Champion and Mays 1991) was the inspiration for this book. Dean John Champion, the original lead author and professor of criminal justice at Texas A&M International University, passed away on February 23, 2009. Much had changed in terms of transfers to adult court since *Transferring Juveniles to Criminal Courts* was originally published, and little of the original content remains. But Dr. Champion's commitment to just and fair outcomes for juveniles motivated us through this project.

Both authors thank Valentina Tursini and Robin Tutt for their advice, support, and patience in the development of this book, and for the copyeditors and others at ABC-CLIO, including Subaramya Nambiaruran whose editorial expertise strengthened our work. In addition, we would like to thank Martin Guevara Urbina for making comments on an early draft of this book, and for his insights and suggestions.

Larry Mays would like to express a debt of gratitude to his patient wife of many years, Brenda, for her continuing support. His long-time "partner in crime," Tom Winfree, has also been a source of encouragement on this and many other projects. Finally, he also would like to reinforce the contribution to the original work, and thus the foundation for this book, of the late Dean Champion.

Rick Ruddell offers special thanks to Renu James for her patience with him in the final months of writing this book, as well as to Alister and Lucie Sutherland for their ongoing support and encouragement. In addition, Rick owes a large debt of gratitude to all of his associates with the

Correctional Service of Canada and would like to specifically thank Brian Grant for his support, mentoring and friendship. Rick had the pleasure of working with a team of skilled research professionals from whom he learned every day, including Marsha Axford, Philippe Bensimon, Ian Broom, Tammy Cabana, Colette Cousineau, Renée Gobeil, Terri-Lynne Scott, and Yvonne Stys-Rosen. In addition, he wouldn't have survived his time with the Service without the support of Andrew Harris, Andrea Moser, Martine Pilon, Lynn Stewart, Kelly Taylor, Kim Vance, and John Weekes. Last, but certainly not least, Rick Ruddell thanks Larry Mays for his encouragement and years of intellectual stimulation, and for inviting him to coauthor this book.

Introduction

On March 1, 2011, a 12-year-old boy killed his parents and critically wounded his five- and nine-year-old siblings. Reporters who interviewed friends of the family and neighbors found that this home-schooled youngster was "pleasant, helpful, a good spirit, a good kid" who actively participated in church activities (Leibowitz 2011). The family's pastor described him as "the sweetest kid," adding that, "He is very helpful; he's got a very pleasant personality" (Nicholson and Steffen 2011). One neighbor stated that "It's shocking" and that "They're good Christian people. They go to church. As far as I know, they had a happy family. You don't expect this to happen in a small town like this" (Harrison, Gathright, and Nguyen 2011). The neighbor was referring to the town of Burlington, Colorado, a 3,700-resident community where violent juvenile offending is rare.

Parricides—where children kill one or both of their parents—are atypical crimes. Heide and Petee (2007, 1389) found that between 1976 and 1999 there were 793 cases of parricide in the United States where the offender was younger than 18—or about 30 cases a year. In 2009, by contrast, the Federal Bureau of Investigation (2010, Table 38) reported that there were 942 arrests of persons younger than 18 for homicide or nonnegligent manslaughter. Juvenile homicide arrests have been declining for years, and Snyder (2000) reported that there were nearly 3,800 arrests of juveniles for murder in 1993. Thus, parricides represent a very small proportion of all murders committed by juveniles, which are also rare crimes.

The involvement of youths in violent crimes and the media's focus on these exceptional events contribute to our fears of juveniles and shape our notions about how these offenders should be treated (Krisberg, Hart-ney, Wolf, and Silva 2009). There is a consensus that something should be done about these offenders but less agreement on how to hold these youths accountable or whether they could be rehabilitated and returned to society to become productive citizens. The public often expresses mixed feelings about the juvenile courts' ability to deal with serious offenders and perceives that juvenile court judges are overly lenient. As a result, about three-quarters of Americans support the transfer or waiver of violent offenders to adult courts, where more severe punishments can be meted out (see Chapter 6).

Yet public opinion polls also show that more than three-quarters of Americans support juvenile offenders' rehabilitation, even for delinquents who have committed serious and violent crimes (see Chapter 6). It is dif-ficult to get agreement on the best course of action to take with cases such as the 12-year-old Colorado youth. Twelve-year-olds are immature, and recent studies show that the parts of our brain that are responsible for higher-level decision making are not fully formed until our 20s, providing a biological explanation for adolescent misbehavior (Maroney 2011; Walsh 2011). Even responsible youngsters sometimes make terrible deci-sions, and their decision-making capability is further compromised when they are exposed to stress or are frustrated or angry. These factors were taken into account when the U.S. Supreme Court decided in the 2005 case of *Roper v. Simmons* that persons younger than 18 at the time of their offense could no longer be put to death.

Under Colorado law this youngster could have been transferred to an adult court and, if found guilty, faced a lengthy prison sentence. There is a long-standing national precedent for severe punishments for youthful offenders, including the execution of juveniles (Streib 2005). Further-more, in 2011 state prison systems held over 70 inmates who had received life without parole sentences for offenses they committed as 13- or 14-year-olds (Liptak and Petak 2011, A13). Colorado also imposes severe sanctions on juveniles: 48 Colorado state prisoners are currently serving life without parole for crimes they committed as juveniles, and two of them were under 15 years of age when the offense occurred (Liptak and Petak 2011, A13). Moreover, both the juvenile and adult incarceration rates in Colorado are above the national average, suggesting a willingness to be tough on offenders regardless of their age (see Chapter 4).

There are limits to the punishments that can be levied in juvenile courts. In most states youths have to be released from the juvenile justice system on their 21st birthday regardless of whether they have been rehabilitated or not. This suggests that in some cases transfers to the adult courts, where youngsters can serve longer sentences are desirable, especially if they are older. Colorado law, however, allows the juvenile justice system to retain jurisdiction of a case until the disposition or sentence expires, which could extend into adulthood (Szymanski 2008b). In some cases, it will take a year or two from the time the offense occurred until the fate of a youth is ultimately decided. In cases that have intensive media scrutiny and life-long consequences for the offender, few officials will make quick decisions. In the meantime, the 12-year old youth discussed at the beginning of the Introduction was held in a juvenile detention facility—typically called a juvenile hall—although Colorado law does allow juveniles to be held in adult jails (Campaign for Youth Justice 2011).

Before a sentence was imposed on September 28, 2011, a number of important decisions were made about the youth's future. Of these decision makers, the most important are the prosecutor, who can request a transfer, and the juvenile court judge, who decides whether the youngster will stay in the youth justice system or will be transferred to a criminal court. The prosecutor had expressed misgivings about the publicity surrounding this case. In a May 2011 article in the *Denver Post*, District Attorney Bob Watson stated that "Half of the community will want me shot if I give a kid anything other than a hug, the other half of a community wants me shot if I don't go as far as life" (Steffen 2011a). As prosecutors are elected officials, however, they cannot afford to be seen as soft on crime. As a result, most will request a transfer to a criminal court and let the judge decide on the most appropriate outcome. Transfers of children to adult courts are relatively rare events: juvenile court statistics showed that 43 children 12 years or younger were transferred to adult courts in the United States in 2008, and most of them (25) were nonviolent offenders (Sickmund, Sladky, and Kang, 2011)

Before deciding to transfer a youngster to a criminal court, the juvenile court judge will weigh the best interests of the youth and the public risk if he or she stays in the juvenile justice system. Because of the seriousness of the crime, reported above, psychological assessments and psychiatric evaluations of the youth are typically conducted prior to a transfer hearing (Grisso 2010). In addition, probation staff will investigate the youth's social history and the family's functioning prior to the murders. It is also possible that the detention facility staff will be asked to write reports about the youth's adjustment to confinement. Even with all this information, the judge's decision about retaining this youth in the juvenile justice system or transferring him will not be an easy one, especially given the age of this youngster when the offense occurred. Whatever decisions are made about this case will likely follow the prosecutor, defense attorney, and judge for the rest of their careers, given the media's scrutiny.

On September 28, 2011 the juvenile court judge imposed a term of seven years of incarceration in a juvenile facility for this youth—the maximum possible disposition in Colorado's juvenile court—with a 21 month probationary sentence to follow (Steffen 2011b). The District Attorney did not seek a transfer to the adult criminal court as a number of assessments showed that the youth was immature, and newspaper accounts suggest that the youth suffered from mental health problems (Steffen 2011b). This decision was controversial, and some extended family members supported the decision to keep this youngster in the juvenile justice system, while others maintained that a lengthy prison term was a more appropriate sentence.

If these Colorado homicides had been committed by a 16- or 17-year-old, there would be considerably less debate about a transfer to an adult court. Older juveniles are seen as more responsible for their actions and are punished accordingly. In fact, Heide and McCurdy (2009) reported that four juveniles were sentenced to death between 1973 and 2005 for killing their parents. Two of these individuals were executed prior to the *Roper v. Simmons* decision, while the death sentences of the other two offenders were commuted to life imprisonment. Altogether, American youths who commit serious adult crimes can receive significant adult time behind bars.

UNDERSTANDING JUVENILE TRANSFERS TO CRIMINAL COURTS

The original juvenile court was first established in 1899 to provide an alternative to youngsters appearing in criminal courts where they were in jeopardy of severe punishments. The founders and supporters of these early courts acknowledged that some youths—by virtue of the seriousness of their offenses, their sophistication, or their inability to rehabilitate themselves—would have to be transferred to adult courts. Transfers were, however, envisioned as a practice that would be rarely used (Mack 1911). Today, however, it is estimated that at least 200,000 persons under the age of 18 years appear annually in criminal courts in the United States (Council of Juvenile Correctional Administrators 2009). While approximately 8,900 youths were actually transferred in 2008, the rest of these youths make their way to adult courts by virtue of their age (e.g., in states where the age of adult criminal responsibility starts at age 16 or 17). Moreover, there are 14 states and the District of Columbia where prosecutors can directly file juvenile cases in adult courts, and 29 state legislatures have excluded certain violent crimes from juvenile court jurisdiction (Griffin 2011). As a result, a great number of youths go directly to adult courts without ever appearing in a juvenile court.

Transfers are an important option for the juvenile justice system and are necessary to deal with youths who have committed violent offenses and with those who have failed to learn from rehabilitative opportunities offered by the juvenile courts and have continued to commit delinquent acts. One question addressed by this book is whether transfers, as currently used, are a rational juvenile justice strategy. In order to answer that question we examine transfer from a national perspective by describing the trends and identifying the key issues associated with this practice. There are six major themes explored in this book; the following paragraphs provide a brief overview of these issues.

First, we explain how social, historical, and political forces have influenced the use of transfers. Like other justice policies, the use of transfers has changed considerably over the past few decades, and Redding (2010) noted that most jurisdictions have amended transfer policies to "get tough" on juvenile offenders—especially after rates of youth violence increased in the late 1980s. Understanding how the founding and historical context of an institution or organization can influence practices a century or more into the future is often overlooked (King 2009). Bernard and Kurlychek (2010) argued that we can pay a significant price in wasted or misplaced efforts when we ignore the lessons of history. Moreover, we also examine how politicians and the media have influenced our notions of juvenile crime and how we should punish or rehabilitate delinquent youths.

Second, we describe transfer statistics over time so that readers can better understand the characteristics of juveniles appearing in criminal courts, the changes that have occurred, and the practices that seem inconsistent with the effective or just operations of justice systems. Before evaluating whether our juvenile justice practices are sound, however, we analyze trends in youth crime over the past five decades. For instance, are transfers to criminal courts and juvenile crime rates related? Moreover, should the use of transfers be driven by violent or nonviolent offenses? Another key question addressed in our analyses is whether there are indicators of racial or gender bias in the use of transfers.

Third, we examine the degree to which transfers have altered the juvenile justice system's boundaries. A number of scholars have suggested that the juvenile court has reconfigured itself to adapt to changing times and circumstances (see Fagan 2008). Such changes included the removal of both serious and status offenders (youths who commit acts that are not crimes for adults, such as being truant from school) from juvenile justice systems. It is possible that these changes have enabled juvenile courts to focus on a core function of processing large numbers of "mid-range" delinquents (youths who have committed less serious violent crimes, as well as property, drug, and public order offenders).[1] Titus (2005) has argued that the juvenile justice system has used transfers in a symbolic manner by sacrificing some youths in order to maintain the system's legitimacy.

The fourth key issue we consider is the due process protections extended to youths in both juvenile and criminal courts.[2] There are both positive and negative implications for youths adjudicated delinquent in juvenile courts contrasted with those who plea or are found guilty in criminal courts. Our practices of "getting tough" on offenders often extend past the expiration of a probationer's or prisoner's sentence. Over the past two decades, a growing number of laws have been passed to make some offenders ineligible for jobs or government benefits. Furthermore, in the past, juveniles' criminal records were sealed when their disposition or sentence was completed. Today, however, these records can be "unsealed" in most jurisdictions, creating a permanent record of a youth's offenses (Szymanski 2010c). As a result, there are now significant long-term consequences to being adjudicated delinquent (Mauer and Chesney-Lind 2003; Wood 2009).

Fifth, we also examine how several key decisions of the U.S. Supreme Court have influenced the juvenile justice system's operations. Many scholars argue that the promises of the legal reforms of the 1960s and 1970s have not been fulfilled (Feld and Schaefer 2010; Kaye 2011). Recent landmark cases, such as *Roper v. Simmons* and *Graham v. Florida*, by contrast, have defined the upper limits to punishing juvenile offenders. *Graham v. Florida* may also establish a legal argument for extending rehabilitative opportunities for juveniles as well as challenging existing transfer legislation (Arya 2010). Current research shows that rehabilitat-ing juvenile offenders is possible and cost effective (Drake 2010). Cohen and Piquero (2009, 25) estimated, for example, that saving one high-risk 14-year-old from a life of crime would save society $2.6 to $5.3 million dollars. Those savings take the form of reduced harms to victims, criminal justice system costs, and the lost opportunities in productivity when an offender is incarcerated.

Last, we analyze the shifting power arrangements between juvenile court judges and prosecutors over the past two decades. Historically, judges held the power in the court, but Zimring (2010) questioned whether legislatures purposely eroded their influence by enacting laws that excluded certain types of offenders from the juvenile justice system altogether (e.g., older violent offenders). Moreover, we explore the issue of prosecutorial discretion and the impact of giving prosecutors in 15 jurisdictions the ability to sidestep the juvenile court by filing juvenile cases directly in adult courts (Griffin 2011).

Altogether, today's transfer policies and practices would not be recognizable to the founders of the first juvenile courts over a century ago. If transfers are used in a manner that is consistent with just and fair outcomes for youths as well as protecting society, then these policies are rational. If, by contrast, transfers are inappropriately used, then we compromise the future of the youths affected by these practices and will suffer a reduction in public safety through increased recidivism.

SUMMARY

We introduced this book with a single Colorado case that illustrates the complexity of the transfer process. In 2008, the last year for which we have data, about 8,900 youths were sent to adult courts (Sickmund, Sladky, and Kang 2011). Transfers of juveniles to adult courts illustrate the tension in the juvenile justice system between acting in the best interests of youths and holding them fully accountable for their delinquent behavior. Both of these positions have merits, and it is often difficult to find the middle ground where the interests of the offender and state are balanced. Understanding the dynamics of transfers is complicated given that America's 51 juvenile justice systems—the 50 states and District of Columbia—have different legislation, crime control priorities, and approaches to youth rehabilitation.

After reading this book you will have a much richer understanding of transferring juveniles to adult courts. In addition, our goal is that readers will develop an appreciation for the challenges confronting juvenile justice systems, including the use of severe sanctions, the impact of race and gender, the influence of media on our perceptions of youth crime, and the relationships among politics, history, legislation, and court decisions on juvenile justice reform.

NOTES

1. Public order crimes are offenses such as driving under the influence, possession of weapons, disorderly conduct, or prostitution.

2. Due process refers to the legal principle that the government must respect the legal rights of citizens.

ONE

Adult Time for Adult Crimes

INTRODUCTION

One of the greatest challenges facing juvenile justice practitioners and policymakers is to develop just and fair responses for youths who have been involved in serious and violent offenses such as homicide or older recalcitrant youths who may not have benefited from the prior rehabilitative efforts of the juvenile court. One option is to transfer these so-called hard cases from juvenile courts to adult criminal courts in order to hold them more accountable for their offenses, remove the more sophisticated offenders from the juvenile justice system, and ensure that they receive rehabilitative services that are more in keeping with their ages or unmet needs.

Juvenile court judges have always had the option of transferring youths to the criminal courts, yet a significant challenge confronting juvenile justice is that we have very little idea about how many youngsters are actually transferred; their demographic characteristics such as age, race, or gender; the types of sentences that they receive in adult courts; their access to treatment or rehabilitative interventions; or whether these transfers or waivers (terms that are used interchangeably throughout this book) have been effective at reducing their likelihood of recidivism. As a result, we cannot really determine whether transferring these youths to criminal courts is sound policy that results in better public safety or responds to the unmet needs of these juveniles and saves them from a life of crime.

We do know, for instance, that the number of youths transferred to adult courts increased along with a juvenile crime wave that occurred in the late 1980s and early 1990s. This resulted in high rates of juvenile arrests for violent crimes (Redding 2010). Yet that factor alone does not explain why the most serious offense for over one-half of the youngsters transferred to adult courts in 2008 was not a violent act (Adams and Addie 2010). In addition, many youths bypass the transfer process altogether as prosecutors in some jurisdictions can directly file the case in a criminal court. Unfortunately, there is very little national-level information on how many of these youngsters actually appear in adult courts each year.

The consequences for some youths waived to criminal courts can be devastating. Prior to the U.S. Supreme Court's *Roper v. Simmons* decision in 2005, juvenile murderers 16 years of age and older were in jeopardy of the death penalty. After that decision it is unconstitutional to execute any offender who was less than 18 years of age when the offense occurred. Yet executions of persons who committed crimes as juveniles occurred with some regularity throughout American history, and Streib (2005) has documented that at least 366 youths were put to death for committing crimes as juveniles between the years 1642 and 2005.

While the death penalty is no longer an option for punishing those who were legally defined as juveniles at the time of their offenses, transfer to a criminal court can result in their sentence to life imprisonment without the possibility of parole (LWOP, which is also called juvenile life without parole, or JLWOP). The Equal Justice Initiative (2007, 20) reported that 73 U.S. prisoners were serving terms of LWOP and all of them were 13 or 14 years of age at the time of their offenses. As a result, unless legislation changes or they are pardoned, all of these individuals will die in prison. Such sentencing is troubling to many scholars, youth advocates, and policymakers as they argue that 13- and 14-year-olds are immature, impulsive, and easily succumb to peer pressure compared to adults. Therefore, there is some question as to whether these youngsters should be held as accountable as adults.

Older youths have also received life sentences. Human Rights Watch (HRW) (2008) has produced one of the most comprehensive and well-regarded studies of this issue, and they estimate that 2,484 Americans had been sentenced to terms of life without the possibility of parole for crimes that they had committed prior to their 18th birthdays. According to HRW (2008, 2), "Youth serving JLWOP across the country are predominately male (only 2.6% are female), and the majority are black (60%). Sixteen percent were 15 or younger when they committed their crimes." HRW points out that a sentence of LWOP sends a message that certain youths are not salvageable; otherwise they would have received sentences that acknowledged the possibility that they could have made some form of rehabilitative change.[1]

Human Rights Watch also reports some of the offense-related characteristics of these juveniles serving sentences of life without the possibility of parole, and their findings add to the debate about the appropriateness of these types of sanctions. First, HRW (2008, 4) found that an estimated 59 percent of these prisoners were first-time offenders who had never been adjudicated in a juvenile court or sentenced in an adult court. Second, approximately one-quarter (26%) of these offenders were convicted of felony murder, meaning that they were committing another crime when a homicide occurred but that a codefendant committed the homicide. HRW reports that in some cases the individuals who committed the actual murder received a *less severe* sentence than the juveniles who accompanied them. Last, HRW (2008, 5) found that in many of these offenses an adult was involved. While they do not report any national-level statistics, they do state that in 70 percent of the California cases adults were involved and that they often received a less severe sentence than the juvenile. Altogether, such findings make us question whether the outcomes for these juveniles were just and fair.

The question of whether JLWOP sentences are appropriate remains controversial, and even the 2010 Supreme Court decision of *Graham v. Florida* illustrates our ambivalence about serious sanctions for juveniles. In this case, the Court held that juveniles could not be in jeopardy of terms of imprisonment of life without parole unless they had been convicted of a homicide. Some of the rationale for the Court's decisions in *Roper* and *Graham* relates to contributions from current research on neurology, which finds that adolescent brains are not the same as those of adults and there is a biological basis for their immaturity (Walsh 2011).

We have always recognized that children and youths are different than adults due to their immaturity, lack of sophistication, and poor decision-making skills. Historically, acknowledgement of these differences resulted in less severe or mitigated consequences based on age, with youngsters less than seven years of age not held criminally responsible. Older adolescents were held less accountable than their adult counterparts, and their dispositions or sentences were mitigated accordingly. This recognition led to the development of a separate juvenile court that was presented as being better situated to help these youths by providing them with more rehabilitative opportunities and acting in the best interests of the child.

Neurological research shows that there is a biological basis to this immaturity and that brain development in the frontal lobes does not finish until individuals have passed their teenage years. According to the American Bar Association (2004, 2) "The evidence now is strong that the brain does not cease to mature until the early 20s in those relevant parts that govern impulsivity, judgment, planning for the future, foresight of consequences, and other characteristics that make people morally culpable." Along with this biological model that holds youths less culpable for their crimes, juveniles have traditionally been seen as more amenable to rehabilitation than their adult counterparts. Maroney (2011, 782) noted that "after *Graham* the diminished culpability/enhanced potential theory of juvenile justice appears to have become not just the near-consensus academic view but the operative jurisprudential one." Only time will tell, however, whether juvenile court judges will limit transfers for youths given the biological basis for their diminished responsibility and immaturity.

In addition to terms of life without parole, thousands of persons under the age of 18 years will be admitted to adult jails and prisons in any given year. Minton (2011, 7) noted that on June 30, 2010, there were 7,560 jail inmates under the age of 18; 1,912 were held as juveniles while the remainder had been admitted as legally defined adults. These youngsters were either awaiting court appearances or serving sentences of less than one year. West (2010, 24) reports that there were 2,778 persons less than 18 years of age in state prisons on June 30, 2009 (2,644 males and 134 females). Of this total, almost one-half (46%) were in Southern penitentiaries, and Florida held 393 of them. This was the highest number for any state. Any state prisoner will be serving a sentence of more than one year, but we do not know the offense or sentence-related characteristics for this population. Prior research conducted by the Bureau of Justice Statistics, however, showed that an overwhelming majority of these juveniles (69%) had been convicted of a violent offense (Strom 2000, 3).

So far, we have focused upon the upper limits of punishing juveniles in criminal courts. There is a body of research, however, that suggests that some juveniles who have been transferred to adult courts serve very light sentences, and property offenders are likely to receive less severe sentences than they would have received in juvenile courts (Feld 1998). This outcome may be due to the fact that they are appearing in a criminal court for the first time and they are treated the same as any other first-time adult offender. Violent offenders, by contrast, tend to receive more severe sanctions. In a study of Maryland offenders, Kurlychek and Johnson (2010) report that juveniles received a harsher sentence than adults, even controlling for offense seriousness and prior criminal history. In the chapters that follow we will take a closer look at the research on the consequences of being transferred to adult criminal courts and offer some potential reasons for these outcomes.

It is possible that the transfer of youths to criminal courts represents our ambivalence toward both adolescents and juvenile crime. Donna Bishop (2006, 656) examined studies about attitudes toward juvenile crime and notes that "the public has strongly and consistently supported rehabilitation as a response to all but the most violent offenders." In terms of these violent juvenile offenders, Bishop (2006, 657) found public support for providing these youths with rehabilitative opportunities:

> It is clear that the American people would like the vast majority of young offenders to be punished for their offenses, to learn from the experience of being punished, and to receive the sorts of treatment that will help them to move through the troubles of adolescence to become productive and law abiding adults.

Such seemingly contradictory feelings point to the public's ambivalence toward juvenile offenders.

Most of our knowledge about juvenile crime comes from the news and entertainment media, and we tend to mix together images of youths and violent crimes, such as homicide, that occur infrequently. Barry Feld (2003b) also draws our attention to the issue of race, juvenile justice, and the media. He suggests that the media has contributed to racial fear and may also have led to our antipathy toward black youths, especially those who receive very severe sanctions in adult courts. These perceptions of the public about juveniles are examined more closely in Chapter 6.

One issue that is of increasing significance to juvenile justice systems is disproportionate minority contact (DMC). DMC refers to the fact that youths of color represent less than one-third of the national population but are overrepresented in all aspects of juvenile justice. While the problem of DMC has long been recognized, there has been comparatively little improvement in the overrepresentation of minority youths in justice systems. Black youths, for example, represented about 16.5 percent of the national population of persons aged 10 to 17 years in 2008 (Puzzanchera, Sladky, and Kang 2010). In the 2007 *Juvenile Residential Facility Census*, however, white youths represented 34.0 percent of the national inmate population, while black youths accounted for 40.8 percent, and Hispanics comprised 20.8 percent (Sickmund, et al. 2011b). Some scholars point out that such overrepresentation may result from justice system failures, such as discriminatory treatment (Kempf-Leonard 2007). Others, by contrast, point to the contextual and organizational factors from which decisions about youth placements are made (Bishop, Leiber, and Johnson

2010). Of key interest in this book are the demographic characteristics of the youngsters being transferred, such as their age, race, and gender. This issue is addressed more comprehensively in the chapters that follow.

There has always been a tension in juvenile justice systems between acting in the best interests of juveniles (such as their rehabilitation) contrasted against punishing them (also called holding youths accountable or acting in the interests of public safety). Over the past three decades, most states have increased the severity of sanctions for youths who have committed delinquent acts (Redding 2010). In New York State, for example, these changes were a result of a single youth who had committed a series of violent offenses (Singer 1996). In other jurisdictions, severe legal consequences for violent offenders were legislated as a response to increased violence, often related to the interconnection of drugs, gangs, and guns—especially in inner-city neighborhoods. Frequently the persons involved in these violent incidents were youths of color, and Feld (2003b, 778) observes that "media coverage . . . disproportionately put a black face on young criminals and reinforced the white public's fear and racial animus." These offenses also contributed to an increased fear of crime, and the public supported get-tough sanctions for juveniles.

While the public favored stricter punishments, rates of serious youth violence have decreased over the past 15 years. Knoll and Sickmund (2010, 2) report that the most serious offense for 1,400 juveniles processed by juvenile courts in 2007 was homicide, which was almost one-half as many as the 2,700 juveniles appearing before juvenile courts in 1993 for the same offense (Scahill 2000). In the 10-year period between 1998 and 2007, the number of juveniles appearing before juvenile courts for aggravated assault and forcible rape also decreased (Knoll and Sickmund 2010). These reductions in violence have also had an impact on the number of youths being transferred to adult courts, and the two measures (violence and transfers) follow a similar trend.

Altogether, the appearance of a juvenile in an adult criminal court is symbolic of our mixed feelings toward juveniles. On the one hand, we want to see these youngsters succeed in a crime-free life. On the other hand, the public also wants safe streets. While some scholars suggest that a youth appearing in an adult court represents a failure of the juvenile justice system, many policymakers and practitioners believe that some youths are too sophisticated to benefit from the rehabilitative efforts of the juvenile court. These youngsters require placement in a system that is better able to manage their risks. Regardless of how one feels about juveniles in adult courts, some are in jeopardy of very serious consequences. In order to develop a deeper understanding of transfers, the following section provides a summary of the prevalence of youths in adult courts and different mechanisms that have been developed to facilitate these placements.

YOUTH IN ADULT COURTS

In an influential statement, Franklin Zimring (1981) likens the transfers to adult courts to capital punishment. Not only is Zimring referring to the fact that youths can receive stricter sentences in adult courts, but he notes that like capital punishment, transfers are rarely used, inconsistently applied, and highly discretionary. Our practices of transferring juveniles are instructive about our views toward youths, their rehabilitation, and juvenile justice system priorities. There are differing perspectives about how many youths appear in adult criminal courts each year. We will present the official estimates, as reported by the Office of Juvenile Justice and Delinquency Prevention (OJJDP), a part of the U.S. Department of Justice. Sickmund, Sladky, and Kang (2011) estimate that approximately 8,900 youths were transferred or waived to adult criminal courts in 2008—the most recent year for which data were available. This number is far below the peak of 13,710 cases transferred in 1994, and this followed the trend in youth violence.

One of the challenges of fully understanding the issue of transferring youths to adult courts is that we do not have an accurate accounting of all of the individuals who are transferred. The Campaign for Youth Justice (2011, 3) reports that "an estimated 250,000 youth under 18 are prosecuted in the adult criminal justice system every year." The Council of Juvenile Correctional Administrators (2009, 1), by contrast, reports that as many as 200,000 persons under the age of 18 years appear in criminal courts annually. That total was originally reported by Amnesty International over a decade ago (1998, 12), but they did not specify how their estimate was obtained. It is plausible that the real total is much less than those estimates, and while the U.S. Department of Justice recently awarded a grant for the study of this issue, the results of that research are not expected for several years. Figure 1.1 shows the use of transfers to adult court from 1985 until the present.

There are five different methods that can result in youngsters under the age of 18 appearing before an adult or criminal court: (1) transfers (also called waivers), (2) directly filing juvenile cases into adult courts, (3) legislative (statutory) exclusion of some types of cases from juvenile courts, (4) blended sentences, and (5) states where juvenile court jurisdiction

Figure 1.1 Juvenile Transfers to Adult Court, 1985–2008

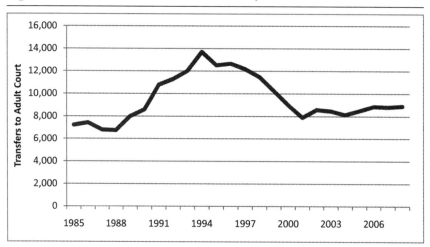

ends prior to the age of 18. Each of these transfer mechanisms is defined in the following pages, with a short explanation of the process, along with identification of who has the decision-making ability in the case.

First, as reported above, approximately 8,900 youths were transferred from juvenile to adult courts in 2008. Transfers represent the oldest mechanism for removing youths from the juvenile court. As Kupchik (2006) notes, each state sets its own guidelines for the transfer or waiver of youths to criminal courts, but the common element in all these transfers is that the juvenile court judge ultimately decides whether youngsters will remain within the juvenile court's jurisdiction. Redding (2010, 1) reports that most states enacted some form of legislative change to make it easier to transfer youths to criminal courts in the past two decades. He observes that "These reforms lowered the minimum age for transfer, increased the number of transfer-eligible offenses, or expanded prosecutorial discretion and reduced judicial discretion in transfer decision making."

Transfers that occur in juvenile courts are perhaps the most transparent method of moving youths to criminal courts. Youths have the right to a transfer hearing, and the defense can present arguments why the individual should stay within the juvenile system, while the prosecuting attorney can challenge those arguments. These rights were extended to youths in the *Kent v. United States* decision of the Supreme Court in 1966 (that case is examined in Chapter 5).

The second mechanism that enables youths to appear in criminal courts is when a prosecutor files the case directly in adult court, bypassing the juvenile court entirely. In addition to the term *direct file*, this process is also called prosecutorial discretion and concurrent jurisdiction. Whatever the name, advocacy organizations have identified a number of limitations with this approach. First, unlike a transfer hearing before a judge, there are few checks or balances on the prosecutor's discretion. Second, the prosecutor's role is inherently political, and decisions may be made on the basis of what is best for prosecutors and their offices rather than what is in the best interests of the youth's future or public safety. This is of particular importance in serious cases where youths have committed crimes that have attracted public attention. While transfer of these youngsters into criminal courts may be appropriate, the prosecutor might not be the most suitable person to make that assessment.

Some states, such as Florida, lead the way in the direct filing of youths into criminal courts, and prosecutors were first granted that ability in 1978. Subsequent legislative amendments in 2000 mandate direct filing for youths who have committed certain violent offenses or who are 16 or 17 years of age and are habitual offenders (e.g., have committed three or more felonies). The Florida Department of Juvenile Justice (2002, 5) notes that 95 percent of youngsters who appeared in criminal court did so after their cases were filed directly by prosecutors, sidestepping the juvenile court altogether. An examination of the Comprehensive Accountability Report from the Florida Department of Juvenile Justice (2010, 6) shows that 4,297 youths were transferred to adult courts in the 2009–2010 fiscal year. Fagan (2008) estimates that approximately 27,000 juveniles each year are sent to criminal courts using this method. If that estimate is correct, then approximately three times as many youth cases are filed directly in adult court than are transferred by juvenile court judges.

The third way that a youth can appear in an adult court is through statutory exclusion. This occurs when the legislature excludes certain cases from juvenile court jurisdiction and youths accused of specific offenses are automatically transferred to criminal courts. When these statutes were enacted, they typically targeted older adolescents who had committed violent offenses. Bishop (2000) notes, however, that in some jurisdictions there has been some creep in both the ages and offenses that can be excluded from the juvenile court, and she points to the example of Illinois, where the legislation was modified four times between 1982 and 1995 to include more offenses and lower the age limits for exclusion. The types of offenses that can be excluded from the juvenile court can be broad, and Fagan (2008, 89) notes that any felony in Mississippi can be excluded for youths who are 17 years of age. At present, 29 states have some form of statutory exclusion (Fagan, 2008).

While the ultimate decision maker in cases of statutory exclusion is the legislature, it is important to recognize that prosecutors make the decision on the charges that will be laid. Thus, it is possible that a prosecutor may charge a juvenile with an offense that is excluded from the juvenile court's jurisdiction and the youngster will appear directly in an adult court. As a result, this method bypasses any review by the juvenile court judge.

A fourth mechanism, used in a number of states, is the blended sentence. This approach straddles both the juvenile and criminal justice systems and is intended to provide a last chance for youths who have committed serious or violent offenses. These dispositions typically involve a juvenile sanction with a criminal sentence that is suspended if the youngsters comply with all of the conditions of their disposition. In the event that a youth does not comply, the sanctions are often very severe. According to Griffin (2011, 1), "blended sentencing generally increases the overall hazard that a juvenile offender will receive an adult criminal sentence, either immediately or eventually. In that sense, although it may be more flexible, it functions somewhat like an expanded transfer law."

In most jurisdictions, once youngsters are transferred to an adult court, they must be treated as adults for future offenses. Szymanski (2011) reports that in 34 states there is a "once-waived, always-waived" provision, although she also notes that several of these states are considering modifications to this practice. Szymanski (2010d, 1) also observes that "these provisions have been criticized because no consideration is given to mitigating factors such as age, possibility of rehabilitation, culpability, or psychological development." Yet these factors have to be balanced against the juvenile's increased sophistication—having experienced the antisocial and criminogenic influences of the adult justice system— one important question is whether they have a negative or adverse influence on the juveniles should they reoffend and be returned to the juvenile justice system.

The last method that may result in a youth appearing in a criminal court occurs in states that have an age limit of criminal court jurisdiction of less than 18 years. For example, in New York and North Carolina an individual becomes a legally defined adult at 16 and thus will appear in an adult criminal court if charged with a crime. In another 10 states an individual becomes an adult at age 17, and in the remaining 38 jurisdictions the upper age limit is 18 years of age. Given the latest neurological research, there is some debate about whether it is appropriate that 16-year-olds in New York and North Carolina should be considered adults, and in both

Figure 1.2 Arrestees Under 18 Years Referred to Adult Courts

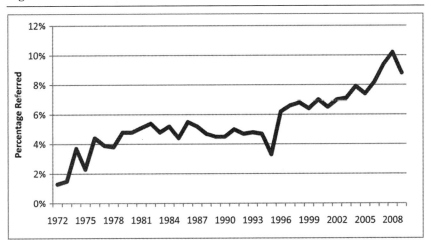

states there is a movement to legislatively raise the upper limit of juvenile court jurisdiction to 18 years (Birckhead, 2008; Citizens Crime Commission of New York City, 2010).

The fact that in 12 states persons under the age of 18 can appear in adult courts may be one reason for the estimate of 200,000 to 250,000 youths appearing in criminal courts each year. To examine that proposition, we used FBI juvenile arrest data to calculate the number of youths who are referred directly to adult courts each year. Figure 1.2 shows the increased number of juveniles who were taken into custody and referred to adult courts from 1972 to 2009. In 1972, slightly over 1 percent (1.3%) of arrestees were referred to adult courts, but that proportion had increased to 8.8 percent by 2009 (FBI 2010, Table 68). The FBI (2010, Table 38) reported that a total of 1,515,586 juveniles were arrested in 2009, and if we apply the 8.8 percent figure to that total, that accounts for 133,371 youths appearing in criminal courts for the year.[2]

The number of youngsters appearing in criminal courts can change depending on the population's demographic characteristics (e.g., a higher number of youths in the general population will typically result in a greater number of youths being taken into custody and facing subsequent court appearances) as well as the involvement of juveniles in crime. In the pages that follow we take a close look at one case to help us better understand the complexities of the juvenile justice system as well as the individual costs associated with transferring a youth to the adult justice system.

THE NATHANIEL ABRAHAM CASE[3]

In order to better understand crime and justice, most social scientists prefer to examine thousands of cases and look for patterns and trends. Yet sometimes it can be instructive to take an in-depth look at a single case as this focus will help us comprehend our attitudes toward juveniles, crime and punishment, and the hope for rehabilitation. Alternatively, a single example of a rare but heinous offense or serious offender has resulted in legislative changes, and some legal scholars refer to these circumstances as "hard cases making bad laws." Juvenile justice is not immune to these types of single crimes that have resulted in legislative changes that toughened state juvenile codes (see Singer 1996). Usually such cases are the result of a serious offense that has somehow fallen through the cracks of the justice system. This might include a youth who commits a homicide, but the punishment in the juvenile court doesn't seem to be appropriate for the seriousness of the act—and decades ago, some youths could not be transferred to adult courts if they were very young (e.g., were 14 or 15 years of age at the time of the offense).

One of the most interesting recent cases of a serious crime committed by a youth is that of Nathaniel Abraham—not only because the case contributed to a national dialogue on juvenile justice, but also because we are able to track what occurred through time and look at his long-term outcomes. Moreover, the case shows the impact of legislative change, the ability of a prosecutor to directly file a juvenile case in an adult court, as well as the judge's sentencing options, including blended sentencing. Altogether, much can be learned about juvenile justice, as well as transfer to adult courts and the debate about rehabilitating juveniles, by reviewing Nathaniel's involvement in a 1997 homicide.

The Facts

While the facts in many juvenile and criminal offenses may be disputed, the actual events in Nathaniel Abraham's case are pretty straightforward: On October 27, 1997, the 11-year-old Abraham, who stood four feet, nine inches and weighed 65 pounds, fatally shot 18-year-old Ronnie Lee Greene Jr. with a .22 caliber Remington semiautomatic rifle—from nearly 300 feet away. At the time of his death, Mr. Greene was standing in front of the Sunset Plaza Party Store in Pontiac, Michigan, with two of his friends. The three individuals heard gunshots, and one of the bullets struck Greene in the head; he died from his wound about 24 hours later.

While nobody disputes the fact that Abraham shot Greene, understanding the motives behind the offense are less clear. Nathaniel's neighbor

Michael Hudack had seen him shooting and had reported the shooting in a 911 call, but the police never responded. The day after the failed 911 call, Hudack confronted Nathaniel about the shooting, and he confiscated the gun and ammunition. At the time, Nathaniel told him that he had been shooting at the fence, the garage, and some trees.

After Hudack read of Greene's death in the newspaper, he again contacted police and gave them the rifle he had taken from Nathaniel. The police arrested the youth on October 31, 1997, in his classroom at school, where he was dressed in his Halloween costume. Nathaniel was interviewed by police, with his mother present, and they waived their *Miranda* rights.[4] When questioned, Nathaniel told the investigators that the rifle confiscated by Hudack was the one he had used to shoot at the garage and trees, but he never admitted to police that he had shot Greene.

By all accounts, Nathaniel Abraham and Ronnie Lee Greene Jr. did not know each other, which gave some credence to the youth's story that he had not intentionally shot Greene. But Nathaniel's involvement in a number of neighborhood crimes prior to the shooting suggests that he was more than a misguided youngster involved in a one-time act of carelessness. Nathaniel had been suspected in a series of property crimes and an assault, although he had only been arrested once—about five weeks prior to the shooting—for his involvement in a burglary. Moreover, it was suspected that Nathaniel committed a burglary in order to steal the rifle and ammunition used in the Greene shooting. Nathaniel's conduct seemed to be deteriorating, and his mother had referred him to community mental health, but after six months on the waiting list he still hadn't received any help.

It was also alleged that Nathaniel had direct knowledge that he had shot Greene. According to a Court TV (2000) summary of the case, he had allegedly told a girl that he "was going to shoot someone," and the day after the shooting Greene had told this girl and another youngster that "he had shot someone." These statements suggest that the shooting was intentional, or at the very least that Nathaniel Abraham was aware of his actions.

Nathaniel's Day in Court

The Nathaniel Abraham case quickly drew national attention, and the case was featured in the media. On the one hand, the juvenile court, first introduced in 1899, was intended to work with immature and impulsive youths such as Nathaniel—who at age 11 and diminutive size could hardly be considered a serious offender that the public should fear. On the other hand, he had also demonstrated an escalating pattern of delinquent behavior, and his actions cost Greene his life. The case provided equal opportunity for those who believed that he should be helped to rehabilitate himself within the protections of the juvenile court and for others who wanted him held fully accountable for his actions in order to maintain public safety and deter other youths from committing similar offenses. One of the questions that relates to the transfer of juveniles to adult courts is how we can best balance these two goals of justice.

At age 11, Nathaniel was charged as an adult with first-degree murder and two counts of illegal use of a firearm. He was charged directly as an adult as the Michigan legislature had amended the criminal code in 1996 (the law took effect in 1997) to allow youths of any age to be charged as adults. At the time, it was one of the toughest juvenile laws in the nation, and prosecutors could decide whether to file the case directly in adult court and avoid the juvenile court altogether—and that is what occurred.

Prior to his court appearances, Nathaniel was held in a juvenile detention facility. Typical of serious cases such as homicide, the actual trial date was far into the future, and Nathaniel was 13 years of age when the case finally went to trial. In fact, the trial started exactly two years after the shooting that claimed Greene's life.

Nathaniel's jury trial lasted several weeks, and during that time the prosecution and defense put forth their arguments: The prosecution took the position that the act was premeditated, Nathaniel's involvement in delinquency was escalating, and his comments to friends that he had shot Greene suggested that the act was not an accident. Yet, despite his apparent involvement in other delinquent acts and his arrest five weeks prior to the shooting, he had not been convicted of any prior offenses.

The defense, by contrast, focused on the fact that Nathaniel was an immature and impulsive youngster with a low intelligence quotient (he was assessed as having an IQ of 75, which is far below the average of 100) and was in a special education class at school—with his teachers assessing his functioning at the level of a six- to eight-year-old. Nathaniel was represented by Geoffrey Fieger, an attorney who had tried a number of high-profile criminal cases including Dr. Jack Kevorkian's (the so-called "suicide doctor") defense. The jury's deliberations lasted four days, which shows the mixed feelings that they must have experienced, but Fieger ultimately had convinced them that the first-degree murder charge was not warranted, and Nathaniel was convicted of second-degree murder on November 16, 1999.

Judge Eugene Moore's Sentencing Options

After Nathaniel's conviction for second-degree murder, Judge Eugene Moore had three sentencing options:

1. To sentence as a juvenile—this option would ensure that Nathaniel could not be kept in custody past his 21st birthday. Moreover, Nathaniel would be housed with other juvenile offenders and benefit from the additional rehabilitative opportunities that juveniles can access;

2. To sentence as an adult and be subject to adult punishments—this option would allow for a lengthy prison term; or

3. To impose a blended sentence, where he would initially be sentenced as an adult but the adult sentence would not be imposed until his 21st birthday. If Nathaniel had rehabilitated himself by his 21st birthday, he would be released; if not, the adult sentence would be carried out. The blended sentencing option also allowed for the early imposition of an adult sentence if Nathaniel committed another offense.

Placing Nathaniel in prison was the most punitive choice of the three options available to the judge. However, the most flexible was the blended sentence as it allowed the justice system to imprison him if he did not make sufficient rehabilitative progress by the time he reached his 21st birthday.

Prior to sentencing, and especially in the case of serious offenders, the judge often orders psychological or psychiatric reports be completed (Grisso 2010). Moreover, pre-disposition reports (for juvenile cases) or presentence reports (for adult cases) are also completed by the probation staff, who examine the individual's social functioning and his or her strengths and weaknesses. These reports typically present information on employment and education, family relationships, the youth's perceptions of the offense and his or her role in the act, and amenability for rehabilitation. Judge Moore ordered that these reports be completed for Nathaniel, and he had the juvenile court workers' recommendations as well as victim impact statements from the Greene family when he was sentenced on January 13, 2000. The purpose of these reports was to get the best possible assessment of the youth's individual needs and potential in order to craft an appropriate sentence.

At sentencing, Judge Moore prepared an extensive review of the three options available to the Court and the strengths and weaknesses of each approach. Moore considered the failure of the adult system to rehabilitate offenders, and he felt that option was a last resort for a juvenile unless public safety was threatened. Placement of Nathaniel in the juvenile system, by contrast, would force the authorities to fully rehabilitate him prior to his 21st birthday, when the juvenile court would lose jurisdiction of the case and he would have to be released. Moore also debated the merits of a delayed or blended sentence, where the decision to release Nathaniel would be postponed until his 21st birthday. Moore (2000, 11) observed that imposing the delayed sentence "take[s] everybody off the hook" but also felt that "the safety net of a delayed sentence removes too much of the urgency." The blended option, he wrote, was a more appropriate sentence for older juveniles, such as 15- and 16-year-olds, who have a shorter time to work toward their rehabilitation.

Given those three options, Moore sentenced Nathaniel Abraham as a juvenile, and this meant that he would be released—at the latest—on his 21st birthday. This sentence effectively forced the juvenile justice system to rehabilitate Nathaniel in eight years. In his remarks in court, Judge Moore made reference to the failures on the part of Nathaniel's caregivers and the educational and justice systems, but ultimately held Nathaniel accountable for Greene's death.

Nathaniel Abraham—Troubled Times Continue

On January 18, 2007, Nathaniel Abraham was released from juvenile confinement, and he moved into subsidized housing where he could continue attending the community college classes that he had started while incarcerated. During his eight years in training schools (the juvenile equivalent of an adult prison) he earned his general equivalency diploma and attended some college classes. These years were not trouble free, and Nathaniel had been involved in some fights. Also, some accounts suggest that he was not always respectful of authority figures and had trouble managing his anger. Despite those challenges, he was not charged with any additional offenses, and, to be fair, it would be difficult for most juveniles to live in correctional settings from age 11 to 21 without being involved in some institutional incidents given the characteristics of juvenile corrections populations (e.g., immature, violence-prone, with high numbers of gang members and risk-takers—see Ruddell and Thomas 2009).

Despite the fact that he had numerous supporters, Nathaniel's adjustment to the community was difficult. He failed to finish his degree, although he did record several rap songs that were featured on a compact disc. Less than 18 months after his release, in May 2008, he was arrested for possessing 254 Ecstasy pills. On January 5, 2009, he was sentenced to a prison term of four to twenty years on the drug offense. At sentencing, Nathaniel acknowledged that a lot of people had tried to help him, and he let them down, but that he wasn't giving up on himself—he felt that he could still be successful in life. Nathaniel's stay in prison has also been troubling, and in January 2011 he was charged with assaulting two correctional officers; each charge carries a potential two- to four-year sentence. Altogether, Nathaniel's future appears to be grim.

What We Can Learn from the Nathaniel Abraham Case?

The Abraham case illustrates contemporary juvenile justice's complexity and the delicate balance between what is in the best interest of a youth and protecting the community, especially from youngsters who have been involved in serious and violent offenses. While these decisions used to be made almost entirely by judges, the Abraham case illustrates how the Michigan legislature enacted a law that enabled prosecutors to charge a juvenile of any age for almost any crime as an adult. However, judges could still decide where a youth could be placed, but these decisions are also complex. While we have the ability to look back at the Nathaniel Abraham case and examine all of the outcomes after a dozen years, judges do not have that luxury.

Sentencing youths of 13 years of age as adults sends a powerful message about their likelihood of rehabilitation, especially given the poor rates of successful community reintegration from adult corrections (Langan and Levin 2002). Likewise, the blended option also posed numerous challenges if a youth was to be rehabilitated. As Judge Moore (2000) stated during sentencing, this might be a better option for older adolescents as the sense of urgency to create rehabilitative opportunities for youngsters might not have been present.

The Nathaniel Abraham case also instructs us about the shifting priorities of juvenile justice and how the Michigan legislature empowered prosecutors by giving them the ability to file an 11-year-old directly into adult courts, bypassing juvenile courts altogether. Having described the difficulties of weighing the different sentencing options for a single case, we now examine how the priorities of juvenile justice have shifted.

SHIFTING JUVENILE JUSTICE POLICIES

For most of the twentieth century, juvenile courts operated as rehabilitative agencies that worked toward the best interests of the youths who came before them. Starting in the 1970s, however, there was a movement to make youngsters more accountable for the offenses that they committed. Some of this shifting policy focus was a result of increased juvenile crime levels and a lack of political and public support for youths. During these years, juvenile court judges transferred large numbers of youngsters to adult courts, and more youths were placed in detention as well as long-term juvenile correctional facilities (Ruddell and Thomas 2009).

While academics and policymakers tend to focus upon the most recent policy shift, Bernard and Kurlychek (2010) observe that there have been at least three cycles of getting tough on juvenile crime followed by eras with more rehabilitative approaches over the past 200 years. Bernard and Kurlychek (2010, 4) contend that three ideas about juvenile justice drive these trends: "[1] that juvenile crime is at an exceptionally high level, [2] that present juvenile justice policies make the problem worse, and [3] that changing those policies will reduce juvenile crime." As disenchantment with the current operations of juvenile justice increases, reforms are developed in response to these perceptions. Historically, these reforms have involved a shift from rehabilitative to punitive interventions, and then the cycle is repeated.

One of Bernard and Kurlychek's (2010) main points is that we fail to learn from history's lessons, and so we keep repeating the mistakes of the past. The second key point is that shifting juvenile justice policies are predictable occurrences and are a function of a number of juvenile justice myths (e.g., that juvenile crime is at historically high levels) that are used by reformers to justify policy changes.

A key obstacle to fully understanding the nature of juvenile justice systems, and the changes within these systems, is that most analyses are based on the notion that juvenile justice systems are fully integrated and that the agencies that comprise these systems work together on a more or less common set of goals. A number of scholars, however, have argued that the juvenile justice system is not really a system but instead a patchwork of procedures, institutions, and agencies that are only loosely coordinated to deal with youthful offenders (Champion and Mays 1991). As a result, many scholars refer to the juvenile justice system as a process rather than a system, while others have used the term "nonsystem" (Bishop, Leiber, and Johnson 2010).

This patchwork of arrangements can make it difficult to deal effectively with some juveniles, especially those with special needs or those who may have committed serious offenses. For instance, the fact that community-based services exist in some jurisdictions to meet the special needs of youthful offenders does not automatically mean that these services will be utilized effectively by judges and others when adjudicating these youths. In addition, the services in youth custody facilities or community-based programs that are said to exist sometimes do not exist, or, when offered, the interventions leave something to be desired because they are not implemented in the manner that the developers of these programs intended (Ruddell and Thomas 2009). Thus, the youths referred to these programs receive services that might not meet their needs. Judges, however, might not be aware of these limitations when deciding on a sentence for a juvenile.

There are other obstacles to ensuring the appropriate treatment of juveniles in existing systems. Sometimes there is a lack of coordination and long-term planning and youths "fall through the cracks" of the system. Even something as simple as a delay in receiving counseling can have a significant impact upon a youth's rehabilitative potential. Furthermore, the challenges of coordination may be increased when there are local as well as state-operated systems within a single jurisdiction (e.g., county-operated detention and state-run juvenile correctional facilities, as in California). Last, during tough economic times, there is increasing demand for services at the same time that programs are being cut.

Recently, there has been increased interest in the factors that are associated with the diffusion of criminal and juvenile justice policies (Bergin 2010) and both how they are implemented and why some are more successful than others. Juvenile justice reforms, including the shifting policies identified by Bernard and Kurlychek (2010), have been stimulated by diverse interests (Bishop 2009). A strong rehabilitation contingent continues to see the juvenile court as mainly serving a treatment function even after almost three decades of a get-tough legal environment. Perhaps more importantly, Piquero and Steinberg (2010) found that the public is also supportive of juvenile rehabilitation and more willing to invest tax dollars in rehabilitative interventions rather than in incarceration.

An analysis of the literature pertaining to juvenile justice reforms suggests that juvenile courts should rely increasingly on a set of graduated sanctions that meet the juveniles' actual risks and needs (Cooley 2011). Some investigators, for instance, emphasize a greater use of community-based treatment, restitution, diversion, and intensive supervised probation in order to keep youths in the community (see Drake 2007, 2010 for reviews of cost-benefit analyses of juvenile intervention programs). In order to facilitate these interventions, effective partnerships need to be established between juvenile courts and community agencies. In some jurisdictions, for example, advocacy groups and other stakeholders are becoming increasingly involved in the operations of both community-based and institutional programs for juvenile offenders.

Juvenile justice systems have been in a state of almost continuous change, and there is a glaring lack of consistency when one compares the 50 state jurisdictions and the District of Columbia. Despite these differences, a key concern of all policymakers is reducing recidivism and determining the types of interventions that will work most effectively to reduce a juvenile's likelihood of reoffending (Drake 2007, 2010). In recent years, evidence-based practices (where interventions are based on what the research has demonstrated to be effective) have emerged as a strong movement within the fields of juvenile justice and corrections. In addition, organizations such as the Washington State Institute for Public Policy are emerging as strong advocates for the careful analysis of justice policies and the application of cost-benefit studies to the debate about the effectiveness of different juvenile justice interventions.

Some academics and advocates for adolescents believe that decisions to transfer youths to criminal court are often reflections of the juvenile court's unwillingness to accept alternative interventions available in communities or to consider less formal strategies. However, a significant segment of a concerned public endorses the use of transfers, especially for the most serious, chronic, and dangerous youthful offenders. One unanswered question is from where these punitive values and attitudes come. Are they are in response to rates of juvenile crime, rare but sensational incidents of youthful violence, political campaigners advocating a tough-on-crime agenda, economic downturns, or the wider social, political, and economic context? These issues are addressed more thoroughly in the chapters that follow.

SUMMARY

The rehabilitative, treatment-centered philosophy that dominated juvenile justice systems for most of the twentieth century gradually gave way to a "just deserts" philosophy. This approach is associated with harsher punishments and administering penalties for offenders according to the seriousness of their crimes, with comparatively less attention paid to the rehabilitative prospects for the youths involved. Starting in the 1970s, the get-tough movement pervaded juvenile justice systems, and an estimated 228,771 youngsters were transferred from juvenile to adult courts between 1985 and 2008 (Sickmund, Sladkey, and Kang 2011). Many more found their way into criminal courts due to legislative exclusion, prosecutors who filed their cases directly in adult courts, or by virtue of the fact that they committed crimes in states that considered them adults at 16 or 17 years of age. Prior to 2005, some of these youths were sentenced to death, and many more were placed in adult prisons, sometimes for the remainder of their lives.

Along with the get-tough movement, there has also been a massive transformation of the juvenile justice system, especially since the mid-1960s. Numerous reforms have been observed in juveniles' rights; juvenile court organization and operations, adjudication, and sentencing; and the sanctions available to judges as sentencing options, including the waiver of youths to adult courts. While we like to think that the juveniles most likely to be transferred to criminal court are serious and persistent offenders, there is ample evidence to lead us to believe that this is not always the case: less than one-half of juveniles transferred between 1985 and 2008 were violent offenders (Sickmund, Sladkey, and Kang 2011). In addition, more than one-half of youngsters sentenced to life in prison without the possibility of parole, for example, were first-time offenders (Human Rights Watch 2008, 4).

Transfers to adult court play an important role in the justice system to ensure that public safety is maintained, although there is less agreement on which juveniles should be transferred. The use of transfers to adult court from 1985 until the present, shown in Figure 1.1, has followed a similar trend as arrest rates of serious youth violence: when juvenile crime decreased after the peak in 1993 and 1994, the number of youths transferred also dropped. This suggests that the use of transfers was rational, although since we do not know the true number of youths who appeared before criminal courts, we will never be able to test these assumptions empirically at the national level.

The juvenile justice system suffers from many of the problems of the adult criminal justice system. After almost two decades of federal government support for reducing disproportionate minority contact, there are still significant challenges concerning DMC and the overrepresentation of youths of color throughout the juvenile justice system. In addition, there is growing concern that although youngsters have been granted a number of rights, including the right to be represented by an attorney, many youths still appear before juvenile courts without the benefit of counsel (Feld and Schaeffer 2010). Community-based sanctions and treatment fail to live up to expectations, which could "set youth up for failure." Moreover, juvenile detention facilities are typically overcrowded and dangerous places for some youths (Holman and Ziedenberg 2009). Also, some long-term youth correctional facilities more closely resemble adult prisons and offer few therapeutic interventions (Ruddell and Thomas 2009).

Because the juvenile justice system is fragmented and diverse among jurisdictions, various professionals have advocated greater harmony and cooperative effort between juvenile courts and community-based agencies to better serve the needs of youthful offenders. Consistent policy decisions are needed. However, before that will occur, there has to be greater consensus about the juvenile justice system's goals and whether they rest with the traditional rehabilitative ideal of the first juvenile courts or with an approach that emphasizes accountability, just deserts, or punishment.

A key objective of the chapters that follow is to inform readers of the major issues surrounding the use of transfers and how transfers fit into the juvenile court's history. Additionally, we describe the political, social, and economic contexts from which the get-tough-on-juvenile-crime movement emerged. Last, we examine the juvenile court's legal context, especially as it relates to transfer and the upper boundaries of juvenile punishment (e.g., the death penalty and sentences of life without parole), the types of juveniles who appear in juvenile courts, as well as their outcomes. Our goal in writing this book is to contribute to the debate about the transfer of youngsters to adult court and how that can help define the boundaries of juvenile justice.

NOTES

1. According to Hechinger (2011, 411 only) six states forbid LWOP for juvenile offenders (AK, CO, MT, KS, KY, and TX).

2. Considerable caution must be used with this estimate as the 8.8 percent figure provided by the FBI was based on police departments that represented about one-third of the national population. It is possible that the 12 states where the age of adult responsibility ends at 16 or 17 years were either over- or underrepresented in that total, which would have a significant influence on the estimate.

3. Information for this case summary was obtained from Court TV (2000) and Moore (2000). Current information on the Abraham case was retrieved from online news sources.

4. *Miranda* refers to the 1966 Supreme Court case of *Miranda v. Arizona* that guaranteed the right against self-incrimination.

TWO

Understanding the System

INTRODUCTION

Juvenile justice systems in the United States are composed of many different agencies and organizations that deal with young people who have violated the law, some of whom have been identified as being at risk for criminal behaviors and others who have been the victims of parental neglect or abuse. Sometimes there is coordination and cooperation among these organizations. At other times they operate as virtually independent bodies. Understanding what has taken place in one juvenile justice system is complicated by the array of judicial- and executive-branch bodies that are involved in the administration of justice, but one also has to consider that there are 51 systems in the United States and these organizations have different philosophies, histories, operational priorities, and funding arrangements.[1] These differences make it difficult to fully grasp what is occurring within juvenile justice at the national level and also makes it hard to make broad generalizations.

Before we examine current trends and issues, however, it is important to acknowledge that what has occurred in earlier periods influences the juvenile justice system's current operations. Thus, it is worthwhile to examine what has happened in the past to determine whether current events are part of larger trends and to better understand the factors that stay the same as well as things that have changed. Bernard and Kurlychek (2010) observed that juvenile justice practitioners and policymakers tend to disregard history's lessons and, because of our short-term focus, are likely to repeat the mistakes that others have made. Every time we introduce policies or practices that have previously failed, we waste resources and lose opportunities to enhance public safety—unless our new approach is fundamentally different than past efforts. But we will not know if our approaches are different unless we understand what occurred in the past and why those interventions succeeded or failed.

Consequently, we start this chapter with an examination of the origins of U.S. juvenile justice systems and focus on how and why the first juvenile court was established. Knowing the motivations behind the development of juvenile justice systems is important because the philosophical tension that existed 200 years ago—between those who wanted to help troubled youth and those who wanted them held accountable—is still present today. This tension illustrates our mixed feelings about wanting to help and to punish juvenile offenders. Public support for the transfer of youths to adult courts, for example, is based on beliefs about holding youngsters accountable, punishing wrongdoers, and maintaining public safety.

Yet there may also be political and organizational reasons why the number of transfers increased along with rates of youth violence in the 1980s and 1990s. In order to understand the need for transfers, one must first learn at what point they occur in a youth's movement through the system as well as the decision makers responsible for these actions. As a result, we explain how youngsters flow through the juvenile justice system and the decision points at which a transfer can occur. Last, we describe the juvenile court's dispositional alternatives and the limits to the court's jurisdiction.

A SHORT HISTORY OF JUVENILE JUSTICE

On July 1, 1899, the first juvenile court was established in Cook County, Illinois, for delinquent, dependent, neglected, and abused children. It had long been recognized that juveniles' needs were not being met in the adult criminal justice system, but it was difficult to establish a way for the state to intervene in the lives of children and their families that would respond to the unmet needs of the youths, acknowledge the parents' interests, as well as protect community safety. Prior to the establishment of juvenile courts, youths who had committed crimes often received treatment that was very similar to that of adults. Yet there was growing dissatisfaction with placing youngsters in adult courts and jails as these placements were seen as making a bad situation worse (Fishman 1923; Mack 1909). In addition, it was widely acknowledged that many of these youthful offenders were economically, socially, and educationally disadvantaged and that they often required support and assistance rather than punishments (Shallo 1947).

The first juvenile court emerged after growing concern and dissatisfaction in the treatment of children in criminal courts. During that time policymakers, politicians, and justice system stakeholders grappled with some of the same issues that we confront today, especially in regards to determining the proper sanctions for juveniles who had committed serious offenses or were persistent offenders. Prior to the introduction of the juvenile court, delinquent youths were treated much the same as adult offenders, with harsh punishments and little formal acknowledgement that sanctions should be mitigated because of their immaturity or dependency. All youths involved in delinquency appeared in criminal courts, and while that concept seems antiquated today, it fit with the attitudes and practices of the time.

Colonial justice systems were based on European practices, as these were familiar and well-established, although they were silent on the issue of children and their care or control. The further back one looks in history, the less care children received, especially when contrasted against children's treatment today and the protections that they receive. Life was harsh for both adults and children, and in the absence of child protection agencies or youth advocates, many were left to fend for themselves, especially if they had been abandoned.

Sullivan (2009, 23) described the desertion of children in Europe, and he noted that "parents deserted their offspring in desperation when they were unable to support them due to poverty or disaster, when they were unwilling to keep them because of their physical conditions or ancestry, because of religious beliefs, in self interest, or interest in another child." Boswell (1988, 16) estimated, for example, that between 15 and 30 percent of all children born in European cities in the late 1700s and early 1800s were abandoned by their parents. Such findings illustrate the need for some form of safety net for these dependent children, but governments were slow to intervene, and religious and charitable organizations took on the challenge of providing care for them.

The social roles and responsibilities of children were also different. Bernard (1992) noted that fertility rates and infant mortality were high: many children were born but many died. As a result, parents may have been hesitant to form attachments with their children until they were older. In addition, youths were often treated as miniature adults, and the expectations placed on them were high. Many 15- and 16-year-olds, for instance, were working and were more or less independent of their parents. Often they were married at young ages and started their own families, leaving them little time for delinquent behavior (Felson 1994). Yet some youths were engaging in crime, and the harsh consequences for unruly behavior can be found in one of the earliest examples of juvenile justice legislation: In 1646 the Massachusetts Bay colonists established their criminal code, which included a section on dealing with stubborn children.

The Stubborn Child Law of 1646

Perhaps one of the best ways to understand the shifting boundaries of juvenile justice is to examine how much legislation has changed over time and the intentions of the policymakers who enacted these laws. When the Massachusetts Bay colonists drafted their criminal code they specified how parents could sanction their children. The Stubborn Child Law, which is almost identical to a section of Deuteronomy from the Old Testament, reads as follows (as cited in Sutton, 1993, 10–11):

> If a man have a stubborn or rebellious son, of sufficient years and understanding (viz.) sixteen years of age, which will not obey the voice of his Father, or the voice of his Mother, and that when they have chastened him will not harken unto them: then shall his Father and Mother being his natural parents, lay hold on him and bring him to the Magistrates assembled in Court and testify unto them, that their son is stubborn and rebellious and will not obey their voice and chastisement, but lives in sundry notorious crimes, such a son shall be put to death.

This law had a popular appeal with the public, and Sutton (1993) reported that variants of this code were adopted in Connecticut, Rhode Island, and New Hampshire. Perhaps more surprising is that the law remained on the books in Massachusetts, albeit in a highly modified form, until 1973.

While Rosenberg and Rosenberg (1976) reported that no children were actually put to death for being stubborn, the legislation is instructive for a number of reasons. Sutton (1993) argued that the law was enacted to control children as well as to define deviance in a politically and economically fragile society. Rosenberg and Rosenberg (1976) also observed that this was the first legislation to make an act a crime for youngsters (being stubborn or out of parental control) that an adult did not have to follow. This is the basis of status offenses, which are offenses for children but are not considered criminal acts if committed by adults. Today, status offenders are youngsters who engage in truancy, curfew violations, running away from home, or incorrigibility. Managing status offenders was a key function in the juvenile court's early days as many of these youth were considered at risk of delinquency (McNamara 2008). One way that these juveniles could be controlled was through their placement in a house of refuge.

The Houses of Refuge Movement

Throughout the 1800s there was increasing concern about the plight of children, and reformers of the era sought to improve their living conditions. There is some debate whether the interests of these reformers was entirely altruistic or if there were other motivations, such as extending formal social controls on juveniles (see Platt 1977). Regardless of their intent, many children were neglected, dependent, and delinquent. Education, for example, was intended for the children of the wealthy, and compulsory public education would not be introduced until the 1850s. As a result, many youngsters were living on the street with few constructive outlets for their energies, and some engaged in larceny and disorderly conduct. Others were abandoned or orphaned, and these youths were sometimes drawn to gangs (Pearson 1983).

Clearly there was a need to develop a solution to the challenges posed by these wayward children. Policymakers and reformers looked to Europe to determine whether any of their practices for managing these children could be introduced in America. One notion that seemed feasible was to develop an institution that would shelter these at-risk or delinquent youths until they had developed the skills to establish their independence.

The English had a long history of placing the poor or dependent in almshouses and poorhouses. While originally intended for adults, by the late 1700s some of these shelters were housing dependent and delinquent youths. Quigley (1996) noted that children from five to 14 years who were drifting into delinquency were placed in institutions, while others were sent to live with wealthy families or farmers as indentured servants. By 1820 a number of public institutions for juveniles had been established throughout England for the supervision of delinquent youths, and these served as a prototype for the development of similar shelters in America.

The earliest American juvenile facilities were introduced before there were juvenile courts. The Society for the Prevention of Pauperism in New York, for example, established the first house of refuge in New York City on January 1, 1825 (Krisberg 2005; Shelden 2003).[2] In addition to housing children who were dependent and neglected, youngsters who had violated the law were also placed in these houses of refuge by criminal court judges. These facilities provided shelter and education and sought to increase employability, which in turn would save children from a life of pauperism and crime. Houses of refuge had a popular appeal, and Shallo (1947, 298) observed that "by 1865 ten states had established separate institutions; by 1900 there were 65 such institutions private and public and in 1933 the American Prison Association listed a total of 111 institutions for the care of juveniles."

Houses of refuge were often operated by charitable and religious groups. In New York, for instance, the house of refuge was privately financed and managed (Shallo 1947). The staff sought to instill in their residents middle-class values relating to discipline, hard work, and education (Feld 2003a; Shelden 2003). The primary goals behind these early shelters were regeneration, restoration, socialization, or more commonly rehabilitation. Despite these admirable goals, however, the treatment of youths in these facilities left a lot to be desired, and there is some debate about whether the individuals admitted to these places were serious offenders.

Bernard (1992, 62–63) noted that during the first year of operations the New York House of Refuge admitted 73 youths and that most of them were minor offenders:

> Nine of the first sixteen children sent to the House of Refuge had not committed any punishable offense at all. . . . The most serious offender had been convicted of grand larceny. Nine additional children had been sent for petty larceny, and the remaining sixty-three for vagrancy, stealing, and running away from the poorhouse.

Shallo (1947, 296) reviewed the 1828 annual report from the Philadelphia house of refuge and found that:

> The youth committed fell into three classes: (1) Those without parents or friends who made their living begging or stealing, (2) Those having parents or guardians but became disobedient, stubborn and intractable, or what appears today in juvenile court records as incorrigible, and (3) Those "who committed overt acts of wickedness."

While houses of refuge were intended to provide a supportive and nurturing environment for at-risk and delinquent youths, they failed to live up to those expectations (Bernard 1992).

Finley (2007, 21–22) observed that children in these houses of refuge experienced conditions that were similar to penitentiaries. Residents were frequently whipped or placed in solitary confinement (Pisciotta 1982). These places were also dangerous: although only 138 youths were admitted to Philadelphia's house of refuge in the 1834–1835 fiscal year, seven of them died (Philadelphia House of Refuge 1835, 10).[3] Moreover, some of these shelters were overcrowded, although many youths fled the facility or ran from their apprenticeships (Finley 2007). Last, while education of the youths was a key objective when these institutions were first established, Finley (2007) noted that residents only received a few hours of instruction a day, while most of their waking hours were devoted to employment. In Philadelphia, for instance, the males made brass nails, bound books, and built furniture, while the females made clothes as well as cooked and cleaned (Philadelphia House of Refuge 1835).

Despite the fact that these houses of refuge were established almost two centuries ago, there are a number of features of their operations that are present in today's juvenile correctional systems. First, unlike adults who received a determinate sentence (i.e., a fixed number of years), youths were held indeterminately—meaning that they would not be released until they were assessed as being rehabilitated or they reached the age of majority, which was 21. Thus, a 15-year-old who was dependent, a status offender, or had committed a relatively minor offense could have been held until his or her 21st birthday. While our treatment of dependent youth and status offenders is far less punitive today, indeterminate dispositions are commonly used in juvenile courts.

Second, youths placed in houses of refuge had few due process protections. An 1838 decision of the Pennsylvania Supreme Court that affirmed the confinement of an "unruly" young woman named Mary Ann Crouse illustrated the prevailing view that these facilities were saving children from pauperism. Bernard (1992, 68–70) noted that the court in the *Crouse* case focused on the rehabilitative nature of these facilities (children were being helped, not punished), the good intentions of the operators of these facilities (compared to their actual performance), and the state's role to respond to dependency or delinquency when the parents were not up to the task (see *Ex Parte Crouse*, 4 Wharton [PA.] 9 [1838]).

One aspect of the *Crouse* case deserves special attention. In order to act in the youth's rehabilitative interests, the court drew upon the concept of *parens patriae*, which reformers had borrowed from England (Pisciotta 1982). The translation of this Latin term literally means "the father of the country," and it referred to Chancery Courts, which were established so that the Crown could become involved in a family's affairs if the welfare of dependent or orphaned children was threatened (Finley 2007). As Forst (1995, 1–2) observed, this created the "responsibility of government to care for persons who are unable to care for themselves or whose family members are unable to care for them," and affirmed that "The court was supposed to act *in loco parentis*, that is, to take the place of the parents if the parents were not doing a proper job of raising their children." The *parens patriae* philosophy would be used in the development of the first juvenile courts and is still widely referenced.

A third aspect of the house of refuge that is relevant today was the paternalistic treatment of girls. Many young women were placed outside the home for being incorrigible or out of parental control—which was not a crime for adults. While status offenders are less likely to be placed in secure training schools today, criminologists such as Meda Chesney-Lind and Randall Shelden (2003) observed that some girls are still being incarcerated for being unruly, which is a codeword for being sexually active—as in the *Crouse* case mentioned above. In order to involve the juvenile court to get treatment for their children, the behaviors of these young women are sometimes criminalized by their parents (e.g., a daughter who pushes a parent during an argument is charged with assault and then can be placed outside the home), a process Feld (2009) called relabeling or bootstrapping (see also Buzawa and Hirschel 2010).

While some of their philosophies and practices are still evident in today's juvenile justice systems, houses of refuge gradually disappeared. By the 1900s many of these institutions had been repackaged as reform or training schools—large facilities that held long-term residents (Sullivan 2009). Others became places of temporary detention where youths accused of crimes would await their day in court. Bernard (1992) observed that the house of refuge movement failed to live up to the reformers' high expectations. While their rehabilitative nature was widely promoted, by the 1860s appellate courts had recognized that their actual performance fell short of this ideal. Youths were arbitrarily placed in these facilities (see *People v. Turner*, 55 Ill. 280 [1870]), and their harsh living conditions were not conducive to rehabilitation (Lindsey 1914; Pisciotta 1982).

Despite their limitations, these early juvenile facilities and the child-saving philosophies that they promoted set the stage for the development of contemporary youth justice systems. Like their work in founding houses of refuge, reformers would play a prominent role in the establishment of the first juvenile courts. While juvenile courts have many critics today, they are an important social institution, although one that the reformers who founded them would hardly recognize today.

Founding the Juvenile Court

We can view today's juvenile court as the centerpiece of the juvenile justice system—since once the court was created, the system developed around it. The juvenile court did not spring suddenly full-blown onto the American judicial scene. In fact, it is possible to view the juvenile court as the result of several centuries of legal evolution on both sides of the Atlantic (Feld 2003a; Mays and Winfree 2006; Merlo 2003).

In the United States two particular events contributed to the creation of a separate juvenile court. First, the Industrial Revolution of the mid-to-late 1800s transformed the nation from a rural, agricultural economy to one increasingly urban and industrial. Many young people were displaced from the rural to urban areas, and jobs for these unskilled and semiliterate laborers were scarce. Along with the Industrial Revolution, the United States experienced a great deal of immigration from both Eastern and Western European countries and from Asia. These newly arrived workers provided labor, often at the lowest possible costs, to fuel the developing industrial economy. Immigrants also brought with them children who sometimes were left to roam the streets. Concern over these children committing crimes and living disorderly lives led many reformers to seek ways to aid them (see Platt 1977). As Judge Julian Mack (1909, 116–17), an advocate for children, observed:

> Most of the children who come before the court are, naturally, the children of the poor. In many cases the parents are foreigners, frequently unable to speak English, and without an understanding of American methods and views. What they need, more than anything else, is kindly assistance; and the aim of the court, in appointing a probation officer for the child, is to have the child and the parents feel, not so much the power, as the friendly interest of the state; to show them that the object of the court is to help them to train the child right.

Analyses of the admitting records from the New York house of refuge support Mack's observations. Shallo (1947, 296) reported that "of 335 admitted during 1856, 103 were of American parentage." The remaining two-thirds of youth admissions were foreign-born, and many of them were from Ireland. Shallo (1947, 296) cited the home's Board of Managers, who had stated that "the evils of delinquency are in a large degree but the natural result of a sudden and foreign increase in population." Mack's (1909) observations and Shallo's (1947) statistics show the court's role in socializing immigrant youths.

A second factor that led to the founding of the juvenile court was the Progressive movement (Krisberg 2005). The individuals and groups associated with this movement were concerned about the quality of life in

America's cities, and from these efforts evolved what was known as the "child saving movement" (Shelden 2003). While a number of scholars have questioned the child-savers' motives (Platt 1977; Schlossman 1977), clearly there were charitable societies and associations in many cities that were dedicated to improving the lives of immigrant children and those of lower social classes, especially those who came into contact with the law (Lawrence and Hemmens 2008, 23).

There were at least two key motivations behind the child-saving movement: (1) a desire to instill proper or middle-class civic and moral values in youngsters—and especially in foreign-born youths, and (2) an equal desire to reduce the law's often harsh treatment of children. For example, in the 1800s courts did not distinguish between children and adults in determining their degree of criminal culpability. This meant that children were punished like adults and, at times, were placed in the same correctional facilities (Fishman 1923; MacCormick 1949).

Child-savers felt strongly that youthfulness should be a factor that reduced the degree of punishment. This unique blending of law and a social welfare philosophy resulted in the founding of the first juvenile court (Merlo 2003). The concept of a rehabilitation-based court for youth was popular, and Platt (1977, 10) observed that "By 1917 juvenile court legislation had been passed in all but three states and by 1932 there were over 600 independent juvenile courts throughout the United States." Lenroot (1923, 217) reported that 175,000 youths had appeared before these courts in 1918. She noted, however, that the performance of these courts was hampered by a lack of probation staff and qualified professionals who could conduct assessments and formal record keeping.

The juvenile court, as initially established, was to have a number of distinctive features. First, juvenile cases had a different terminology than adult proceedings. There no longer would be warrants, trials, and sentences. In their place were petitions, hearings, and dispositions (Feld 2003a). Children would not be found guilty. Instead, they would be found or adjudicated delinquent and were viewed as needing the court's help. As a result, these courts were said to act in the best interests of the child.

Second, delinquency hearings were to be private and confidential. Unlike adult criminal trials, these hearings were closed to the public. This was done to reduce stigma and emphasize the courts' rehabilitative nature (Snyder and Sickmund 2006). In most instances, this meant that both the public and the media were excluded. Consequently, there was no publicity surrounding these hearings, and the names of accused delinquents were not published.

Third, delinquency hearings were informal. In some courtrooms this informality was shown by the lack of judges' robes and a trial bench. Hearings might be conducted around conference tables where the chief question was, "How can we help this child?" Judge Mack (1909, 119) articulated the qualities of a good juvenile court judge:

> He must be a student of and deeply interested in the problems of philanthropy and child life, as well as a lover of children. He must be able to understand the boys' point of view and ideas of justice; he must be willing and patient enough to search out the underlying causes of the trouble and to formulate the plan by which, through the cooperation, ofttimes, of many agencies, the cure may be effected.

All of the parties present were assumed to be acting on the child's behalf. Often many of the normal courtroom rules of procedure and evidence were absent. This feature in particular caused a number of problems for the juvenile courts, which resulted in appellate court reviews of juvenile procedures.

Finally, delinquency proceedings were not intended to be adversarial. One of the guiding principles of American law is that there are two opposing parties in any case, and one side wins and the other loses. Juvenile cases, however, were not to be adversarial as the youth was not supposed to be in jeopardy of punishment. The reality was that children were very much at risk of being deprived of their liberty as these courts offered few due process protections. Early critics of the court argued that the due process protections were not being respected (Lindsey 1914), but it wasn't until the U.S. Supreme Court cases of *Kent v. United States* (1966), *In re Gault* (1967), and *In re Winship* (1970) that juveniles' rights were formally defined.

Between 1966 and 1975 a great many changes occurred in the legal environment of the juvenile court. The Supreme Court's "due process revolution" had an impact on the juvenile courts, and accused delinquents received many of the due process rights guaranteed for adult criminal defendants (see Chapter 5). Expanding due process protections changed the juvenile court's informal and nonadversarial nature. Attorneys appeared more frequently, and the differences between adult courts and juvenile courts became less clear. As a result of the reduced distinctiveness, over the years some critics have called for an end to separate adult and juvenile courts (see Ainsworth 1999; Feld, 1997; Lindsey 1914).

Changes in juvenile court procedures from the mid-1970s through the 1980s resulted in two lines of criticism. Youth advocates view juvenile courts as excessively punitive, and they want to reaffirm the rehabilitation philosophy (e.g., the "Books not Bars" campaign; Ella Baker Center 2011). The second group, while not necessarily larger, has been vocal about the potential risks that juveniles pose (DiIulio 1995; Fox 1992). These crime control critics have been heard, and the result has been that the juvenile court's general nature has moved in the direction of more punitive or just deserts–oriented dispositions. Overall, these competing views of youth justice show the tensions between implementing policies that are in the best interests of the child and holding youths accountable for their delinquency (Merlo and Benekos 2010).

AN OVERVIEW OF THE JUVENILE JUSTICE SYSTEM

One criticism regarding the use of the term *system* is that it implies a coordinated effort with agreement on goals and purposes. While there is a general lack of coordination within the juvenile justice system, we will still treat it as a system throughout this book. However, it is important to acknowledge that the individual components we will identify sometimes operate at cross purposes with one another. The three primary components of the system are law enforcement (the police), courts, and correctional agencies. Figure 2.1 illustrates the flow diagram of justice system processes—from the commission of an offense until the final outcome for the case—that was created by the Center on Criminal and Juvenile Justice (2011).

The following pages highlight how a juvenile moves through the system. The approach we present is somewhat generic, as there are some significant variations in the manner that a case proceeds in the 51 different U.S. jurisdictions. Much of the data that follow are reported from Puzzanchera, Adams, and Sickmund's (2010) analyses of *Juvenile Court Statistics: 2006–2007*, produced for the Office of Juvenile Justice and Delinquency Prevention, and our examination focuses on delinquency rather than cases of abuse, neglect, or dependency.

Referrals to the Juvenile Court

In order for the juvenile court to hear a case, there must first be a referral. Most referrals to the juvenile court for delinquency are made by law enforcement, and in 2007 about 83 percent of all cases were referred by the police; that proportion has been stable since 1985 (Puzzanchera et al.

Figure 2.1 Juvenile Justice Flowchart

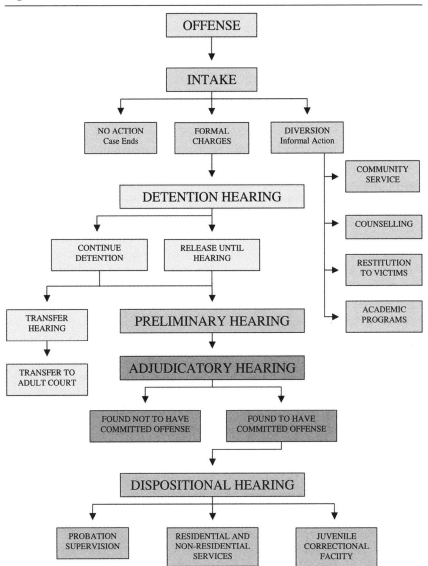

2010, 31). Referrals are also made by officials in health, educational, or social service organizations. Cases of truancy, for example, are likely to be referred to the court by a school official. In addition, parents, guardians, or family members sometimes contact juvenile court officials to request assistance in managing a youngster who is out of control, incorrigible, or requires support. Because most referrals are the result of law enforcement, this section highlights some of the controversies surrounding interactions between the police and juveniles.

For the most part, police procedures are much the same no matter a suspect's age. The police have considerable discretion, and minor acts are often dealt with informally: the officer gives a youth a verbal warning and then sends him or her home, or in some cases an officer escorts a juvenile home and warns the youth with his or her parent(s) present. Some suspected delinquents, however, are more likely to result in a referral to the juvenile court. These include instances when juveniles have committed a serious or violent offense, if the youth is uncooperative or at risk of harming himself and others, or if the officer cannot find a parent, guardian, or responsible adult who can take custody of the youth.

When a youth is taken into custody, there are only a few distinctions between juvenile and adult offenders, and most of the procedures used by the police are much the same no matter a suspect's age. There are two major areas of differences: (1) identification of suspects (fingerprinting, photographing, and DNA evidence) and (2) interrogation techniques.

In keeping with the juvenile court's original rehabilitative orientation, most states had prohibited fingerprinting and photographing juvenile suspects. By the 1990s, however, most jurisdictions had changed their laws regarding identification procedures for juvenile suspects. In fact, a report by the National Institute of Justice (1995, 1) dealing with the use of juvenile records by prosecutors and judges recommended that "states should consider mandating police fingerprinting of juveniles charged with felonies or weapons violation misdemeanors." Szymanski (2010a, 1) reported that by the end of the 2009 legislative session, 10 states placed some form of age restriction on fingerprinting juveniles, with North Carolina and Wisconsin setting the minimum age for fingerprinting at 10 years. In addition, a number of states now take DNA samples from certain adult and juvenile suspects, and these samples can be entered into the state's criminal records database (see Shepherd 2000; Szymanski 2009a).

The fear historically was that handling juvenile suspects in such a routine "criminal" manner would highlight the stigma associated with formal justice system processing. However, as the National Council of Juvenile and Family Court Judges (2005, 40) noted, "Most youth openly share their situations with peers, school, and community so that before even appearing before the court, their alleged illegal activity is well-known to those in the youth's life." Thus, relatively little additional stigma seems to result from police identification and record keeping procedures.

In addition to identification processes, the police traditionally have used different interrogation procedures for adults and juveniles. The issue always has been to what extent the *Miranda* rights apply to juvenile interrogations. Over the years appellate courts have decided a number of cases dealing with the interrogation of juvenile suspects (see, for example, *Haley v. Ohio* 1948; *Gallegos v. Colorado* 1962; *Fare v. Michael C.* 1979). The Supreme Court expanded the *Miranda* rights of juveniles in the *J.D.B. v. North Carolina* case, which was decided in June 2011. This ruling forces police officers to take into account the age of a youth in their interrogations, and as a result juvenile suspects must receive a *Miranda* warning in situations where adults would not have to be warned.

Juveniles can be interrogated, and like adults they have the right to have an attorney present during questioning, although some youths are interviewed with their parent or guardian present. Also, while youngsters can waive their right to an attorney, the courts will apply the "totality of circumstances" test to decide whether such a waiver was freely, knowingly, and voluntarily given (Feld 2003a; Hemmens, Steiner, and Mueller 2004). There is, however, considerable concern that many youths still waive their right to an attorney, which may place them at considerable disadvantage in these proceedings (Feld and Schaefer 2010).

Intake Decision Making

The degree to which a youth will be involved in the justice system is decided at the intake stage, with the determination of whether a formal petition to the court will be made. This decision is influenced by several distinct, but connected, sets of actors, including police officers, juvenile probation officers (or other court intake workers), and juvenile court judges. The initial decision made by the police and intake workers is whether to detain the juvenile temporarily. In most cases, suspected offenders are held only long enough to process paperwork and contact their parents. Detention for longer periods of time is justified if the juvenile has committed a serious violent crime (such as homicide, rape, or armed robbery), there is an immediate danger to the public, if there is a risk of flight prior to scheduled court hearings, or when the accused might be in danger from the public (Feld 2003a, 159–62).

At the same time intake workers are deciding whether to detain the juvenile, they along with the prosecutor's office will consider what charges, if any, seem justified. In some cases the police will have a major impact on this decision, but usually intake workers and prosecutors control the charging decision (Bishop, Frazier, and Henretta 1999; Feld

Figure 2.2 Case Flow for Delinquency Cases

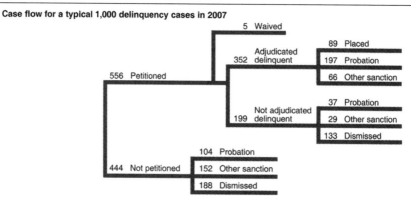

Case flow for a typical 1,000 delinquency cases in 2007

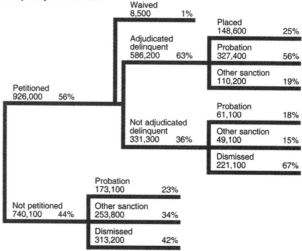

Case flow for 1,666,100 delinquency cases in 2007

Notes: Cases are categorized by their most severe or restrictive sanction. Detail may not add to totals because of rounding. Annual case processing flow diagrams for 1985 through 2007 are available at www.ojjdp.ncjrs.gov/ojstatbb/court/faqs.asp.

1999b; Sanborn 2003). Figure 2.2 shows the outcomes for youths referred to juvenile courts. According to Knoll and Sickmund (2010, 4) for every 1,000 cases that were referred to courts in 2007, about 444 never appeared before the juvenile court. Of that total, 104 were placed on informal probation, while 152 received some other sanction, and 188 cases were dismissed entirely.

Much like a funnel, Figure 2.2 shows that many of the youths are filtered out of the system before there is a formal disposition or sentence. Slightly less than one-half of all cases that are referred to juvenile courts do not result in an appearance. A number of factors influence the process.

Most juvenile courts have an intake staff—often juvenile probation officers or deputy juvenile officers—and they decide whether a case justifies issuing a petition. For much of the juvenile court's history, intake decisions were made by these officials, but with the juvenile court's increasingly adversarial nature, prosecuting attorneys are playing a larger role earlier in the decision-making process. The result has been that prosecutors now tend to dominate juvenile court processes in some jurisdictions, especially in cases of serious offenders (Lawrence and Hemmens 2008; Sanborn 2003).

Throughout its early history, juvenile court intake workers used social and legal considerations in determining whether to file a delinquency petition (Merlo 2003; Snyder and Sickmund 2006, 94). Social factors relate to juveniles' background characteristics and include family stability, whether the youth's parents or guardians can supervise the juvenile, as well as the child's academic record and employment history. By contrast, legal factors relate to what the child has done. These elements concern the nature of the present offense, the role played in the act (i.e., as a leader or follower), and the youth's previous offense history. Of the two, social factors traditionally played the leading role. Currently, legal factors dominate the intake process.

Intake Dispositions

Since about one-half of cases do not go beyond intake, it is important to consider the options that are available to intake decision makers. As previously mentioned, one alternative is to file a petition on behalf of the child. This normally will be done in three types of cases: those involving persistent offenders, those involving juveniles who have committed a single very serious offense, and those where the parents are unable or unwilling to exercise appropriate control over the child. Situations arising out of lack of parental control typically involve dependent or neglected children. Aside from filing a petition, however, the court has a number of other options.

Unlike adult courts, juvenile courts may use a sanction known as informal probation (Mays and Winfree 2006, 174–76; Snyder and Sickmund 2006, 104), and earlier we noted that about 104 youths out of every 1,000 referrals to the court in 2007 were placed on informal probation (Knoll and Sickmund 2010, 4). With adults, probation is a sentence imposed by courts following a conviction. This is true for formal probation with juveniles as well. However, some juvenile probation officers, acting under statutory or court authority, use informal probation to handle minor offenders such as shoplifters or vandals. Informal probation also may be used for first-time offenders if the cases do not involve crimes against persons and where it is apparent that the child has done something but legal sufficiency has not been clearly established (Bortner 1988, 107–9).

Informal probation allows the probation staff to place youngsters under a very lax form of community supervision and to serve notice on them that future law violations will result in more severe punishments. The juvenile probation staff takes this approach to place a hold on the request for a petition for some specified period of time (generally three to six months). This allows them to see whether there will be additional facts discovered or charges filed. If not, the charges may be dismissed, but court records concerning the nature of the child's court contact and involvement in the offense remain.

One of the criticisms of informal probation is the amount of coercion present during the process. In some jurisdictions informal probation and other alternatives to delinquency hearings are handled through consent decrees (Snyder and Sickmund 2006, 104). These orders require that the child admit to the charges in exchange for leniency. In such situations, due process protections may be minimized in order to promote a rapid, informal disposition. These offers are difficult to refuse for many children and their parents.

In addition to informal probation, courts also use diversion. Diversion was designed to remove first and relatively minor offenders from the formal legal process as quickly as possible to avoid the stigmatizing effects of delinquency hearings. Such interventions were consistent with labeling theories that posited that youths who were labeled as delinquents would be more likely to engage in subsequent delinquency. Diversion programs emerged from the federal government's Juvenile Justice and Delinquency Prevention Act of 1974 (Schwartz 1989). In some ways, these programs were returns to the juvenile court's original nonstigmatizing goals. Some scholars have been satisfied with the results of diversion efforts, while others are critical (Patenaude 2003; Schwartz 1989).

One intended consequence of diversion programs was the removal of large numbers of relatively minor offenders from juvenile court processing. A variety of community-based programs and agencies have been created in order to meet the treatment needs of these youths, most of whom have not faced juvenile court delinquency hearings. Broad-scale application of diversion, however, has left the juvenile courts to deal with the most serious delinquency cases.

An unintended consequence of diversion, by contrast, has been the development of "wider, stronger, and different nets" (Austin and Krisberg 1981), which is also called "net-widening." Thus, some youngsters diverted from the formal juvenile justice system have been captured in informal "nets" and are supervised or treated by community-based agencies. As a result, it is possible that more youths are now under some form of control as a result of diversionary programs than before these programs existed. It is therefore likely that juveniles who have had one label removed as a result of diversion will now be relabeled through placement in community mental health and private psychiatric care facilities or treatment programs (Snyder and Sickmund 2006, 225–28).

Puzzanchera, Adams, and Sickmund (2010) observed that waiver determinations in some states are made at intake. In these jurisdictions, the decision to transfer a youth is made by the officials mentioned above. However, in some cases, the juvenile might be charged with an offense that places him or her outside of the juvenile court's jurisdiction. If youths' offenses and age place them outside the jurisdiction of the juvenile court, the only role of the judge is to confirm the charges and approve the transfer to a criminal court.

In summarizing intake decision making, it is important to note that intake is not simply a "yes–no" determination. Decisions can occupy a number of possible places along a continuum. The least severe outcomes require some action short of filing a petition, with no further legal action being taken on the case. The two most severe outcomes are filing a petition with the juvenile court and setting the youngster's case for a delinquency hearing or initiating a transfer to an adult criminal court. For each option and each alternative there are consequences for the juveniles involved, especially regarding the possible penalties facing them (Redding 2003; Singer 2003).

Adjudicatory Hearings

Slightly more than one-half of all youths referred to juvenile courts in 2007 for delinquency matters had a hearing before a judge. For every 1,000 youths who were initially referred to the court, 556 appeared, 352 were adjudicated as delinquent, 199 were not adjudicated as delinquent, and five were transferred to adult courts (Knoll and Sickmund 2010, 4). Of special interest are the 199 who were not adjudicated as delinquent and the five waived to adult courts.

The fact that only five of every 1,000 youths who are referred to juvenile courts are transferred affirms our earlier observations that these are relatively rare events, although these figures do not include youth who appear directly in adult courts (either through direct file of prosecutors, legislative exclusion, or in the case of juveniles who had previously been transferred and are now considered adults in the eyes of the court, or "once-waived, always-waived"). In terms of the 199 who were not adjudicated delinquent, a total of 133 cases were dismissed, 37 were placed on probation, and the last 29 youths were given some other sanction (Knoll and Sickmund 2010, 4).

Although there is substantial variation in the manner that hearings take place across the country, they can be described in two ways. First, many are less formal than adult court proceedings, and concern for the child typically dominates the decision-making process. Second, delinquency hearings are much more formal than they traditionally were. This means that with attorneys present for both sides, careful application of the rules of evidence, and a stricter weight of proof, juvenile courts operate under much more of a due process legal model than they previously did. In some ways this has made juvenile courts more like the adult criminal courts.

The dilemma for some juvenile court observers is over whether due process or rehabilitation will be the court's guiding philosophy. Weisheit and Alexander (1988) do not believe that this has to be an either–or choice. In fact, given the two-part nature of juvenile court processes, it is possible to have an adjudicatory hearing governed by due process principles and dispositional hearings influenced by rehabilitative principles. This is not a new suggestion, and Lindsey (1914) advocated for juvenile hearings that occurred in adult criminal courts, where the due process rights of the accused would be guaranteed, and if the youths were found guilty they would be sentenced in a juvenile court that could craft a disposition based on each youth's risk and needs.

To summarize the adjudicatory processes for delinquents, two important trends have been developing simultaneously. The first is the diversion of status offenders and less serious offenders from the formal adjudicatory process (Feld 2003a; Patenaude 2003). This has removed many minor offenders from juvenile courts. By contrast, the most serious offenders are increasingly being transferred to adult criminal courts. When these two trends are considered together, one could conclude that the juvenile justice system's boundaries are shrinking and that the juveniles who remain are likely to comprise "regular delinquents;" property, public order and drug offenders; and a smaller percentage of violent offenders. These shifting boundaries have enabled the juvenile justice system to focus on youths who are at risk of future delinquency and are seen as salvageable.

Dispositional Alternatives

Of the 556 youths (of every 1,000 referred to the court) who had been petitioned in 2007, 352 were adjudicated delinquent (Knoll and Sickmund 2010). Each of these youths received a disposition of some type. Juvenile court judges have a wide range of possible punishments when dealing with youngsters who have been found to be delinquent. The National Advisory Committee on Criminal Justice Standards and Goals (1976) placed these alternatives into four categories: (1) nominal, (2) conditional, (3) suspended, and (4) custodial dispositions (see also Gardner 2009, 270–80). In this section we describe each of these options.

The best way to understand a nominal disposition is to recognize that at times the juvenile court may decide not to continue its control and supervision over adjudicated delinquents. This would be punishment in name only. For example, a youth who has been found to be delinquent may be given a verbal reprimand by the judge and warned not to commit further delinquent acts. If the case involves relatively minor offenses and the juvenile probation office lacks the resources to supervise them, children can be released without community supervision. This approach is considered a passive form of probation.

As a result of the key role played by probation in juvenile court processes, conditional dispositions are the most frequent sanctions imposed on delinquent youngsters. For example, in 2007 there were an estimated 926,000 cases petitioned to juvenile courts, and of that number 586,200 were found to be delinquent and 327,400 were placed on formal probation (Knoll and Sickmund 2010, 4). This did not include youths placed on informal probation, which would bring the total to 561,600 juvenile probationers (Knoll and Sickmund 2010). Thus, as Snyder and Sickmund (2006, 174, 176) noted, "Probation is the oldest and most widely used community-based corrections program."

Conditional dispositions involve some form of community supervision and a number of requirements that must be met in order to remain on what is considered "privileged" status. These dispositions may include any or all of the following (Rogers and Mays 1987, 425–26; Snyder and Sickmund 2006, 176):

1. *Financial sanctions*—these may include fines and restitution. Many juvenile court judges hesitate to impose fines knowing that juveniles often are unable to pay and this can place a financial burden on some families. Restitution, however, has become a fairly common probation condition, especially in cases involving theft or property damage.

2. *Community service*—this may be imposed in the case of relatively minor offenses such as vandalism. The service might include cleaning city parks and recreational facilities, working at animal shelters, or assisting in hospitals and clinics. One of the difficulties

associated with imposing community service as a conditional disposition is that someone must monitor the work. This may be a probation officer, and when it is, there will be an additional burden on an already overworked probation staff.

3. *Remedial services*—these include receiving treatment for educational deficiencies and substance abuse as well as individual and family counseling. Such services usually are provided by community-based organizations.

4. *Alternative residential placements*—other housing arrangements must be made in situations where a juvenile cannot or should not be left in the home. These placements may include foster or group homes, shelters, and halfway houses. In some cases, parents arrange for their children's placement in psychiatric facilities, residential treatment centers, or privately operated wilderness and boot camps.

In most instances, conditional dispositions are administered by the juvenile probation office. When judges place juveniles on probation, they attach a set of conditions to the probation order, and the youth's compliance with those conditions is monitored by a probation officer. If the youth violates the probation conditions, he or she can be returned to court, and the judge can suspend probation and impose a custodial sanction. One shortcoming of this approach, however, is that many probation officers have large caseloads and find it difficult to closely supervise their clients.

Much like nominal dispositions, suspended dispositions may involve the threat of court action more than the action itself. For some youngsters, the judge may be willing to withhold adjudication or disposition if the juvenile is willing to refrain from law-violating behavior or to engage in prosocial behavior. This is most likely to occur with first-time offenders or with minor property offenders. Occasionally, when juvenile courts have jurisdiction over traffic offenses, judges will withhold fines or other punishments if a juvenile does not receive another citation within six months to a year.

Custodial dispositions involve short- or long-term incarceration, and Knoll and Sickmund (2010, 4) estimated that 148,600 youths were placed outside the home in 2007. These dispositions are often ordered as a last resort by juvenile court judges. As a result of the widespread application of the juvenile court's rehabilitative philosophy, most judges and juvenile probation officers will try traditional probation or alternatives to incarceration as many times as possible. While incarceration should be reserved for the most serious offenders, a review of the 2007 *Census of*

Juveniles in Residential Placement shows that the most juvenile inmates were not violent offenders. Sickmund, Sladky, Kang, and Puzzanchera (2011a) reported that 35.8 percent of the residents were violent offenders, 24.3 percent were property offenders, 12.7 percent were public order offenders, 8.2 percent were drug offenders, 15.1 percent were placed in custody for violating their probation conditions, and 3.9 percent were status offenders.

Juveniles can be incarcerated in a variety of correctional facilities (Ruddell and Thomas 2009). These settings range from locally operated minimum-security facilities that resemble college dormitories to state-run training schools for delinquents that are modeled after adult prisons. The length of time for confinement is determined by state statutes. Szymanski (2008b, 1) reported that in seven states the juvenile court loses jurisdiction upon the youth's 19th birthday, while in 33 states the juvenile court jurisdiction ends at the offender's 21st birthday, and several states extend jurisdiction until the individual's 24th or 25th birthdays.

Juvenile courts historically have used indeterminate sentencing. Under this approach, juveniles are sent to correctional facilities for a period to be determined by correctional authorities. A juvenile's release date is set once he or she is "rehabilitated." Thus, sentences can range from a few weeks to years, or when the juvenile reached the age of majority.

Recently, some states have shifted from indeterminate to determinate sentencing for juveniles (Mears 2002). This change means that open-ended sentences have been replaced by fixed-duration commitments. This transformation in sentencing procedures is similar to many of the other changes in juvenile courts and illustrates a more adult-like treatment of youthful offenders.

SUMMARY

In an influential statement, King (2009) observed that law enforcement organizations have a life course, and that every agency passes through a number of stages that starts with its creation or founding. King (2009) claimed that these founding effects shape the organization's functioning long into the future. Applying that notion to juvenile justice, we can see that the introduction of the Stubborn Child Law, the houses of refuge, and the establishment of the juvenile court represent our attempts to control status offenders and delinquents, as well as responding to the unmet needs of dependent and neglected youth. These changes did not occur in a vacuum but were in response to a number of historical events and social factors, including the end of the Civil War, the beginning of the Industrial

Revolution, immigration from Europe and the Orient, and the influence of the Progressive movement. The juvenile court, with its *parens patriae* philosophy and its intention to act in the best interests of the child, proved to be the cornerstone upon which the American juvenile justice system was built.

One of the challenges of these fledgling juvenile justice systems was that reformers made promises that were difficult to meet, especially since many of them were operated by charitable and religious organizations that received little government funding. Despite that shortcoming, many of the philosophies introduced by reformers such as the child-savers are present today and still influence what occurs in contemporary juvenile justice systems.

For most of the twentieth century, the treatment of juveniles as a distinct category of offenders was intended to be informal, confidential, non-stigmatizing, regenerative, and caring. The reality was that in return for these supposed benefits juveniles received few legal rights and protections. Starting in the 1960s, when constitutional rights were expanded dramatically for adults, the issue of due process rights for accused juvenile offenders became more prominent. With adult cases such as *Gideon* and *Miranda*, the disadvantaged status of most criminal offenders became apparent, and when juvenile court procedures were measured against these standards, the differences became even more dramatic.[4] As a result, from 1966 to 1975 a new set of constitutional rights was extended to accused delinquents by the United States Supreme Court and other federal and state appellate courts, a subject covered in Chapter 5.

With the benefits of the due process revolution in juvenile procedures there also came costs. Some policymakers felt that if juveniles were going to receive adult-like protections, they should face adult-like punishments (Bennett, DiIulio, and Walters 1996; Regnery 1985). In most jurisdictions the result has been increasingly punitive sanctions aimed at serious, violent, and persistent youthful offenders.

Before reaching the conclusion that juvenile procedures have become more adult-like for all offenders, however, it is important to note that the juvenile justice system is becoming more and less punitive at the same time. While we have seen more severe measures like mandatory or determinate sentences and transfers to adult courts, some youngsters are punished less severely by juvenile courts. Less harsh treatment has been experienced, especially by status offenders, many of whom were treated as delinquents prior to 1974. Today, relatively few status offenders are incarcerated. The same can be said for minor property offenders. For example, the percentage of property offenders held in residential placements dropped from 56 percent in 1985 (Snyder and Sickmund 2006, 174) to 24.3 percent in 2007 (Sickmund et al. 2011b).

A number of states have limited the capacities of their juvenile correctional facilities, or they have been financially unable to expand them. This causes institutional bed space to be reserved for the most serious or persistent offenders. A few states have actually reduced the number of public facilities or bed spaces available for adjudicated offenders: Hockenberry, Sickmund, and Sladky (2009) reported that there were 2,658 juvenile residential facilities in October 2006, compared to 3,061 facilities in 2000 (Sickmund 2002).

The result has been an increasing reliance on diversion of juvenile offenders from the formal legal process into community-based treatment programs. Even many youngsters found to be delinquent are placed in alternatives to incarceration because of lack of space or funding. Moreover, there has been a philosophical shift in some jurisdictions to treat juvenile offenders, whenever possible, in the least restrictive environment (Daleiden, Pang, Roberts, Slavin, and Pestle 2010).

Several summary points can be made based on this brief overview of the juvenile justice system. First, juvenile justice procedures no longer resemble those envisioned by the founders of our first juvenile courts. Juvenile records often are no longer confidential (since some states allow routine publication of juvenile suspects' names, and proceedings in many states are now open to the public); informal (since rules of procedure must be applied); or nonadversarial (since attorneys are present in many cases, and some states provide for a nonwaivable right to counsel by juvenile suspects). Ironically, the philosophy of *parens patriae* treatment and rehabilitation persist as features of the juvenile justice system (Benekos 2003; Russo-Myers 2003). The outcome often has been a confusing approach to meting out justice to juveniles. It is as if we have tried to put new wine into old wine skins, and the old philosophies have had trouble accommodating the new procedures.

NOTES

1. The federal government also prosecutes a relatively small number of juveniles each year—primarily those involved in offenses occurring on Indian lands and military bases—although some juvenile offenders are also prosecuted for their involvement in felonies. Motivans and Snyder (2011, 1) reported that in 2008, 152 persons under the age of 18 years were prosecuted in federal courts.

2. According to Bernard (1992, 60), paupers were perceived to be "undeserving poor people—those undeserving of charity because of their wicked and dissolute ways. Paupers were deceitful, traitorous, hostile, rude, brutal, rebellious, sullen, wasteful, cowardly, dirty, and blasphemous."

3. Snyder and Sickmund (2007, 8) reported that in 2000, 2002, and 2004, an average of 27.7 juveniles died in all of the U.S. youth custody facilities in each of those years. In addition, the Bureau of Justice Statistics' *Deaths in Custody Reports* show that in 2007 a total of five juveniles died in all of the U.S. adult jails and state prisons (Noonan 2010a; Noonan 2010b). Thus, the Philadelphia house of refuge was a very dangerous place for youngsters.

4. The *Gideon v. Wainwright* case was heard by the U.S. Supreme Court in 1961, with the Court ruling that indigent defendants be given state-funded counsel when charged with a felony.

THREE

Juvenile Crime and Transfer Trends

INTRODUCTION

There is widespread agreement that transfers to adult court have a place in the juvenile justice system. There is much less consensus about how many youths should be exposed to the adult criminal justice system and the mechanisms used to waive them to criminal courts. Individuals who believe in holding juveniles accountable for their actions argue that public safety is jeopardized if we fail to rehabilitate repeat or violent offenders in the juvenile justice system (Rossum 1995). Advocates for children, however, believe that transfers should be used sparingly and only for the small number of youths who represent the biggest threats to public safety (Arya 2010). Because our ability to predict future reoffending is incomplete, it is difficult to distinguish between offenders who will go on to commit more crimes and those who have "learned their lesson" and will lead crime-free lives in the community.

We described in Chapter 1 that placing youths in adult criminal courts exposes them to the possibility of severe punishments, including lengthy adult prison terms. But even a misdemeanor conviction in a criminal court can permanently affect an individual's lifelong employment opportunities, access to government housing, admissions to higher education, as well as student funding (Colgate Love 2011; Mauer and Chesney-Lind 2003). Moreover, young people who are placed in adult facilities are sometimes physically and sexually abused, and there is the possibility that exposing impressionable young people to sophisticated adult offenders will pull them further into crime once released (Leigey, Hodge, and Saum 2009). Some suggest that the experiences of these young offenders make it difficult for them to successfully reintegrate into society. If we make these ex-offenders ineligible to pursue legitimate education and employment opportunities, for example, then they might feel pushed into illegitimate means of sustaining themselves. As a result, by transferring some youths to adult courts we can make a bad situation worse (Hahn et al. 2007).

The starting point for debates about the purposes and effectiveness of transfers should be informed by what the research demonstrates about the number of transfers, where and when they occur, and who is impacted by these policies. Bernard (1992, 12) observed that there are three ways that the public looks at juvenile delinquency: (1) that it was more serious in the past than today ("things have progressed"), (2) that delinquency rates are about the same as they were in the past ("nothing has changed"), and (3) that it was less serious than today (the "good old days"). Even after almost two decades of declining crime rates, the public often has a pessimistic view about juvenile crime and believes that things are getting worse (Dorfman and Schiraldi 2001; see also Chapter 6). When it comes to violent crime, however, juveniles today are far less likely to be involved in serious and violent crimes than they were two decades ago. In order to better understand youths' involvement in crime, it is important to look as far back as practical to see how juvenile crime levels have changed to detect trends and patterns.

Consequently, in this chapter we take a closer look at crime and transfers to adult courts and their relationship over time. First we examine juvenile crime trends using Federal Bureau of Investigation (FBI) arrest data as well as information from the FBI *Supplementary Homicide Reports*. Second, we use National Crime Victimization Survey (NCVS) data—collected by the U.S. Census Bureau for the Bureau of Justice Statistics—to provide a supplementary source of information to the law enforcement data. The second part of the chapter examines the characteristics of juveniles transferred to adult courts using court data collected and reported by the Office of Juvenile Justice and Delinquency Prevention (OJJDP).

Our goal in this chapter is to help readers better understand the context from which tough-on-crime policies emerged, such as the increase in the number of serious and violent crimes committed by juveniles starting in the 1980s. If, for example, the use of transfers is a rational policy, there should be a strong relationship between juveniles' involvement in serious and violent crimes and the number of youths who are waived to adult criminal courts. The second part of this chapter examines the characteristics of juveniles who were transferred to criminal courts from 1985 to 2008. Of special importance to our analyses are the types of offenses that trigger transfers to criminal courts, whether these youths are detained, as well as offenders' demographic characteristics.

JUVENILE CRIME TRENDS

Violent juvenile crime increased throughout the mid-1980s, peaked in 1994, decreased substantially over the next decade, and has since remained stable. We base this observation on two sources of crime data. The first is the FBI's annual reports on arrests and crimes reported to the police. The second source is the NCVS, a national-level survey of Americans that asks respondents about being victimized. Both of these crime measures have their strengths and weaknesses, and these are briefly highlighted in the paragraphs that follow.

The FBI has been collecting data on crimes reported to the police since the 1930s in annual publications called the *Uniform Crime Report* (UCR). The UCR also reports on the characteristics of persons arrested, including their ages, and this provides us with an annual snapshot of juvenile crime. There are a number of limitations to the use of these data—especially in terms of its accuracy in the early years of the *Report*—but critics would suggest that the quality of the *Report* has improved, as most police departments (covering 96.3 percent of the population in 2009) provide annual information to the FBI. As a result, we are basing our analyses of juvenile crime on official police sources that, though incomplete, give us a reasonably accurate picture.

One consideration is that not all offenses are reported to the police. As a result, a second information source about juvenile involvement in crime is the NCVS. The NCVS collects self-reported information about victimization, and Truman and Rand (2010, 2) noted that, "In 2009, 38,728 households and 68,665 individuals age 12 and older were interviewed for the NCVS." The NCVS is an important information source about crime because many crimes go unreported, what criminologists call the "dark figure of crime." There are many situational, offense-related, and demographic reasons why crimes are not reported to the police. In some cases the victims might not think that reporting a crime is worthwhile (e.g., the theft of an inexpensive item), or they may be too embarrassed to report an offense because of their role in an incident (e.g., a person who is robbed by a prostitute). Other victims do not report their victimization because they do not trust the police or are fearful of law enforcement (Baumer and Lauritsen 2010). Moreover, crime also occurs in family settings or between acquaintances, and these acts are seldom reported. Regardless of the reasons why victims do not report crimes, the NCVS is a good resource because it gives us information about crimes not captured by police statistics.

Scholars have compared police-reported crime to the NCVS results and have found that the trends tend to be parallel—they both rise and fall at approximately the same rate—although self-reported victimization levels are always higher (see Catalano 2006). Thus, by using both officially reported arrests and crimes as well as self-reported victimization, we will have a more complete picture of juvenile crime in the United States.

The following figures depict juvenile crime rates from 1960 to 2009 using FBI (2010) data. In order to facilitate comparisons between years and account for the changing national population these arrests and offenses are all reported as rates per 100,000 U.S. residents. The FBI classifies crimes into two categories: Part I includes the most serious offenses (homicide, rape, robbery, aggravated assault, burglary, motor vehicle theft, larceny/theft, and arson), while Part II offenses include 21 less serious crimes, such as simple assault, drug and weapons offenses, prostitution, driving under the influence, and fraud. As the intent of transfers is to place serious and repeat youthful offenders in criminal courts, we focus upon the Part 1 offenses.

Figure 3.1 shows that arrests for Part I offenses increased throughout the 1960s and 1970s, peaked in 1978, dropped somewhat, and then rose again until 1994. Since that time, the number of Part I offenses has decreased to 1960s levels. This indicator, however, includes all arrests, and it is possible that some crimes have increased while others remained stable or decreased at the same time. As a result, Figure 3.2 looks at crime based on three types: property, public order, and violent. Juvenile arrest

Figure 3.1 Arrests per 100,000 Juveniles, 1960–2009

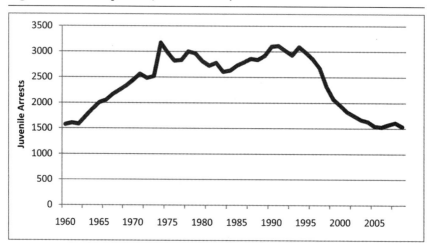

Figure 3.2 Violent, Property and Drug Arrests, 1960–2009

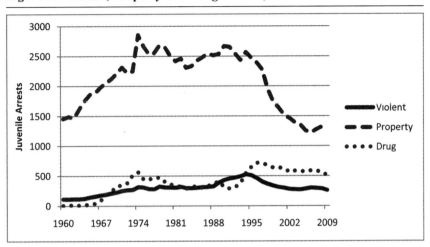

rates for violent crimes (homicide, robbery, rape, and aggravated assault) and property offenses (burglary, larceny, and auto theft) show a similar pattern. Arrests for drug offenses (both misdemeanor and felony drug offenses), by contrast, have increased. One limitation of our knowledge about drug offenses, however, is whether increased arrests are the result of changing law enforcement practices (e.g., "crackdowns" on juvenile drug use). It is plausible, for example, that adolescent drug use has remained relatively constant but that enhanced enforcement has increased arrests.

One important trend to feel positive about is that the numbers of juvenile arrests have decreased while the youth population has been increasing. From 1985 to 2008, the OJJDP reported that the at-risk population (the number of youths from 10 to 17 years) has increased from 26.2 to 32.9 million (Puzzanchera, Sladky, and Kang 2010). Thus, given the population increase, the reduction in the overall juvenile arrest numbers for serious offenses is even more noteworthy.

There are a number of factors to consider when examining arrest rates, and especially for those involving juveniles. First, Puzzanchera (2009) noted that juveniles are more likely than adults to commit crimes in groups, and a single offense could result in a number of arrests (e.g., when five youths commit a robbery and all are arrested). Second, the FBI considers only the most serious offenses in the reporting of their statistics, and thus some minor crimes will not be counted. Third, it is likely that some youths will be arrested more than once in a calendar year, thus both inflating the arrest numbers and suggesting that more juveniles are taken into custody than is the actual case. Fourth, some crimes are never reported to the police, and so no suspects will ever be investigated or arrested for these unreported offenses. Last, as these are arrest statistics, it is important to acknowledge that some juveniles will never be arrested for the offenses that they committed so the arrest statistics will underestimate the true number of youths involved in crimes as well as the extent of crime.

Our second series of analyses examines the involvement of juvenile offenders as described by crime victims in the NCVS. Some of the questions in the NCVS pertain to the crime event and the victim's perceptions about the incident, including the age and number of offenders involved. One question asked of victims of serious and violent crimes (which includes rape, robbery, and aggravated assault) is whether they could determine the age of the offender. Based on this information, the NCVS (2011) estimated that juveniles accounted for about 20 to 25 percent of these offenses. The peak and decline in youth crime depicted in the FBI arrest data listed above corresponds with the self-reported responses of victims shown in Figure 3.3. The NCVS statistics revealed that juvenile involvement in crime decreased from over one million incidents at the peak of youth arrests in 1994 to slightly more than one-quarter million incidents in 2007 (1,013,000 and 277,000 incidents respectively).

Several other indicators of juvenile involvement in crimes are also reported by the NCVS, and these help explain juvenile crime characteristics. For example, victims reported that in 18 percent of all violent crimes the offenders were thought to be under 18 years of age (Rand and Robinson 2011, Table 39). Most of these victims of juvenile offenders

Figure 3.3 Serious and Violent Incidents Committed by Juveniles, 1973–2007

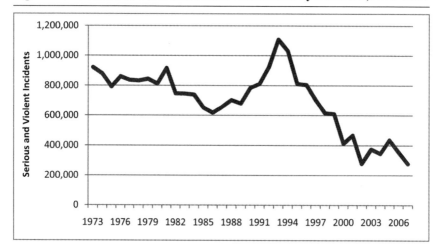

were themselves adolescents. For victims of violent crimes aged 12 to 19, for example, juveniles accounted for 58.5 percent of offenders, but this decreased to 14.4 percent for victims 65 years and older and 4.7 percent for victims aged 20 to 34 (Rand and Robinson 2011, Table 41). Offenses with multiple offenders show a similar pattern, and most individuals who were victims of groups of offenders were themselves young (aged 12 to 19). The exception to that generalization was robbery victims 65 years and older, who estimated that 62.8 percent of the offenders who victimized them were less than 18 years of age.

There are several limitations to accurately estimating the extent of juvenile offending using self-report surveys. Correctly categorizing the age of one's assailant, for example, is a difficult task when one is being victimized, and given the stress that those encounters produce it is possible that some victims do not correctly classify an offender's age. Some scholars are also critical of self-report methods as the accuracy of responses is sometimes questionable. Others are critical of the samples that are used. These include only persons above 12 years of age and those who have residences and phones—which excludes groups that might be prone to higher levels of victimization, such as young adults who do not have landline phones or the homeless. Last, the survey itself has been criticized for failing to track white-collar crimes such as identity theft. Despite these limitations the NCVS further confirms the accuracy of the FBI reports.

While the NCVS does not collect homicide information, juveniles' involvement in that offense is of special interest. Not only is it the most serious crime but cases involving juveniles are often overreported or sensationalized in the media, which contributes to the public's uneasiness and fear (Krisberg, Hartney, Wolf, and Silva 2009; Soler 2001). Juvenile offenders are sometimes vilified in the media: Titus (2005, 124) noted that the two preteen offenders in the murder of James Bulger, an English toddler, were labeled as "animals, beasts, freaks of nature, savages, and monsters." These sentiments are common in the United States, despite the fact that juvenile involvement in homicide has decreased, as illustrated in Figure 3.4.

Figure 3.4 shows the arrest rates for homicide from 1960 to 2009 for persons 17 years of age and younger. This chart shows that the trend is very similar to the one for all Part I violent crimes, but there was a more pronounced increase after 1987, peaking in 1993, and then dropping sharply after that time. Consistent with arrests for all Part I offenses and Part I violent offenses reported above, arrest rates for juvenile homicide had dropped to 1960s levels by 2002. In terms of the actual numbers of homicide arrests, there were almost 3,800 arrests at the peak of the

Figure 3.4 Youth Homicide Arrests, 1960–2009

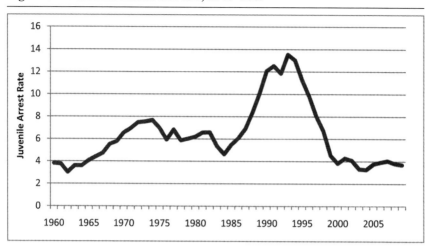

violence epidemic in 1993 (Snyder 2000), but this had decreased by almost two-thirds, to 1,280 homicide arrests, in 2008 (Puzzanchera 2009).

A review of the 2009 FBI arrest data reported in the UCR shows that there were 923 juvenile homicide arrests (FBI 2010, Expanded Homicide Table 3). Of that total, most (92.1%) were male, and black youths were overrepresented in these arrests (58.4%) compared to their proportion of the national population, which was approximately 16.4 percent of all persons aged 10 to 17 years in 2009 (Puzzancherea, Sladky, and Kang 2010). Homicide also tends to involve older youths, and of the 923 juvenile arrestees in 2009, slightly over one-half (51.6%) were under the age of 17 years, while 17-year-olds alone accounted for the remaining murders. The FBI (2010, Table 5) data also show that juvenile offenders were almost twice as likely to be arrested for killing persons older than themselves. In the 355 incidents where there was a single victim and offender, 107 of the victims were juveniles, while 246 victims were over the age of 18 (the ages of two victims were unknown).

One of the key findings that emerged from these analyses was that the proportion of the murders committed by racial groups differed significantly: from 1993 to 2001 the arrest rate of white youths dropped from 2.8 arrests per 100,000 residents to 1.1 (FBI 2003, 59). For minority youths the rate dropped from 19.7 to 4.9 arrests per 100,000 residents during the same time (FBI 2003, 59). Thus, the most recent arrest data show that males, older juveniles, and minority youths were more likely to be arrested for their involvement in homicide.

Fox and Swatt (2008, 1) examined juvenile murder trends and noted that while the overall national rate was stable, the number of black youths arrested for homicide increased by 43 percent from 2002 to 2007. An examination of juvenile court data shows similar results to the homicide arrest statistics reported above, and the Office of Juvenile Justice and Delinquency Prevention (2000, 4) summarized their findings as follows:

Between 1980 and 1997, the large majority (93%) of known juvenile homicide offenders were male. More than half (56%) were black. Of the known juvenile homicide offenders 42% were age 17, 29% were age 16, and 17% were age 15; 88% of homicide offenders were age 15 or older.

In addition to the demographic characteristics of these populations it is useful to more closely examine whether other factors are associated with juvenile homicides.

It is important to examine the underlying patterns of violence within the national trends. A number of scholars, for instance, have argued that much of the youth violence that started in the 1980s was gang-related. Curry, Maxson, and Howell (2001) reported that an inordinate number of youth gang homicides in the 1990s occurred in large cities such as Los Angeles or Chicago and that these cities influence the entire nation's homicide rates. In a review of the data from the National Youth Gang Survey, Egley (2005, 2) reported that, "These findings provide evidence that, in large part, gangs, gang members, and gang-related homicides are predominately concentrated in larger cities" (see also Egley and Howell 2011). While some scholars point to the relationships between youth gangs, guns, and drugs as driving gang-related murders, Howell (2007, 42) noted that "youth gang-related violence mainly emanates from inter-gang rivalries, turf protection and expansion, and interpersonal disputes or beefs."

An examination of current homicide statistics confirms Howell's (2007) comments as well as the observations made by Curry and his colleagues (2001), who reported that gang activities resulted in an elevated homicide rate. The FBI (2010, Expanded Homicide Table 10) reported that 715 homicides in 2009 were juvenile gang killings. In terms of the actual characteristics of these crimes, 680 offenders were male, and firearms were used in 665 of these offenses. Thus, gang violence plays a significant role in the overall juvenile murder rate.[1]

Our review of juvenile crime trends for the past half century shows that a rapid increase occurred in the late 1980s, which was followed by a drop in arrests of almost two-thirds and a plateau that exists today. Yet we present public opinion information in Chapter 6 that shows that the public is still fearful of juvenile crime and thinks that crime has been increasing (Krisberg et al. 2009). Creating rational juvenile justice policies in an environment of public fear is difficult, especially when one considers that most of those fears are unfounded: one's likelihood of victimization from juveniles generally decreases as one ages (an exception to this generalization is the robbery of persons 65 years and older) and diminishes significantly if one is not involved in a gang or associating with other offenders.

While there are some limitations to the data that are collected by federal agencies and are reported in this chapter, they provide us with a fairly accurate representation of juvenile crime. These findings suggest that we have much to be optimistic about when it comes to youthful offenders. The second part of the chapter questions whether we can share that optimism in the manner in which the system handles delinquents. Earlier we speculated that if transfers were used in a rational manner, they would be closely related with crime rates, and that we should expect that if serious and violent juvenile crimes increase, so should the use of transfers.

TRANSFERS TO ADULT COURTS

The following pages report the outcomes of our analyses of juvenile court statistics published by the OJJDP. According to Puzzanchera, Adams, and Sickmund (2010, ix), juvenile court data have been collected since the late 1920s, although only since 1985 has it become more reliable due to more uniform methods of data collection, a greater number of agencies participating, and the use of computers to organize these data. Sickmund, Sladky, and Kang (2011) reported that the 2008 juvenile court statistics were estimates based on information received from over 2,200 courts from 41 states (representing 82 percent of the national juvenile population).

As the OJJDP data used in this chapter have been collected and reported for decades, they enable us to examine the use of transfers and identify the key trends. In addition to reporting the total numbers of juveniles waived to adult courts, the OJJDP reports on the youths' demographic characteristics as well as the nature of the offense that triggered the transfer (e.g., whether the crime was a person (violent), property, drug, or public order offense). We are somewhat constrained in our analyses, however, by the things that we do not know about these offenders, including the actual offense that led to their court referral. A violent offense, for example, could be a homicide, robbery, rape or sexual assault, kidnapping, or aggravated or simple assault. We are further limited by the fact that we do not know these youths' prior criminal history, which is a good predictor of sentencing outcomes. Generally speaking, those with a greater number of contacts with the juvenile courts should be waived to criminal court at a higher rate, but the research on this proposition has produced mixed results (Campaign for Youth Justice 2011; Jordan and Myers 2011). Moreover, these are national-level data, and we do not know the variations among the states or which states have the most punitive justice practices. One of the biggest limitations, however, is that the OJJDP statistics do not report the outcomes of these cases after their transfer to adult courts. We address that challenge in our examination of transfer outcomes in Chapter 7.

A number of organizations have suggested that anywhere from 200,000 to 250,000 youths are prosecuted in adult courts each year (Campaign for Youth Justice 2011; Council of Juvenile Correctional Administrators 2009). It is possible that most of these juveniles resided in states where they become legally defined adults upon their 16th birthdays (New York and North Carolina) or at age 17 in 10 states.[2] Furthermore, as noted in Chapter 1, some youths are statutorily excluded from the juvenile court, meaning that if they commit serious or violent crimes, such as homicide, they automatically appear in adult courts. Last, prosecutors in 15 jurisdictions can directly file cases in adult courts and thus circumvent the juvenile courts entirely. We do not have any national-level measures of the numbers of youths in the three categories listed above, but we do have estimates of the numbers of youths transferred by juvenile courts from 1985 to 2008, as reported by the OJJDP (Sickmund, Sladky, and Kang 2011). Unless otherwise noted, all of the analyses reported below use those data.

Transfers by Offense Seriousness

Transfers are a relatively rare event. In 2008, an estimated 1.653 million cases were referred to juvenile courts, and of that number, 8,898 were transferred to adult courts, representing about 0.5 percent of all cases. From 1985 to 2008 there were 228,771 transfers of youths to adult courts. The OJJDP data report four broad offense categories that led to waiver: person (violent), property, drugs, and public order. During the 24-year era for which we have data, 138,434 youths (60.5%) were transferred to adult courts for their involvement in nonviolent offenses, and juveniles who committed violent offenses accounted for only 90,337 (39.5%) transfers. Most of the nonviolent delinquents had committed property crimes (88,482) followed by drug (29,725) and public order offenses (20,227). As noted earlier, one possible explanation for a lower volume of transfers for violent offenders is that these juveniles might bypass the juvenile court entirely through legislative exclusion or if charged by the prosecutor as an adult. One limitation of these data is that these categories are very broad, and a violent offense could range from a simple assault to a homicide, while a drug offense could range from possession to trafficking. As a result, it is difficult to make sweeping generalizations about transfers based on these data. Figure 3.5 illustrates the offenses that precipitated the transfer.

In order to see if the proportion of juveniles waived due to a violent offense has changed over time, we examined their involvement from 1985 to 1989 and compared this with the percentage of youths transferred from 2004 to 2008. We found that the proportion of transferred youths with a violent offense increased from 30.6 percent during 1985 to 1989 to 47.5 percent from 2004 to 2008 (in 2008 the proportion of violent juveniles was 49.8%). This finding suggests that transfers may be used more rationally today than in the past by placing the most dangerous youthful offenders in adult systems. Earlier we speculated that if the use of transfers was rational, they should be related to crime seriousness. In order to examine this proposition more carefully, we compared juvenile homicide arrest rates, cases of homicide handled by juvenile courts, and the use of transfers from 1985 to 2008; the results are shown in Figure 3.6.

The national transfer trend closely mirrors the juvenile arrest rates for homicide (which was multiplied by 500 to better illustrate the relationship in the figure) and juvenile court homicide cases. These factors were all

Figure 3.5 Major Offense Leading to Transfer, 1985–2008

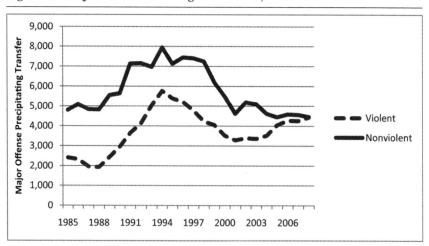

Figure 3.6 Juvenile Homicide Arrests and Transfers, 1985–2007

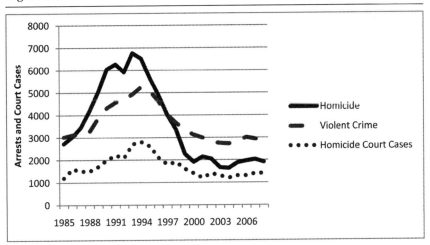

strongly interrelated: when arrests for violent crime increased, so did the number of juvenile court homicide cases, as well as transfers.[3] In Chapter 6 we examine the relationships between public opinion and the use of tough-on-crime strategies, including transfers to adult courts, and we find that there is a strong relationship between the public's perceptions of a juvenile crime problem and desire for more severe sanctions for youths. The results presented above suggest that when youth involvement in violent crime is high, there will be a greater use of transfers, and this, in turn, may also contribute to a higher number of juveniles transferred for nonviolent offenses by creating a climate of fear of all youthful offenders.

Transfers by Gender

A closer look at the data reveals that male offenders as well as older and minority youths are overrepresented in transfers. First, males represented 92.6 percent of the 228,771 juveniles transferred between 1985 and 2008. This result is not surprising given their higher involvement in crime. FBI (2010, Tables 39–40) arrest data from 2009, for example, showed that there were slightly more than a million arrests of males less than 18 years of age while females had less than half that number. Furthermore, males had a much higher involvement in violent crime, with 55,690 arrests for homicide, robbery, rape, and aggravated assaults, whereas 12,384 females were arrested for the same offenses (FBI 2010, Tables 39–40).

Very little has been written about young women transferred to adult courts. One reason why this might be the case is that their numbers are relatively low. Over the entire 24-year era for which we have data, a total of 16,879 females were transferred—approximately 700 per year—although the annual number has been higher in recent years. The offenses that resulted in a transfer for almost two-thirds (64.9%) of these females were nonviolent. Of these nonviolent offenders, most had committed property crimes (38.8%), followed by drug (13.3%) and public order offenses (12.8%). In terms of the racial composition of these female delinquents, over two-thirds (68.2%) were white, which was a greater proportion than the white males who were transferred (56.3%).

Like their male counterparts, most of the transferred females were older, and those 16 years and over accounted for 83.1 percent of the total. Fourteen- and 15-year-olds represented 13.2 percent of the total number of females transferred. There were, however, 620 girls who were 13 years of age or younger who were transferred to adult courts between 1985 and 2008.

The number of females transferred to adult courts has increased significantly since the statistics were first reported in 1985. In the five years from 1985 to 1989, for instance, a total of 1,913 females were transferred to adult courts, but this number more than doubled to 4,320 in the five-year period from 2004 to 2008. We speculate that some of this increase may have been due to their involvement in violent offenses, but the proportion of violent female offenders increased from 26.6 to 40.6 percent. Further examination of the data reveals that the number of females transferred for drug and public order offenses almost tripled. Drug offenses led to the transfers of 214 females in the five years from 1985 to 1989, and this increased to 585 females from 2004 to 2008, while the number of females waived for public order offenses grew from 219 to 612 juveniles in the same time period. A slightly higher proportion of females than males were transferred for their involvement in drug and public order offenses. In 2008, for example, these offenses led to the transfer of 24.1 percent of females and 21.1 percent of males.

Transfers by Age

Figure 3.7 shows the distribution of transfers by age. Almost 9 of 10 youths transferred between 1985 and 2008 were 16 years or older (16-year-olds represented 27.4 percent of the youths transferred, while those 17 years and older accounted for 58.6%). Of the remaining juveniles, 9.4 percent were 15 years old, 3.1 percent were 14 years old, and the remaining 3,610 youths (representing 1.6% of the total) were 13 years of age or younger. Of special interest are the 1,529 youths who were 12 years of age or younger at the time of their transfers.

Figure 3.7 Juveniles Transferred by Age, 1985–2007

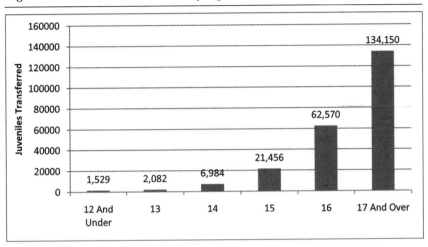

Transferring preteens to adult courts is a controversial subject. Deitch, Barstow, Lukens, and Reyna (2009) suggested that only the "worst of the worst" juvenile offenders should be transferred and questioned whether children 12 and younger should ever be sent to adult courts. Placing these children in adult courts and facilities puts them at very high risk of victimization, self-harm, and psychological injuries as well as the negative socialization from adult offenders (Campaign for Youth Justice 2007; Leigey et al. 2009). Given these risks, we question whether transfers for these children are a sound juvenile justice practice.

Of the 1,529 preteens who were transferred between 1985 and 2008, only 622 (40.7%) had been transferred for a violent offense, while 651 (42.6%) had committed a property offense, 36 (2.4%) had been charged with a drug offense, and the remaining 219 (14.3%) had committed public order offenses. In terms of these preteens' demographic characteristics, 84.3 percent were males, and from 1985 to 2008 most of the 1,529 preteens were white (71.6%), followed by blacks (25%), American Indians (3.3%), and Asian/Native Hawaiian/Pacific Islanders (hereafter: Asians), who accounted for less than 1 percent.

Our analyses showed that the number of preteens who were transferred has increased in recent years. The proportion of these children who were charged with a violent offense, however, has decreased. In the five years between 1985 and 1989, for instance, a total of 87 youths 12 years and younger were transferred, but this increased to 249 in the five years from 2004 and 2008. The involvement of these preteens in violent offenses remained fairly stable during this time, from 43.1 percent of the total number transferred from 1985 to 1989 to 44.4 percent of those transferred from 2004 to 2008. Of these youths, only 19.5 percent had been detained prior to their transfer, suggesting that they did not pose much of a risk to the community.

We also examined the characteristics of 13- through 15-year-olds and found a similar pattern of increasing transfers. Using the same five-year time periods (1985 to 1989 and 2004 to 2008), we found that the number of 13- to 15-year-olds had almost doubled, from 3,013 to 5,978. Unlike their younger counterparts, however, a higher proportion (65.1%) of these youngsters had been referred to the court for committing a violent offense from 2004 to 2008. Between 1985 and 1989, by contrast, less than one-half (44.9%) of these 13- to 15-year-olds had been transferred for a violent offense.

The practice of transferring older juveniles to adult courts seems to be rational, especially when a youth is close to the juvenile court's maximum age jurisdiction. If jurisdiction ends at 18 years, as it did in seven states at the end of the 2008 legislative session, the judge may not feel that 17-year-old offenders can rehabilitate themselves (or be held fully accountable for their actions) in the time before they have to be released from custody.[4] Consequently, a transfer to the adult system may be seen as an attractive alternative to a short-term juvenile disposition.

While most youths transferred to adult courts from 1985 to 2008 were nonviolent offenders, there could have been aggravating factors that contributed to the judge's decision to transfer. Many of them could have been repeat offenders, and some may have been involved in prior acts of violence or were on probation at the time of the offense. In addition, some of these nonviolent offenders may have been involved in gangs or acted as the leader or instigator in a crime with multiple offenders. These explanations, however, are speculative, and in the absence of more detailed information we will never know the reasons behind the transfers of these nonviolent youths.

Detention

One indicator that suggests the potential for dangerousness is detaining youths prior to their court appearances. In most jurisdictions detention facilities are used to hold youths on a short-term basis, much like an adult jail. Typically, youths are detained because they present a risk to the community or are thought to be at risk of failing to appear in court (Holman and Ziedenberg 2009). For the 24-year era for which we have data, our analyses showed that about one-half of the juveniles who were transferred

(49.9%) had been detained. Of the juveniles who had been detained, less than one-half (47.9%) had been charged with a violent crime, while the remainder were youths with property (32.7%), drug (12.3%), and public order (7%) offenses.

Examination of the characteristics of juveniles detained from 1985 to 1989 compared with those detained from 2004 to 2008 shows some significant changes. While the actual numbers of youths placed in detention were similar for the two eras, the proportion of detained youths who had been involved in violent acts rose from 35.6 percent to 60.4 percent, and in 2008 the total was 65.2 percent. While almost one-half (47.3%) of all detainees from 1985 to 1989 had been charged with a property crime, this had decreased to 22.6 percent in the 2004-to-2008 time period. The proportions of youths detained for public order and drug offenses, by contrast, were relatively stable during these two time frames.

We also examined the racial characteristics of youths who were detained and found that more nonwhites had been detained than their white counterparts. Of the 114,079 juveniles who were detained, 57,687 (50.6%) were minority youths. Further analyses revealed, however, that white detainees had the lowest involvement in violent offenses (42.4%) compared with black (53.3%), American Indian (46.6%), and Asian youths (66.2%).

Transfers by Race

In Chapter 1 we addressed the issue of disproportionate minority contact (DMC) and the fact that minority youths are overrepresented in the juvenile justice system. Of all the youths who were transferred from 1985 to 2008, 57.2 percent were white, followed by blacks (39.8%), American Indians (2.2%), and Asians (0.8%). In terms of their numbers in the national population, however, blacks 10 to 17 years old represented slightly more than 5.4 million persons, while there were over 25.5 million whites and Latinos of the same age group in 2008 (Puzzanchera, Sladky, and Kang 2010). Thus, while the white and Latino youths outnumbered black youths by more than four-to-one in the national population, the overall number of blacks transferred to adult courts was close to the number of whites transferred between 1985 and 2008 (91,123 and 130,876, respectively).

Our examination of the transfer trends revealed that the overall percentage of minority youths who were transferred had decreased somewhat. In the five-year period from 1985 to 1989, for example, minority youths (blacks, American Indians, and Asians) represented 43.7 percent of all

Figure 3.8 Transfers by Race, 1985–2008

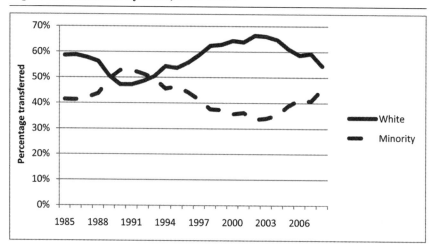

juveniles transferred. In the five years from 2004 to 2008, by contrast, minority youths accounted for 40.4 percent of all transferred youths—suggesting that juvenile justice officials are making some progress in addressing DMC. In terms of transfers by race, Figure 3.8 shows the transfer trends for minority and white youths and reveals that the proportions had fluctuated somewhat. What is not shown in Figure 3.8 is the growth in the numbers of American Indian and Asian youths who were transferred. By comparing the first five years of the series (1985–1989) to the last five years of the series (2004–2008), we found that both of these populations grew by over three-quarters (from 832 to 1,493).

In order to better understand the disparity in the use of transfers, we examined the offense that triggered the transfer. We speculated that since the arrest rate for black juveniles in violent crimes was higher, that could account for the greater use of transfers. These analyses revealed the following involvement in violent offenses: whites (33.8%), blacks (47.5%), American Indians (36.4%), and Asians (58%). These findings suggest that a higher involvement in violent crimes might be a contributing factor that explains some of the racial disparities in juvenile transfers.

We also scrutinized the ages at which minority youths were transferred. This analysis revealed that blacks had a greater number of transfers of 13- to 15-year-olds compared to whites (15,511 and 14,197 youths respectively). While the size of the 16-year-old white and black populations were similar (31,436 and 29,591 youths respectively), there were fewer transfers of older black youths. From 1985 to 2008, for example, 45,639 black youths who were 17 years and older were transferred, compared to 84,148 white juveniles. This finding suggests that blacks are more likely to leave the juvenile justice system at a younger age than their white counterparts.

Altogether, our analyses of youths transferred between 1985 and 2008 have raised additional questions about the use of transfers. Our findings suggest that transfers to adult court may be used in a manner that was inconsistent with the aims of the juvenile courts' founders—as we are not sending the "worst of the worst" but instead preteens as well as a high number of property, public order, and drug offenders. Yet, as we lack a full accounting of the factors that led to transfers, we cannot make any definitive assessments about the appropriateness of transfer decisions, but we do speculate, in the following pages, on whether transfers are used in a rational manner.

SUMMARY

In this chapter we examined two key issues: the extent of serious juvenile crime and the characteristics of youths transferred to adult courts. While we have a good understanding of youth crime, our knowledge about the factors that lead to transfers to adult courts remains incomplete. As a result, a lot of our interpretations are speculative. What we do know, however, is that while transfers that originate in juvenile courts are a relatively rare event, the cumulative number of young persons affected by these practices has resulted in a large number of individuals whose lives have been significantly impacted, as convictions in criminal courts can have lifelong consequences (Colgate Love 2011; Mauer and Chesney-Lind 2003).

We examined the characteristics of almost one-quarter of a million juveniles transferred to adult courts from 1985 to 2008 in order to evaluate whether transfers were being used in a rational manner. Our analyses produced a number of noteworthy findings. We found that the annual number of transfers is highly related to incidents of serious and violent juvenile crime, suggesting that they are used appropriately. But, when we examined the national trends more closely, the findings suggest that transfers may not always be used in a suitable manner, and our interpretations of these outcomes are summarized in the following paragraphs.

First, transfers have been labeled as a mechanism to remove the most serious cases from the juvenile court. After reviewing the major offense that led to the waiver for the entire 24-year era from 1985 to 2008, we found that only 39.5 percent of youths were transferred after committing violent offenses. Upon closer examination, however, our analyses revealed that transfers of violent offenders have increased over time, and between 2004 and 2008 a violent offense led to almost one-half (47.5%) of transfers. This signifies that transfers are now being used to handle more serious cases, but most youths are still being transferred for property, drug, and public order offenses—suggesting that waivers have not been reserved for the most serious offenders.

In Chapter 1 we observed that DMC was an entrenched problem in justice systems. Our initial analyses showed that minority juveniles were waived to adult criminal courts at a rate that was disproportionate to their representation in the juvenile population. While black youths aged 10 to 17 years represented 16.5 percent of the juvenile population, they accounted for 41.9 percent of the juveniles who were transferred in 2008. One plausible explanation for this disparity is the higher arrest rates for black youths for violent crimes (Fox and Swatt 2008; Snyder and Sickmund 2006). In 2008, for example, 60.2 percent of all black youths were transferred on the basis of a violent offense, compared with 42.3 percent of white juveniles. This suggests that transfers are being used appropriately, especially given that the fact that the number of black juveniles who were transferred as a result of drug or public order offenses has decreased substantially over time. Comparatively little attention, however, has been paid to American Indian and Asian youths who are transferred, and this is a limitation in the juvenile justice literature, as the number of these youths who were transferred has increased by over 75 percent when the five year period of 1985 to 1989 is compared to 2004 to 2008.

Because the upper limits of juvenile court jurisdiction end before age 21 in most states, the transfer of older youths seems to be a rational practice. Juvenile court judges, for example, might perceive that the limited time available for 17-year-olds to rehabilitate themselves might make it preferable to send them to adult court. Our review of the data showed that the overwhelming majority of offenders were 16 or 17 years old when transferred. But we also found that a growing proportion of juveniles who were transferred were preteens or less than 15 years old. In fact, these numbers almost doubled, while the offenses that triggered the transfers of these youngsters were primarily nonviolent.

The percentage of females transferred to adult courts has also increased over time. Our analyses revealed that most of this increase was triggered by their involvement in drug and public order offenses, and the number of females transferred for these offenses almost tripled from the first (1985–1989) to the second time frame (2004–2008). Inconsistent with the findings for males, there was a smaller proportion of black females transferred to adult courts. In 2008, for instance, blacks represented about one-quarter (25.8%) of the female juveniles, while black males accounted for 43.5 percent of the transfers. There has been increasing interest in females' offending and considerable speculation about the reasons for higher arrest levels. Some scholars, such as Barry Feld (2009) as well as Meda Chesney-Lind and Randall Shelden (2003) have argued that females' behaviors have been criminalized in order for parents to exert more control over them.

Altogether, our assessments on whether transfers are used in a rational manner are tempered by the fact that our knowledge of the factors that contribute to the transfer decision is incomplete. Our analyses have, however, revealed some troubling practices. First, while the proportion of nonviolent offenders who are transferred has decreased over time, many youths are waived to adult courts as a result of property, drug, or public order offenses—which suggests that these are not the most serious cases before the court. Second, transferring preteens to adult courts seems to be a very inappropriate use of the sanction, given the length of time these children have to work toward their rehabilitation. These transfers are especially disconcerting given that most of these youngsters were nonviolent offenders. Third, the proportion of females transferred to adult courts for public order and drug offenses almost tripled between the periods 1985 to 1989 and 2004 to 2008. Again, we question whether these youths pose a significant risk to public safety, especially since most of them were not detained prior to their transfers.

NOTES

1. Attempting to reduce youth gang homicides, however, is a complex challenge, as aggressive law enforcement approaches to gang suppression can exacerbate tensions between minority populations and the police. Duran (2009, 143) observed that "equating gangs as synonymous with crime allows for differential policing that ... is over-inclusive and embedded with practices that create opportunities for abuse of authority."

2. Szymanski (2008b) observed that the juvenile court jurisdiction extended to age 17 years in GA, IL, LA, MA, MI, MO, NH, SC, TX and WI at the end of the 2008 legislative session.

3. In order to examine this relationship more closely, we conducted a bivariate correlation between the number of transfers, the rates of juvenile arrests for violent crimes (homicide, rape, and aggravated assault), juvenile homicides, and juvenile homicide court cases. We found that the relationship between annual transfers and all violent crime arrests

was r = .803; transfers and murders was r = .586; and transfers and juvenile homicide court cases was r = .815. These are all very strong relationships.

4. According to Szymanski (2008b) the upper limit for juvenile court jurisdiction in the 2008 legislative session was age 18 in seven states (AK, IO, KY, NE, OK, RI, TN); age 19 in two states (MS, ND), age 20 in 32 states and the District of Columbia (AL, AZ, AR, CT, DE, DC, GA, ID, IL, IN, LA, ME, MD, MA, MI, MN, MO, NV, NH, NM, NY, NC, OH, PA, SC, SD, TX, UT, VA, VT—effective January 2009—WA, WV, WY), age 21 in FL, age 22 in KS, and age 24 in three states (CA, MT, WI). In four states (CO, HI, NJ, OR) the court's jurisdiction ends with the full term of the dispositional order. There have been some recent legislative changes that have increased the limits of juvenile court juris-diction in a number of states, including CT, IL, and MS (Campaign for Youth Justice 2011).

FOUR

Transfers and Public Policy

INTRODUCTION

Public opinion polls about the transfer of juvenile offenders to adult criminal courts have generally produced mixed findings. In some polls the public supports punitive sanctions for juveniles while in others they express interest in rehabilitating these offenders in the youth justice system (Steinberg and Piquero 2010). Such findings reinforce our earlier observations that the public has mixed feelings toward youthful offenders and what constitutes just and fair responses to juvenile crime. The problem is that academics, legislators, directors of funding agencies, and practitioners often have very different ideas about the terms *just* and *fair*, and this returns us to the debate about rehabilitating youths versus holding them accountable, especially when they have committed serious offenses. Most jurisdictions have made it easier to punish juveniles, and this is demonstrated by the number of laws aimed at juvenile offenders and the punitive focus of many of these laws that have been enacted over the past 30 years (Merlo and Benekos 2010). There has been comparatively less attention paid to investing in services that provide more rehabilitative opportunities for at-risk or delinquent youths, despite the fact that cost-benefit analyses have demonstrated that some interventions are very effective in reducing the risk that these youngsters pose (Drake 2007; 2010).

A core element of a get-tough-on-youth agenda is the removal of juveniles who have committed serious offenses from the juvenile court. These changes did not occur overnight but were a result of a long-term process where all states increased the severity of sanctions for juvenile offenders

(Merlo and Benekos 2010). In order to better understand these philosophical and policy changes, this chapter highlights the major pieces of national-level juvenile justice legislation and state policy initiatives from the past three decades. One theme explored in both Chapters 1 and 2 is that the boundaries of juvenile justice are shifting and that, in some ways, minor offenders (e.g., those involved in status offenses) as well as the more serious offenders are being removed from the traditional juvenile courts. This leaves these courts to deal with regular delinquent youths who have been involved in public order offenses, property offenses, and minor violent offenses such as simple assaults. While acknowledging that juvenile courts still routinely deal with thousands of cases of serious youth violence, including homicide, the core function of these courts seems to have shifted to the processing of "middle range" offenders.

One of the key points concerning the juvenile justice system's evolution is the way that juvenile offenders, especially status offenders, have been viewed. Historically, these youngsters represented a significant part of the institutional corrections population. Schwartz (1989, 16) estimated that "more than 40 percent of all youth confined in adult jails, juvenile detention centers, youth prisons, and training schools were status offenders and, to a lesser extent, dependent and neglected children." There were significant risks of placing status offenders in these facilities, including the likelihood of self-harm, suicide, or victimization from other youths. Moreover, status offenders were commonly mixed with delinquent youths—some of whom had committed serious offenses, were gang-involved, or were persistent offenders—and there is a risk that placing impressionable youngsters with their older and more sophisticated counterparts will have a negative impact on them (DeLisi, Hochstetler, Jones-Johnson, Caudill, and Marquart 2011). Status offenders are now less commonly encountered in juvenile detention facilities or correctional facilities. One reason for this change is that in order to receive federal funding for juvenile justice programs states are limited in their ability to place status offenders in secure facilities.

While status offenders still come to the attention of juvenile justice systems, they are commonly referred to as persons in need of supervision (PINS) or children in need of supervision (CHINS). In other words, these youths are seen as needing guidance and support to help them avoid delinquency in the future. While it could be argued that these youths are at some risk of delinquency, their treatment has now been relegated to the periphery of the juvenile justice system in most jurisdictions.

As status offenders are not considered delinquent or in jeopardy of incarceration, they are not afforded constitutional due process protections and thus are cared for using an approach based on the *parens patriae* philosophy. As a result, Kim (2010, 867) argued that these offenders' treatment is unequal and unpredictable, and that there are two possible solutions: extend the rights and protections to status offenders that are consistent with delinquent youths, or remove them from the juvenile court's jurisdiction entirely. It is unlikely that either of these recommendations will come about as both solutions threaten the status quo and represent a significant financial burden to the juvenile justice system (e.g., in providing state-funded counsel for status offenders or establishing a bureaucracy to treat status offenders).

There has also been a 30-year movement to remove the more serious offenders from the juvenile court's jurisdiction. Indicators of this punitive orientation include the increasing numbers and types of offenders transferred from juvenile to adult criminal courts, the direct filing of their cases in adult courts, and the blended sentences that keep the juvenile in the juvenile justice system but in jeopardy of adult sentences if they reoffend. There is some evidence that this punitive orientation has softened in recent years. Merlo and Benekos (2010, 21) attributed these changes to decreased levels of youth violence, the growing success of juvenile justice interventions, recognition of the biological causes of adolescent immaturity, and the impact of state budget crises that make it difficult to sustain punitive justice practices.

This chapter examines changes in federal- and state-level policies that resulted in the changing boundaries of juvenile justice. While the federal government generally had a passive role in juvenile justice until the mid-1970s, state-level legislation removed multitudes of youths from the juvenile justice system, which enabled the courts to focus their attention on middle range offenders. The following pages highlight the key legislative trends at both the federal and state levels of government as well as describe the current philosophies and operations of state juvenile justice systems and how these factors might influence the treatment of delinquent youths.

FEDERAL JUVENILE JUSTICE LEGISLATION

While the first juvenile courts emerged at the turn of the twentieth century, the federal government took a hands-off approach to the operations of these systems—meaning that it was reluctant to intervene in these state-level activities. One fledgling step toward federal government involvement in delinquency prevention was the creation of the Children's Bureau in 1912, which reported on youth-related issues, including juvenile court operations (OJJDP 2011). The federal Interdepartmental Committee on Children and Youth followed in 1948, and this organization was formed to facilitate more effective interrelationships between agencies that were involved with issues pertaining to youngsters. Neither the Children's Bureau nor the Interdepartmental Committee, however, played an active role in the delivery of delinquency prevention programs.

After World War II, federal politicians became increasingly interested in the causes of delinquency and reducing juvenile crime. One outcome of this interest was a series of Senate hearings by the Special Subcommittee on Juvenile Delinquency that were initiated in 1953 and continued until 1971. While much of the focus of these hearings was related to factors typically associated with the causes of delinquency, such as poor socialization, poverty, and gang involvement, the senators were particularly interested in how cultural values and moral decay contributed to delinquency. One of the issues related to the Senate's study of cultural values was the 1954 examination of comic books as a source of delinquency; an Internet search will reveal that these hearings remain a very popular area of interest today.

Ohlin (1983, 463–67) described the federal government's growing involvement in delinquency with the introduction of the 1961 Juvenile Delinquency and Youth Offenses Control Act and the 1967 Presidential Crime Commission. The 1961 legislation gave the federal government a toehold in delinquency prevention by providing states with leadership and financial support to prevent and respond to juvenile crime. Much of this assistance was related to disseminating information about federally sponsored demonstration projects to reduce delinquency based on employment, strengthening family relationships, and accessing social, educational, and recreational services (Ohlin 1983).

The federal juvenile justice legislation enacted in 1974 can be traced to the President's Commission on Law Enforcement and the Administration of Justice (1967). The Commission's influential report, *The Challenge of Crime in a Free Society*, clearly expressed the nation's concern with crime generally, and especially with delinquency. The Commission's (1967, 55) report noted, for example, that "America's best hope for reducing crime is to reduce juvenile delinquency and youth crime." A Task Force on Juvenile Delinquency was created as a result of the work of the President's Commission, and it issued a 1967 report entitled *Juvenile Delinquency and Youth Crime*. The report focused on delinquency prevention and the relationships youths have with their families and schools, as well as the impact of economic conditions on juvenile crime. Reforms based on these findings were aimed at making juvenile justice less stigmatizing and punitive. However, the policy goals were painted in very broad strokes and lacked specific details on how they would be achieved.

The legislation that came from the Commission's work was primarily aimed at adult crime reduction. The Omnibus Crime Control and Safe Streets Act of 1968 initiated the "war on crime," but most of the "enemies" were adult criminals. Ohlin (1983, 465) observed that the following six youth-related priorities were identified by the Commission:

(1) decriminalization of status offenses, (2) diversion of youth from court procedures into public and private treatment programs, (3) extending due process rights to juveniles (in anticipation of the *Gault* decision that guaranteed those rights), (4) deinstitutionalization (use of group homes or non-residential treatment facilities rather than large training schools), (5) diversification of services, and (6) decentralization of control.

Federal legislation aimed at delinquency prevention would be based on these priorities, although it would take another six years before the Juvenile Justice and Delinquency Prevention Act (JJDPA) would be enacted.

One of the reasons for the lengthy period before the introduction of federal delinquency prevention legislation was conservative opposition to the recommendations of the Commission. Ohlin (1983, 466–67) called this the "Law and Order Reaction," and conservatives supported mandatory sentencing, determinate sentences for juveniles, lowering the upper age of juvenile court jurisdiction, greater use of transfers to adult courts, and increasing the access to juvenile records. Ironically, by the 100th anniversary of the juvenile court's founding in 1999, all of those tough-on-crime initiatives were in place.

The conservative opposition to juvenile justice reform, however, was not successful in stopping the federal government from introducing as series of legislative initiatives (or reauthorizing previous legislation) that raised its involvement in juvenile justice. The OJJDP (2011, 1–2) noted that the Juvenile Delinquency and Youth Offenses Control Act was extended in 1964 and the 1968 Juvenile Delinquency Prevention and Control Act was introduced to develop a national approach to delinquency prevention, rehabilitation, training, and research. Although not a delinquency program *per se*, the 1968 Omnibus Crime Control and Safe Streets Act authorized funding for juvenile justice interventions. The Juvenile Delinquency Prevention and Control Act of 1968 was reauthorized in 1971, and in that same year the Omnibus Crime Control and Safe Streets Act was amended to include programs that responded to delinquency. The Juvenile Delinquency

Prevention Act was introduced in 1972 to enable the Department of Health, Education, and Welfare to fund delinquency prevention programs, and in 1973 the Omnibus Crime Control and Safe Streets Act was again amended to require states to include a delinquency component in their plans to improve the administration of justice. Altogether, these acts and amendments signaled the federal government's intention to become more involved in delinquency prevention, a process that culminated with the introduction of the JJDPA in 1974.

The JJDPA was the first major piece of juvenile justice legislation following the work of the President's Commission. This act has set the tone for federal efforts dealing with juvenile offenders (Krisberg 2005, 77–78). Soon after its passage, the National Advisory Committee on Criminal Justice Standards and Goals issued a report entitled *Juvenile Justice and Delinquency Prevention* (1976). Much like the President's Commission earlier, many of the National Advisory Committee's recommendations were aimed at making the juvenile justice system less punitive. Major policy initiatives included diversion, deinstitutionalization, and decriminalization (Snyder and Sickmund 2006).

Deinstitutionalization and Diversion

The enactment of the JJDPA led to the creation of the federally operated OJJDP, which is intended to support local and state organizations, both private and public, to prevent delinquency and improve the juvenile justice system. This support comes in the form of providing funds to the states for juvenile justice programs, collecting and disseminating juvenile justice statistics, acting as a clearinghouse for research, and providing financial and technical assistance in the development of pilot or demonstration projects. The OJJDP identified the four main goals of the JJDPA as the (1) deinstitutionalization of status offenders (DSO), (2) sight and sound separation (to separate juvenile from adult detainees if placed in an adult detention facility), (3) removal of juveniles from adult jails, and (4) confronting disproportionate minority confinement (which was later changed to disproportionate minority contact, or DMC). While DSO and sight and sound separation were in the original 1974 legislation, the removal of juveniles from adult jails and DMC came later (in 1980 and 1988 respectively).

In terms of DSO, federal officials attempted to reduce the stigmatization believed to accompany formal processing and adjudication, which is a key component of labeling theory. Labeling theorists proposed that reducing this stigmatization reduced the likelihood that the youths perceive themselves to be delinquent and adopt that identity (as well as the labels that others attach to someone who has committed an offense). One outcome of DSO was the removal from the juvenile justice system of large numbers of status and minor delinquent offenders (Mays 2003).

As the name implies, diversionary programs are intended to divert first-time minor offenders from the court, thus reducing the stigmatization that might occur when youths are brought before juvenile courts. Instead of a court appearance, most diversionary programs require youths to participate in some form of treatment (e.g., alcohol or family counseling) or provide some type of community service, such as picking up litter on a roadway. These diversionary programs are operated by a variety of different agencies, including local police departments, local or state-operated probation services, as well as nonprofit, religious, or charitable organizations.

While the numbers of status offenders who are placed in secure custody or an adult jail have decreased since the 1970s, Arthur and Waugh (2009) noted that the 1980 amendments to the JJDPA enabled courts to confine status offenders who violated court orders (VCO). For example, a truant is referred to the juvenile court where he or she receives a disposition that has school attendance as a probation condition. If the youngster does not attend school he or she has violated the probation conditions and could be placed in detention. As a result, it was not the status offense *per se* that led to the youth's placement but his or her violation of the court order.

According to the 2007 *Census of Juveniles in Residential Placements*, 3,412 juveniles were held on status offenses, although this total had decreased from 6,242 status offenders held in 1997 (Sickmund, Sladky, Kang, and Puzzanchera 2011b). Moreover, another 13,141 youths were incarcerated because of technical violations, and some of those were undoubtedly status offenders. Further analyses revealed that more than almost three-quarters (71.8%) of these status offenders had been in the facility three weeks or longer (Sickmund et al. 2011b). In terms of their demographic characteristics, in 2007 most of these status offenders were males (61.3%), whites (49.1%), and older (only 21.4% were 14 years of age or younger).

One statistic that is unknown, however, is how many status offenders were placed in group homes, boarding schools, wilderness programs, residential substance abuse treatment centers, privately operated boot camps, shelters, and assessment centers or psychiatric facilities. While some of these programs are government-operated, many are run by proprietary enterprises or faith-based organizations, and they offer a less restrictive and more therapeutic environment than traditional custodial placements. Given the large number of facilities that deliver these services, it is a fair estimate that tens of thousands pass through them every year, and many of them are status offenders.

Removing Juveniles from Adult Jails

The second main policy goal of the JJDPA was the sight and sound separation of juveniles from adult jail populations. This priority was based on the proposition that incarcerating adults and youths together places juveniles at risk of victimization as well as the exposure to procriminal or antisocial values (DeLisi et al. 2011). This problem has long been recognized, and Fishman (1923, 26), a federal jail inspector who worked at the turn of the twentieth century, wrote that:

> I visited the jail at Welch late at night, as I had but a comparatively short time to stay. The prisoners were all asleep. With a lantern the jailer took me down along the row of cells. In one cell into which he flashed his light I saw a prisoner of about forty-five years of age, whose face indicated that he had run the gamut of dissipation, actually occupying the same bunk or hammock with a boy who was not over fourteen years of age. What can one expect of prisoner possibilities when conditions such as this are allowed to exist?

While Fishman wrote about these problems almost 100 years ago, juveniles are still being detained in adult jails, usually facilities in rural counties, and separating them from adults is a considerable challenge for county sheriffs and jail administrators.

This leads us to the third legislative priority, the removal of juveniles from adult jails in most, if not all, circumstances. The results of this policy have been somewhat mixed. For instance, Minton (2011, 7) noted that in 2010 the one-day midyear number of jail inmates under the age of 18 years held for juvenile charges was 1,912, which is a very small proportion of the overall jail population (0.3%) but an increase from the 1,489 juveniles held at midyear 2000. By contrast, the 2010 one-day count of inmates under the age of 18 years held for adult charges was 5,647, which was fewer than the 6,126 held as adults in 2000 (Minton 2011). Thus, the JJDPA mandate of removing juveniles from adult jails presents a muddled picture, at best.

There are a number of possible reasons why juveniles are held in adult jails. Some of these young persons could be from New York and North Carolina where 16- and 17-year-olds are considered adults. In addition, juveniles whose cases are heard in adult court can be held in adult jails as they are considered legally defined adults regardless of their actual age. Szymanski

(2010b, 1) found that 48 states and the District of Columbia allowed the placement of juveniles who have been transferred to adult criminal courts in adult jails, and only two states (Kentucky and West Virginia) prohibited this practice. Last, many rural areas do not have juvenile detention facilities, and in the rare event that a juvenile is detained, the jail becomes the default option for holding these youths. Regardless of the cause, the jail removal initiative has been backed by the federal government's power. States are required to monitor the use of juvenile detention in adult jails and report this information to the OJJDP. Federal juvenile justice funding is tied to the degree to which juvenile detainees have been kept out of adult facilities, which is a powerful incentive for complying with the jail removal initiative.

Disproportionate Minority Contact

The last major policy issue is DMC, which was previously known as disproportionate minority confinement. As mentioned in Chapter 1, DMC is the overrepresentation of minority group members in the juvenile justice system. In order to receive federal juvenile justice funding each jurisdiction is expected to develop a strategy to minimize the number of youths of color entering the system. However, this goal has proven to be very difficult to achieve. Knoll and Sickmund (2010, 2) examined the 2007 delinquency statistics and noted that while black youths represented approximately 16 percent of the national population, they accounted for 33 percent of delinquency cases appearing before juvenile courts, and that:

The rate at which referred cases were petitioned for formal processing was 12% greater for black youth than for white youth. The rate at which petitioned cases were adjudicated was about 8% less for black youth than for white youth. The rate at which petitioned cases were waived to criminal court was 9% greater for black youth than the rate for white youth. The rate at which youth in adjudicated cases were ordered to residential placement was 27% greater for black youth than for white youth, but the rate at which they were ordered to probation was 14% less for black youth than for white youth.

While the Knoll and Sickmund (2010) study did not provide any possible answers for this overrepresentation, the researchers did note that the involvement of black youngsters in violent offenses was high. Black youths accounted for 41 percent of all delinquency cases for violent offenses, and their involvement in more serious offenses might result in higher levels of out-of-home placements. One limitation of this federal research, however, is that it did not account for Latino and Latina youths (who were added to the white youth population), so we do not have a clear idea of their representation in juvenile courts.

DMC has long been recognized, but responding to this challenge has been vexing. Kempf-Leonard (2007, 72) noted that "state officials were encouraged to identify the disparities, locate the sources—which would probably involve the discretion of officials—and then implement policies to restructure the process in a way that would eliminate discretion and bias." One barrier to achieving proportionate minority involvement in the system, according to Kempf-Leonard (2007), is that there is no single explanation for these disparities. DMC could be the result of differential involvement in crime, bias on the part of officials (at any part of the process—from being taken into custody through intake or during court appearances), the local culture, or the juvenile court's location, what Barry Feld (1991) has called justice by geography (see also Macallair, McCracken, and Teji 2011). Moreover, the economic disadvantage of many members of minority populations gives them few options other than relying on public defenders, who are overworked and underresourced (Puritz and Majd 2007). Last, many middle-class parents can afford to have their children placed in treatment facilities instead of custody, an option not available to those with low incomes. DMC could also be a consequence of all of these factors acting together. While Cabaniss, Frabutt, Kendrick, and Arbuckle (2007) have identified a number of possible solutions to DMC, their first recommendation is to use research to fully understand the problem.

The four policy challenges of deinstitutionalization, diversion, jail removal, and disproportionate minority contact are long entrenched, and there are no easy answers to resolving them. By providing funding for states that attempt to overcome these issues, the federal government can demonstrate juvenile justice leadership without the burden of mandating specific solutions to these challenges.

Federal Government Priorities

An examination of the Federal Register (2011, 2136) showed the priorities of the OJJDP, and they include:

1. Empower communities and engage youth and families
2. Promote evidence-based practices
3. Require accountability
4. Enhance collaboration

In order to achieve these goals, the OJJDP funds a large number of initiatives, including research into violent crime, girls' delinquency, mentoring, substance abuse, juvenile drug courts, and community reentry. Most of these initiatives are pilot or demonstration projects that are researched and the results disseminated in publications placed on the OJJDP website. Furthermore, the OJJDP has recently introduced a journal of juvenile justice practice to promote delinquency research.

At yearend 2011, the JJDPA is in the process of being reauthorized by Congress. The JJDPA was last reauthorized in 1992, and it expired in 2007. Hornberger (2010, 15) observed that over 360 organizations had provided input into the reauthorization. These organizations include local stakeholders such as the Franklin County, Ohio, Public Defender's Office along with well-established national-level associations that advocate for youth justice, such as the American Bar Association. Many youth advocacy groups are using reauthorization as an opportunity to lobby for changes to the Act that extend federal funding to the states, strengthening the role of the OJJDP as well as using federal resources to support delinquency prevention, provide stronger treatment-oriented interventions for youths, and confront DMC. Despite this optimism, however, there are indications that the OJJDP will suffer from significant cuts to their budget in future years (Kelly 2011).

STATE TRANSFER PROFILES

Up until the 1960s, there had been comparatively little scholarly or political attention paid to the transfer of juveniles to adult courts. Transfers were a low-visibility event, and a review of scholarly work published prior to 1965, for example, shows that articles about transfers were rarely published. The *Kent v. United States* case in 1966 (which is highlighted in the following chapter) drew attention to the question of due process protections for juveniles, and that stimulated academic interest in juvenile justice. Yet there was also growing public and political concern over rising juvenile crime rates. Bernard (1992, 33) noted that in each decade from the 1920s to the 1960s there was the perception of "a rising tide of juvenile delinquency and crime, and that it had not been a serious problem only forty or fifty years ago." Ohlin (1983) reported that this concern over delinquency increased even during eras when juvenile crime was decreasing.

For the most part, these public perceptions did not drive any wholesale changes in juvenile justice legislation. Transfers to adult court were relatively rare events, which was in keeping with the juvenile court's original philosophy. Judge Julian Mack (1911, 678), an early juvenile court advocate, foresaw the need for transfers but only for serious or habitual offenders:

> The law recognizes the fact that some children under seventeen or eighteen are criminals in whatever sense you may define the word criminal; and the power is therefore given to the judge of the juvenile court to determine, as to any child, whether or not it shall be dealt with in the juvenile court or turned over to the criminal court. It sometimes but very rarely happens that a child at sixteen has become a habitual criminal, and it must be dealt as such.

Mack's (1911) admonition that waivers to criminal courts be used sparingly seems to have been consistent with practice. A 1962 survey of 50 juvenile courts showed that waivers were rarely used, although some juvenile court judges transferred youths to adult courts for very minor acts, such as traffic tickets (Advisory Council of Judges 1963).

At the same time that the federal government was enacting legislation to support the diversion and the deinstitutionalization of status offenders a get-tough movement on juveniles was also gaining momentum. This resulted in legislation in each state that increased the severity of juvenile delinquency sanctions. Snyder and Sickmund (2006, 96–97) reported that, between 1992 and 1997, 47 states enacted one or more changes in the following areas. First, 45 states altered their laws to make it easier to transfer juveniles to adult courts. Second, 31 states expanded the sentencing options for youthful offenders in both adult and juvenile courts. Third, 47 states changed in some ways or completely removed juvenile court confidentiality requirements. The result of these changes has been juvenile proceedings that are less confidential and greater openness for juvenile records. Fourth, 22 states had expanded victims' rights in cases involving juvenile offenders. Finally, several states have expanded their correctional program offerings as a result of having offenders under 18 years of age in adult facilities.

These legislative changes to get tough on some youthful offenders have resulted in altering the juvenile justice system's nature without eliminating it altogether. In fact, most jurisdictions have successfully adapted to these changes while keeping juvenile justice a separate entity. One way that this could be achieved was to transfer the most serious or recalcitrant youths into the adult justice system. The National Center for Juvenile Justice has tracked the different ways that juveniles can be transferred to adult courts, and Table 4.1 presents the state transfer

Table 4.1 State Transfer Mechanisms

| Total States | Judicial Waiver | | | Direct File | Statutory Exclusion | Reverse Waiver | Once/Always | Juvenile Blended | Criminal Blended |
| | Disc. | Presumptive | Mandatory | | | | | | |
	45	15	15	15	29	24	34	14	18
AL	x				x		X		
AK	x	x			x			x	
AZ	x			x	x	x	X		
AR	x			x		x		x	x
CA	x	x		x	x	x	X	x	x
CO	x	x		x		x		x	x
CT			x		x	x			
DE	x		x		x	x	X		
DC	x	x		x			X		
FL	x			x	x		X		x
GA	x		x	x	x	x			
HI	x						X		
ID	x				x		X		x
IL	x	x	x		x		X	x	x
IN	x		x		x		X		
IA	x				x	x	X		x
KS	x	x					X	x	
KY	x		x			x			x
LA	x		x	x	x				

(continued)

Table 4.1 (continued)

Total States	Judicial Waiver			Direct File	Statutory Exclusion	Reverse Waiver	Once/Always	Juvenile Blended	Criminal Blended
	Disc.	Presumptive	Mandatory						
	45	15	15	15	29	24	34	14	18
ME	X						X		
MD	X	X				X	X		
MA					X	X		X	X
MI	X			X	X		X	X	X
MN	X	X			X		X		
MS	X				X	X	X	X	
MO	X						X		X
MT				X	X	X		X	
NE				X		X			X
NV	X	X			X	X	X		
NH	X	X					X		
NJ	X	X	X						
NM					X	X		X	X
NY					X	X		X	
NC	X		X				X		
ND	X	X	X				X		
OH	X		X				X	X	
OK	X			X	X	X	X		X
OR	X				X	X	X		
PA	X	X			X	X	X		
RI	X	X	X				X	X	

84

State								
SC	x			x		x		
SD	x		x	x		x	X	
TN	x		x	x		x	X	
TX	x	x				x	X	x
UT	x	x		x		x	X	
VT	x		x	x	x	x	X	x
VA	x		x	x	x	x	X	x
WA	x		x		x	x		
WV	x			x	x	x		
WI	x		x	x		x	X	x
WY	x		x	x		x	X	x

Source: Griffin, Addie, Adams, and Firestine 2011.

mechanisms, which were current at the end of the 2009 legislative session (Griffin, Addie, Adams, and Firestine 2011).

Officials in all 51 jurisdictions have more than one method of trying juvenile cases in adult court. First, in terms of transfer laws, 44 states and the District of Columbia still retain judicial or discretionary waiver, where a juvenile court judge decides whether the youth will be transferred to an adult court. This is the traditional mechanism for transfer, and only six states (CT, MA, MT, NE, NM, and NY) had not retained this method.

The criteria for transfer vary among jurisdictions, but in most cases the court assesses the youth's amenability for rehabilitation and will consider the offender's age, prior criminal history, and role in the offense (i.e., as a follower or leader) as well as the seriousness of the current offense. In most states the prosecution bears the burden of demonstrating that young-sters should be transferred to adult courts, and in some jurisdictions the prosecution must initiate the transfer hearing (Griffin, Torbet, and Szymanski 1998). In addition to considering legal factors such as the seriousness of the offense and prior record, the judge typically orders that probation officers investigate the youth's strengths and weaknesses. As noted in Chapter 2 these investigations typically take the form of pre-disposition or presentence reports. Psychological or psychiatric reports are also used to help the judge in deciding whether a youth remains in the juvenile justice system (Grisso 2010).

Griffin et al. (2011, 3) noted that 15 states have presumptive waiver laws, which means that the burden is on the juvenile to demonstrate why he or she should remain in the juvenile court. Fifteen states also have man-datory waiver provisions; these are for juveniles who have committed serious offenses, such as homicide, that are excluded from the juvenile court's jurisdiction. In these cases, the juvenile court judge's only role is to confirm that the characteristics of the case warrant the transfer.

The ability of prosecutors to directly file a case in adult criminal courts exists in 15 jurisdictions. This is a controversial method because the pros-ecutor effectively bypasses the juvenile court altogether, preventing youths from arguing that they could benefit from the juvenile justice sys-tem's rehabilitative efforts and supports. The prosecutor's ability to directly file cases is very broad in some jurisdictions. Florida prosecutors, for instance, are mandated by state legislation to directly file cases where the juvenile has committed any one of 17 different crimes, ranging from murder to trafficking in illegal drugs. Moreover, the Florida Department of Juvenile Justice (2008, 1) noted that prosecutors must direct file cases "for youth who are age 16 or 17 who have three prior felony adjudications withheld occurring at least 45 days apart."

In order to provide youths with some due process protections, all but four of the jurisdictions with direct file provisions (DC, FL, LA, and MI) have a reverse waiver option, which gives youngsters the opportunity to demonstrate to a criminal court judge why their case should be returned to the juvenile court.

Youths who have been involved in serious or violent offenses can be statutorily excluded from the juvenile court's jurisdiction. The 29 states that have statutory exclusion also bypass the juvenile court (Griffin 2011). In these states, the legislature has established the limits of juvenile court jurisdiction, and this method typically excludes older youths as well as those involved in serious violent crimes. One of the challenges of these provisions, however, is that the prosecutor decides the charge and thus can bypass the juvenile court by charging a youth with a more serious offense (Zimring 2010).

Thirty-four jurisdictions have some form of once-waived, always-waived juvenile stipulation, which means that once a juvenile has been convicted and sentenced in an adult court, any subsequent criminal charges will be heard in an adult court. While there is a sound rationale for this practice (i.e., juveniles who have been incarcerated in an adult jail or prison will not return to the juvenile justice system with the procriminal or antisocial values they learned in the adult system), some youths who had been transferred will be returned to the adult system for very minor offenses. In acknowledgement of this possibility, Indiana changed its once-waived, always-waived legislation in 2008 to ensure that once-transferred youths would not appear in a criminal court unless they had committed a felony (Campaign for Youth Justice 2011).

Last, two types of blended sentencing laws exist. According to Griffin (2011, 1) "juvenile blended sentencing schemes empower juvenile courts to impose adult criminal sanctions on certain categories of serious juvenile offenders." As in the Nathaniel Abraham case highlighted in Chapter 1, a judge can suspend the adult criminal sentence, which serves as an incentive for youths to comply with their disposition. If they do not abide by these conditions they are in jeopardy of the adult sanction, which could be very severe, such as terms of life imprisonment.

Eighteen states, by contrast, have criminal blended sentencing laws. Griffin (2011, 1) observed that "Criminal blended sentencing provides a mechanism whereby individual juveniles who have left the juvenile system for criminal prosecution may be returned to it for sanctioning purposes." Like juvenile blended sentencing, the intent of these schemes is to provide an incentive for prosocial behavior and to punish youths who do not take advantage of the opportunity to make those changes.

While six states had both blended sentencing options, there are 26 states that have at least one type of blended sentence (Griffin et al. 2011).

All 51 jurisdictions within the United States have developed different approaches to transferring youths to adult courts. Writing about transfers, Fagan (2010, 49) described "the current statutory landscape is an elaborate game of chutes and ladders, with some youths automatically transferred to the criminal courts only to be "reverse waived" back to the juvenile courts." The complexity of these different approaches—and what occurs both informally and formally in courts—makes it difficult for researchers to accurately summarize waiver legislation or to make national-level generalizations based on the limited information that we have about transfers.

Some states, such as Florida, are considered to be more punitive due to their high rates of placing juveniles in adult courts. The Florida Department of Juvenile Justice (2002, 8) reported that it transferred 45,940 youths in the 10 years from 1991 to 2000. As approximately 95 percent of these occurred through direct filing, those cases are not included in the *Juvenile Court Statistics* reports prepared by the OJJDP. To put the Florida statistics into perspective, judicial transfers for *all* U.S. juvenile courts during the same time frame showed that there were 115,861 transfers (Sickmund, Sladky, and Kang 2011). In the following section we examine the extent to which the juvenile justice system's philosophy as well as its organization and administration shape the treatment of youths.

STATE JUVENILE JUSTICE SYSTEMS

In the previous chapters we have observed that there is no formal juvenile justice system but a patchwork of different agencies that can intervene in the lives of dependent and delinquent youths. In the following pages we examine the purposes of state juvenile justice systems and a number of different approaches to the delivery of juvenile services. Knowing these state-level differences in philosophy, organization, and administration is important in order to better understand how and why transfers occur. An agency mission that is based on public safety and holding youngsters fully accountable for their delinquent behavior, for instance, is more likely to have stricter controls on the youths in its care than an organization whose stated purpose is rehabilitation and acting in the best interests of the child.

Table 4.2 shows the juvenile court's guiding philosophy, or what the authors termed the purposes of their juvenile justice systems (Griffin and King 2006). These investigators used five classifications: balanced and

Table 4.2 State Juvenile Philosophies and Out-Of-Home Placement Rates

Total States	Juvenile Philosophy					Juvenile Placement and Adult Incarceration Rates	
	Balanced Rest. Justice 17	Standard Juv. Court 17	Legislative Guide 12	Public Safety 6	Child Welfare 3	Juvenile Rate (2007)	Adult Rate (2007)
AL	X					325	615
AK	X					383	447
AZ						208	554
AR		X	X			261	502
CA	X	X				329	471
CO						339	465
CT				X		148	410
DE						401	482
DC	X					588	NA
FL	X	X				315	535
GA		X				286	563
HI				X		101	338
ID	X					298	483
IL	X	X				204	350
IN	X					382	426
IA		X				294	291
KS	X					370	312

(continued)

Table 4.2 *(continued)*

Total States	Juvenile Philosophy					Juvenile Placement and Adult Incarceration Rates	
	Balanced Rest. Justice 17	Standard Juv. Court 17	Legislative Guide 12	Public Safety 6	Child Welfare 3	Juvenile Rate (2007)	Adult Rate (2007)
KY					X	247	512
LA		X				321	865
ME		X	X			150	148
MD	X					149	404
MA		X			X	167	249
MI		X				274	499
MN	X	X				230	181
MS		X				131	734
MO		X				218	506
MT	X		X			204	356
NE						359	243
NV		X				348	486
NH			X			125	222
NJ	X	X	X			176	308
NM			X			170	313
NY			X			239	322
NC				X		144	361
ND			X			322	221
OH			X			341	442

State						Out-of-home placement rate	Adult incarceration rate
OK						219	665
OR	X					330	369
PA	X					344	365
RI		X				282	235
SC		X				292	524
SD						513	413
TN			X			191	424
TX			X	X		287	669
UT				X		262	239
VT			X			69	260
VA						261	490
WA	X					218	273
WV					X	320	333
WI	X					269	397
WY					X	443	394

Sources: Juvenile court philosophy (Griffin and King 2006); out-of-home placement rate (Sickmund 2010); adult incarceration rate (Sabol, West, and Cooper 2009).

restorative justice (BARJ), the standard juvenile court, legislative guide, public safety, and child welfare. The usefulness of these classifications is somewhat limited. First, these definitions were current at the end of the 2005 legislative session, which is somewhat dated. Second, classifications for eight states were missing (AZ, CO, DE, NE, NY, OK, SD, and VA). Third, some jurisdictions have more than one guiding purpose or philosophy (terms that we use interchangeably), which further demonstrates the often conflicting perspectives that we have toward youth justice. In 10 states, for example, two purposes of the court were listed (AR, CA, FL, IL, ME, MA, MN, MT, TX, and WY) and New Jersey had elements of three different philosophies. The fact that there may be more than one philosophy or purpose is not surprising given that legislators often value more than one purpose of juvenile courts, and a single juvenile code will sometimes articulate elements of youth rehabilitation as well as holding youngsters accountable for their actions.

BARJ is one of the newest philosophical approaches to juvenile justice, and it is based on balancing public safety, individual accountability, and an offender's skill development. With 17 states incorporating elements of this approach, it was tied with the standard juvenile court philosophy that also was also present in 17 states. The standard juvenile court approach emerged in the 1920s and is based on a balance between the individual needs of the juvenile and the state's interests. Perhaps the most significant difference between these two approaches is BARJ's emphasis upon maintaining public safety and victim involvement. While the victim's involvement had traditionally been overlooked in juvenile justice systems, restorative justice initiatives have increased victim participation and are based on the BARJ philosophy.

Table 4.2 also shows that 12 states incorporate elements of the legislative guide philosophy. This model came about in the late 1960s and emphasizes the care and rehabilitation of youths along with protection of their rights. One of the cornerstones of this approach is that juveniles will be removed from their homes only as a last resort. As such, this philosophy is consistent with the current practice of graduated sanctions and placing youths in the least restrictive settings.

The public safety and child welfare models have fundamentally different approaches to the care of juveniles. The six states that emphasize public safety (CT, HI, NC, TX, UT, and WY) typically refer to punishment, holding youths accountable for their actions, and ensuring public safety in their juvenile codes. Forst (1995, 101) noted that in the 1970s many state legislatures modified their juvenile justice legislation to add elements of accountability to the best interests of the child philosophy that guided youth justice since the juvenile court's founding. Washington was the first state to add the terms *accountability* and *punishment* in a 1977 amendment to its juvenile code (Forst 2005). By the end of the 2005 legislative session, however, Washington State had adopted a BARJ approach toward juvenile justice. Last, three states (KY, MA, and WV) retained the child welfare model that emphasized the best interests of the child, which is consistent with the guiding purposes of the original juvenile courts.

Table 4.2 also shows the incarceration rates for juveniles and adults from 2007. The juvenile data were obtained from Sickmund (2010, 2) and represent "the number of juvenile offenders assigned a bed in a public or private facility on the census date per 100,000 youth ages 10 through the state's upper age of original juvenile court jurisdiction in the general population." The adult imprisonment rate for 2007, by contrast, is the rate of sentenced state prisoners per 100,000 residents in the general population; these data were obtained from the Bureau of Justice Statistics (Sabol, West, and Cooper 2009, 30).

A comparison of juvenile out-of-home placements and adult imprisonment rates shows some interesting findings. First, the rate of out-of-home placements ranges from a low of 69 (in Vermont) to a high of 588 in the District of Columbia, and the average is 271.5 juveniles per 100,000 youths in the population. The adult state imprisonment rate, by contrast, ranges from a low of 148 to a high of 865, while the average incarceration rate is 413.3 per 100,000 residents in the population. When looking at the national averages, it appears as though we hold adults more accountable than juvenile offenders. In ten states, however, the out-of-home placement rate for juveniles was actually higher than the state adult imprisonment rate (IA, KS, ME, MN, NE, ND, RI, SD, UT, and WY), suggesting that these states may have a more punitive orientation toward youths.[1]

A state's juvenile justice system philosophy should be a sound indicator of the use of out-of-home placements. States that are guided by public safety, accountability, and punishment, for instance, are apt to use youth incarceration more than states that define their system's purpose as acting in the best interests of the child. In order to examine this relationship, we averaged the juvenile incarceration rate for each of the five approaches; the results are summarized in Figure 4.1.

Figure 4.1 shows that the highest average out-of-home placement rates occur in states following the BARJ philosophy, with 300 juveniles per 100,000 youths, while the lowest average take place in the legislative guide states, with an average of 228 juveniles. The states that have philosophies based on the standard juvenile court act, by contrast, are

Figure 4.1 Average Out-of-Home Placement Rate by Philosophy

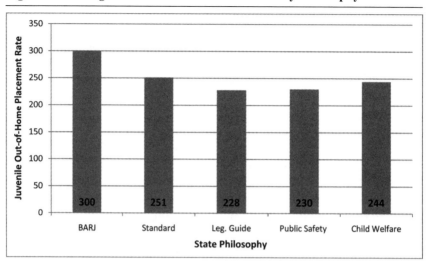

the second highest, with 251 per 100,000 youths in the population. Surprisingly, the six states that emphasized accountability, punishment, and public safety have a *lower* average juvenile incarceration rate than the child welfare states (230 and 244 respectively).

These findings suggest that there is considerable variation in the use of out-of-home placements and that a state juvenile justice system's guiding philosophy may influence the use of youth incarceration. This finding, however, must be tempered by a number of factors. First, these categories are not mutually exclusive, which means that 10 states have more than one indicator and that they were counted more than once. Second, it is possible that some states have transferred the most serious offenders to adult courts so they would not be counted in the youth incarceration rates. Furthermore, data for nine states were missing, so this would reduce the validity of this observation when making generalizations about the entire nation. Last, comparisons including other variables, such as the juvenile arrest or crime rates, were not used in these analyses, and it is possible that states with higher out-of-home placements also had higher rates of juvenile crime. Despite these limitations, however, these analyses suggest that a jurisdiction's justice system philosophy influences the use of punitive sanctions.

Table 4.3 shows the organization of delinquency services and how state delinquency institutions such as secure correctional facilities are administered. In terms of the centralization of delinquency services, Griffin and

Table 4.3 Juvenile Justice Agencies: Centralization and Administration

Total States	Centralization: Delinquency Services			State Delinquency Institutions Administered				
	Centralized	Decent.	Combination	Social/Human Services Agency	Juvenile Corrections	Adult Corrections	Child Protection/ Juv. Corrections	Other
	12	18	21	16	16	10	8	1
AL		X			X			
AK	X			X				
AZ		X			X			
AR		X		X				
CA		X				X		
CO		X		X				
CT			X				X	
DE	X						X	
DC			X	X				
FL	X				X			
GA			X		X			
HI			X	X				
ID		X			X			
IL		X			X			
IN		X				X		
IA			X	X				
KS		X			X			
KY	X				X			

(*continued*)

Table 4.3 *(continued)*

Total States	Centralization: Delinquency Services			State Delinquency Institutions Administered				
	Centralized 12	Decent. 18	Combination 21	Social/Human Services Agency 16	Juvenile Corrections 16	Adult Corrections 10	Child Protection/ Juv. Corrections 8	Other 1
LA			X			X		
ME	X					X		
MD	X				X			
MA			X	X				
MI		X				X		
MN			X	X				
MS			X	X				
MO			X	X				
MT			X			X		
NE			X	X				
NV		X		X				
NH	X			X				
NJ			X					X
NM	X						X	
NY		X					X	
NC	X				X			
ND			X			X		
OH		X			X			
OK			X		X			
OR		X			X			

PA			X			
RI	X	X				X
SC	X			X		
SD		X			X	
TN		X				X
TX		X		X		
UT		X	X			
VT	X	X				X
VA		X		X		
WA		X	X			
WV		X			X	
WI					X	
WY		X				X

Source: Griffin and King (2006).

King (2006) have identified three different administrative approaches: centralized, decentralized, and a combination of those two models. Table 4.3 shows that there are 12 centralized states, which means that the key components of the juvenile justice system (e.g., detention, probation, training school operation, and parole) are operated by a single state-level agency. In these jurisdictions, responses to juvenile crime are more likely to be integrated and interventions delivered in a more seamless manner than in jurisdictions that feature a blend of county- and state-level services.

Table 4.3 also shows that 18 states have a decentralized approach to the delivery of juvenile services. In these states, probation services are administered locally (typically at the county level), and in most of these jurisdictions youth detention facilities are operated by local governments. The third classification is similar to the second and represents a blend of local and state delinquency services. According to King (2006, 5) these 21 jurisdictions "feature a mix of state controlled and locally operated delinquency services. For instance, they may have largely state-run systems— but with significant local control in the more populous, urban areas." King (2006) also observed that in some of these jurisdictions oversight for juvenile justice agencies was split between the executive and judicial branches.

One of the challenges posed with the combined approach is that while local jurisdictions have more autonomy to handle delinquency cases, they often lack the state's larger tax base and therefore find it difficult to properly fund their juvenile justice programs. As a result, one might logically argue that the best approach to manage the operations of local youth justice systems is to consolidate them into the state-run operations. Because this move would have significant financial implications for the state it is unlikely that integrating these services will occur. A review of the 12 centralized states shows that five (DE, ME, NH, RI, and VT) cover relatively small geographical areas and populations, making it far easier to contain costs than in large states such as Florida and Texas.

Figure 4.2 shows the average out-of-home placement rate by the organization of state delinquency services. The 12 states with the centralized services had the lowest use of out-of-home placements, with an average juvenile incarceration rate of 227 per 100,000 youths and range from a low of 69 to 401 youths. This contrasts with the 18 decentralized states, which had an average of 298 juvenile inmates per 100,000 youths (with a minimum of 204 and maximum of 382 inmates), and the 21 combination jurisdictions, which had an average of 274 youth placed outside the home for every 100,000 youths in the population and a range of 101 to 588

Figure 4.2 Average Out-of-Home Placement by Organization of Delinquent Services

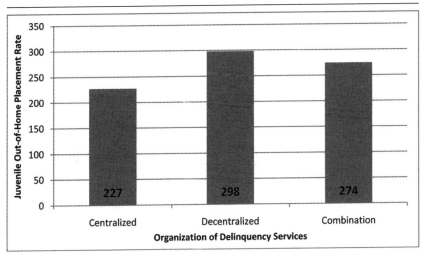

residents. This finding suggests that jurisdictions that centralize their responses to delinquency are organized in such a manner that it reduces incarceration.

The second set of columns in Table 4.3 shows how state delinquency institutions, such as training schools, are administered. These facilities provide long-term placements for youths adjudicated delinquent. The treatment that these juveniles receive may be shaped, in part, by the governing agency's philosophy. It is possible, for instance, that in the 15 states and the District of Columbia where the operations of these facilities fall under the auspices of social service or human service agencies youth treatment will be different than in those where they are administered by an adult corrections agency, which occurs in 10 states.

Two other arrangements account for almost one-half of the remaining jurisdictions, and these are the 16 states that operate a separate or stand-alone juvenile corrections agency and the eight states that oversee their delinquency institutions using a blended child protection and juvenile corrections agency. In the remaining state, New Jersey, the juvenile facilities are administered by the Department of Law and Public Safety.

Figure 4.3 shows the average out-of-home placement rate by the agency that oversees the state delinquency institutions. The average incarceration rates in states where juvenile services are overseen by an adult correctional agency are the highest, with 304 inmates per 100,000 youths in the population (with a range of 150 to 513 incarcerated youths).

Figure 4.3 Average Placements by Administration of Delinquency Services

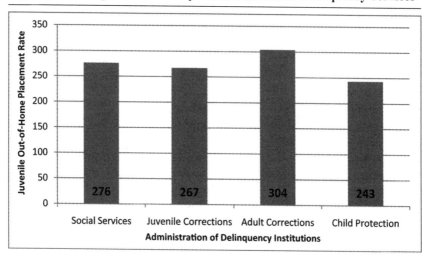

Delinquency institutions overseen by social or human services agencies, by contrast, have the second highest average rate at 276 inmates, with a minimum of 101 and a maximum of 588 juveniles per 100,000 youths in the population. This rate is almost identical to jurisdictions that administer their training schools through juvenile corrections agencies, with an average rate of 267 juveniles placed outside the home and a range of 144 to 370 youths. The lowest average rate of juvenile incarceration, with 243 inmates, occurred in institutions that fall under the auspices of child protection or juvenile correctional agencies, and these states range from 69 to 433 inmates per 100,000 youths in the population. New Jersey has its own classification, which is administered by the Department of Law and Public Safety, and it incarcerated 176 juveniles per 100,000 youths.

Another factor that may influence outcomes in juvenile justice is whether juvenile probation operations are supervised by the executive or judicial branch. Youth probation services are often overseen by the local juvenile court, and Table 4.4 shows that 20 states and the District of Columbia have adopted this approach. Operating juvenile probation agencies under the auspices of executive agencies is the second most common model, with 14 of these arrangements. Last, in 16 states there is a blend of local executive and judicial agencies responsible for juvenile probation operations—with the state executive and local judicial model being the most commonly encountered.

The agency responsible for the operations or oversight of juvenile services plays a significant role in the treatment of delinquent youths.

Table 4.4 Administration of Juvenile Probation

	Judicial Agencies (n = 21)			Executive Agencies (n = 14)			Judicial and Executive Agencies (n = 16)			
	State	Local*	State and Local Judicial	State	Local	State and Local	State Exec. and Local Judicial	Local Exec. and Judicial	State Exec. And Judicial	Local Exec. and State Judicial
Total States	10	10	1	12	1	1	9	5	1	1
AL			X							
AK				X						
AZ		X								
AR		X								
CA		X						X		
CO		X								
CT	X									
DE				X						
DC		X								
FL				X						
GA							X			
HI	X									
ID		X								
IL		X								
IN		X								
IA	X									
KS		X								

(continued)

Table 4.4 (continued)

Total States	Judicial Agencies (n = 21)			Executive Agencies (n = 14)			Judicial and Executive Agencies (n = 16)			
	State	Local*	State and Local Judicial	State	Local	State and Local	State Exec. and Local Judicial	Local Exec. and Judicial	State Exec. And Judicial	Local Exec. and State Judicial
	10	10	1	12	1	1	9	5	1	1
KY				X						
LA							X			
ME				X						
MD				X						
MA	X									
MI							X			
MN							X			
MS							X			
MO										X
MT	X									
NE	X									
NV								X		
NH				X						
NJ	X									
NM				X			X			
NY					X		X			
NC				X						
ND									X	
OH								X		

	C1	C2	C3	C4	C5	C6
OK						
OR		X				
PA			X		X	
RI				X		
SC				X		
SD						X
TN		X				
TX					X	
UT						X
VT				X		
VA		X				
WA	X					
WV						X
WI	X					
WY		X				

*The District of Columbia is included in this column although it was classified as a "district judicial" operation by the investigators.

Source: Griffin and King (2006).

Figure 4.4 Average Out-of-Home Placements by Organization of Juvenile Probation

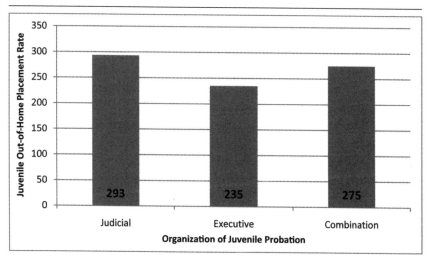

Anecdotal accounts suggest that courts that are tightly coupled with agency service providers are more likely to accommodate those agencies. For example, if a county-level agency operates both the juvenile court and the detention facility, juvenile court judges might be more sensitive to issues such as facility overcrowding and may moderate the severity of their dispositions (e.g., giving youths another chance on probation rather than detaining them) to help manage facility overcrowding. By contrast, if the state government operates detention facilities, the county-level juvenile court may not be as accommodating when these facilities are overcrowded.

Figure 4.4 shows that the 21 jurisdictions that organize and administer their probation agencies through the judicial branch have the highest average youth incarceration rate, with 293 inmates per 100,000 youths (with a range of 101 to 588 inmates). The next highest average out-of-home placement rate is 275 youths in states that combine judicial and executive oversight, and these agencies have a minimum of 131 and a maximum of 443 juveniles placed outside the home. In states where juvenile probation is administered through executive agencies (whether that is state, local, or a combination of the two in Oregon), the average out-of-home placement rate is 235 inmates, with a minimum of 69 and a maximum of 401 juveniles per 100,000 youths in the population.

Altogether, we have found that there are several predictors of higher-than-average youth incarceration rates: (1) states that have a balanced and restorative justice guiding purpose or philosophy, (2) states where delinquency institutions are overseen by adult correctional agencies, (3) states with decentralized delinquency services, and (4) jurisdictions where juvenile probation is administered by the judicial rather than executive branch of government. Although the significance of these findings is tempered by the fact that other factors, such as the youth crime rate, were not considered, these results show that the philosophy, organization, and administration of state juvenile justice services influence the use of punitive sanctions. Consequently, it is plausible that they also influence the use of transfers, although since state-level data for all transfers does not exist this proposition cannot be tested.

SUMMARY

This chapter started with an examination of the federal government's role in the development of national-level juvenile justice legislation. The federal government, through the OJJDP, has supported the states in their efforts to deinstitutionalize status offenders, divert the least serious delinquents from the juvenile justice system, remove youngsters from adult jails, and support efforts in reducing DMC. While the federal government has basically remained silent on the issue of transfers to adult court, it does provide funding for state juvenile justice systems to make it easier to hold violent juvenile offenders accountable for their offenses. However, by the time the federal government started funding the Juvenile Accountability Block Grant Program in 1998 most states had already increased the severity of sanctions (Redding 2010).

One of the primary mechanisms for getting tough on juveniles is the use of transfers to adult courts. Juvenile court judges have always had the ability to transfer the most serious cases, or the most recalcitrant youths, to adult criminal courts. While there is a lack of data prior to the 1980s about the number of transfers, a review of the literature suggests that they were relatively rare events (Advisory Council of Judges 1962; Champion and Mays 1991). As noted in Chapter 3, the number of transfers increased along with the involvement of juveniles in serious and violent crimes starting in the mid-1980s. Our review of the transfer literature showed that most jurisdictions have made it easier to transfer juveniles to adult courts, and in 15 jurisdictions prosecutors have the ability to directly file cases in criminal courts, effectively bypassing the juvenile justice system altogether. Furthermore, in 29 states, some offenses are removed from the juvenile court's jurisdiction, and youths charged with such offenses will appear in criminal courts.

Our examination of state juvenile justice systems found that jurisdictions that have adopted a balanced and restorative justice philosophy, deliver services in a decentralized manner, rely upon adult correctional agencies to oversee state training schools, and administer probation agencies by the judicial branch have a greater use of punitive sanctions, as indicated by the average number of youths placed outside the home. While the importance of these results is somewhat limited, they do suggest that the philosophy, administration, and organization of juvenile services influence the use of sanctions for youths. Inconsistent with our expectations, however, there is not a strong relationship between states that have a high rate of adult imprisonment compared to out-of-home placements for juveniles.

Singer (2011) noted that there are two broad approaches to deciding the sanctions or interventions that a juvenile receives: a case-by-case approach and a categorical rule. Traditionally, juvenile courts have adopted a case-by-case approach, which is based on substantive or individualized justice. Horwitz and Wasserman's (1980, 104) examination of juvenile courts noted that:

In systems of substantive justice, the ideal is to decide particular cases on their individual merits or to refer to substantive goals, rather than to abstract rules. In the juvenile court, this ideal has been to treat each offender as unique and as deserving of individual treatment. Decision making demands a case-by-case consideration and resists standardization into a formal body of rules. Legal officials have a high degree of discretion so that they may, in theory, act in the best interests of the juvenile.

Juvenile justice systems that base their decision making on the juvenile's circumstances may be less punitive than those that have established categorical rules, such as legislative exclusion that results in the automatic transfer of juveniles who meet specific criteria (i.e., are 16 years of age or older and charged with a serious violent offense). One of the challenges of using an individualized approach, however, is that some offenders (e.g., girls, whites, or the middle class) may receive less severe sanctions than minority youths. We describe in the next chapter, however, how categorical rules established by the Supreme Court have been used to place limits on the severity of sanctions that can be imposed on juvenile offenders.

Reducing the number of both serious and status offenders from the juvenile courts' jurisdiction has changed the juvenile justice system's boundaries. Most policymakers would agree that reducing the number of status offenders appearing in juvenile courts is a move in a positive direction. McNamara (2008, 21) noted that these arguments acknowledge that "their experience with the legal system further stigmatizes already troubled youths, exposes them to the influence of 'true' delinquents, and enmeshes them in the system that cannot really help them." Yet some of these status offenders require assistance, treatment, and support, and the juvenile court is ideally situated to help many of them.

While acknowledging that the federal and state governments played an important role in establishing the boundaries of the juvenile justice system, four decisions of the U.S. Supreme Court were also instrumental in ensuring the due process protections for youths (*In re Gault*), clarifying the state's role in transferring juveniles to adult courts (*Kent v. United States*), as well as establishing the boundaries of punishment (*Graham v. Florida*; *Roper v. Simmons*). The following chapter examines these four cases and their contribution to contemporary juvenile justice practice and the use of transfer.

NOTE

1. Surprisingly, the state juvenile and adult incarceration rates were weakly related to each other. In order to measure their relationship, a correlation between these two was computed, and $r = .192$ (which is a weak relationship considering that $r = 1.0$ would be a perfect correlation). We had thought that states that were more punitive toward youths (as indicated by higher out-of-home placement rates) would also have higher adult imprisonment rates, but that was not the case.

FIVE

The Supreme Court Defines the Boundaries of Juvenile Justice

INTRODUCTION

In Chapter 2 we described how juvenile courts emerged as a result of a number of social and political forces. In this chapter we examine how legal decisions of appellate courts have influenced the practice of juvenile justice. The *People v. Turner* (1870) decision of the Illinois Supreme Court, for instance, provided a legal obligation to develop the first juvenile court. At the time, the Illinois Court was concerned about the due process protections that youths received, as it had become clear that placing a juvenile in a house of refuge was closely akin to punishment. Bernard (1992) noted that by this time, appellate courts were considering the actual performance of juvenile institutions and their staff rather than focusing upon their good intentions.

The juvenile court that was founded in Illinois in 1899 used the *parens patriae* philosophy to provide the legal framework to handle abused, neglected, and delinquent youths in a civil court setting. As we noted earlier, juvenile justice systems were built around this court, and its establishment enabled these fledgling systems to continue operating more or less as usual. The staff members working within these agencies generally believed that they were working in the best interests of the children and did not see the need to provide due process protections for them (Bernard 1992; Van Waters 1922).

We noted in Chapter 2 that juvenile courts spread quickly throughout the United States, although many of them left a lot to be desired in terms of their effectiveness (Lenroot 1923). Many were underfunded, staffed completely with volunteers, and lacked access to psychologists or other professionals to help assess and work with difficult cases. In addition, few rural counties had these courts at all—which suggests that juveniles from these counties had little access to the juvenile court's rehabilitative benefits. These public social agencies were given almost complete autonomy to act in a juvenile's behalf, taking whatever action was deemed necessary. Usually, the "action deemed necessary" was closely aligned with some form of rehabilitation or had this as a key objective. Yet critics of these courts maintained that they failed to provide youths with necessary due process protections (Lindsey 1914).

Like today, there was disagreement about the juvenile court's purposes, philosophy, and functions, and these debates often centered on the degree to which youths were being helped or punished. Van Waters (1922, 64) wrote that juveniles should be extended the "primary right to shelter, protection, and proper guardianship" and that official legal action threatened the court's ability to fully understand the strengths and weaknesses of the youth. Waite (1923, 234) observed that the court's goal:

is not to do something *to* the child as an enemy of the social order, but something *for* him, as the erring ward of the state—always correction, never retribution. This view, of course, does not dispense with punishment, but insists that it be administered in the true parental spirit, as an obligation due the child, not as a penalty exacted from him.

By the 1950s and 1960s, however, there was growing concern that some youths, particularly status offenders, were dealt with in a very punitive manner, including long-term placements in state training schools (Schwartz 1989). Some of these youths were incarcerated because of their *potential* to become delinquents rather than for engaging in any specific criminal act.

Caldwell (1961, 499) questioned the amount of due process protections that delinquents required, and noted that:

In general the courts have held that the procedure of the juvenile court is not criminal in nature since its purpose is not to convict the child of a crime, but to protect, aid, and guide him, and that, therefore, it is not unconstitutional if it denies him certain rights which are guaranteed to an adult in a criminal trial.

Extending juveniles greater due process protections, it was argued, would erode the court's traditional informality and had the potential of making it more adversarial and less rehabilitative.

This disregard for due process protections was a prevailing view of the reformers who established the original juvenile court. Children were considered to be an asset to the state, and this required the state—in the form of the juvenile court—to intervene when the parents had failed (Van Waters 1922). Consistent with that philosophy, juvenile courts had a free hand in regulating minors' affairs. Most of this was related to the *parens patriae* doctrine. Whenever the police arrested juveniles for alleged infractions of the law, they were turned over to juvenile authorities or taken to a juvenile hall for further processing. They were not advised of their rights to an attorney, to have an attorney present during an interrogation, or to remain silent. They could be questioned by the police at length without parental notification or legal assistance. In short, they had few, if any, constitutional protections from law enforcement officers and other officials.

When youngsters appeared before juvenile court judges, they seldom had an opportunity to rebut evidence presented against them or to test witness reliability through cross-examination. This was justified by arguing that juveniles did not understand the law and had to have it interpreted for them by others, such as juvenile court judges. Past investigations of the knowledge youths have of their rights seems to confirm this claim (Grisso 1980; Lawrence 1984). In addition, prosecutors were seldom present in juvenile proceedings since they were nonadversarial and juvenile court judges handled most cases informally depending upon the youth's needs and offense seriousness.

Because of juvenile proceedings' informality there were abuses of judicial discretion. These occurred primarily because of the absence of consistent guidelines for case adjudication. Juvenile probation officers might casually recommend to judges that particular youths "ought to do a few months" in a training school or other secure facility, and the judge might be persuaded to decide accordingly. If judges decided that secure placement would best serve the interests of justice and the juvenile's welfare, then the youth would be placed for an indeterminate period in a secure facility. These decisions were seldom questioned or challenged.

However, during the 1950s and 1960s several forces were at work that would eventually result in making juvenile courts more accountable for specific adjudications of youthful offenders. One of these elements was increased parental and public recognition of the liberty taken by juvenile courts in administering juveniles' affairs. The abuse of judicial discretion was becoming increasingly apparent and widely known. Additionally, there was a growing conservative opposition for the rehabilitation ideal

(Ohlin 1983), although this disillusionment was not directed solely at juvenile courts.

Disenchantment with the lack of due process protections resulted in a growing number of appellate challenges to juvenile court decision making. Paulsen (1966, 174–75) wrote that "over forty state supreme courts have upheld the local variants of such laws against the claim that the statutes violated both state and federal constitutions in each case" and, "how could it be, they asked, that the legislature could take away the right to jury trial, to a public hearing, the right to appear and defend in person, the right to counsel and the rest?" Paulsen speculated that the state appellate courts sided with the *parens patriae* philosophy because these youths were not considered criminals and because, in the case of status offenses, no crime had been committed.

An additional reason for the silent acceptance of these appellate decisions was that the U.S. Supreme Court had demonstrated its reluctance to intervene in juvenile court affairs. In the case of *In re Gault* (discussed below), Justice Stewart typified the traditional orientation of the Supreme Court by declaring:

> The Court today uses an obscure Arizona case as a vehicle to impose upon thousands of juvenile courts throughout the Nation restrictions that the Constitution made applicable to adversary criminal trials. I believe the Court's decision is *wholly unsound* [emphasis added] as a matter of constitutional law, and sadly unwise as a matter of judicial policy. . . . The inflexible restrictions that the Constitution so wisely made applicable to adversary criminal trials have no inevitable place in the proceedings of those public social agencies known as juvenile or family courts.

A number of sweeping changes, however, were about to be made in the juvenile justice system and the way in which cases were to be handled.

The debates over the extent to which youths should receive due process protections were heard before the U.S. Supreme Court starting in 1966, and a number of landmark juvenile cases were decided over the next decade. Rights for juveniles resulted in a gradual merger of juvenile and adult protections, and this led to a growing bureaucratization and formalization of juvenile proceedings. This chapter examines these changes and focuses upon three distinct issues: (1) the Court's decision in *Kent v. United States* that established the rights of juveniles being transferred to adult courts; (2) the extension of due process protections in three subsequent decisions, what Feld (1999a) called the juvenile court's constitutional domestication; as well as (3) establishing the limits to juvenile punishment in the Court's decisions about the constitutionality of the death penalty and life without parole for crimes committed by juveniles.

KENT: THE SUPREME COURT ADDRESSES TRANSFERS TO ADULT COURTS

Juvenile court judges always had the ability to transfer youthful offenders to adult criminal courts, although Mack (1911) suggested that this rarely be done and then only for the most serious cases. When Flexner and Baldwin (1914, 264) first proposed a model juvenile court law, there were no conditions for transferring youths to adult court other than the judge's desire to do so:

> The court may, in its discretion, in any case of a delinquent child brought before it as herein provided permit such child to be proceeded against in accordance with the laws that may be in force in this State governing the commission of crimes, and in such case the petition, if any, filed under this act shall be dismissed and the child shall be transferred to the court having jurisdiction of the offense.

These principles served as a basis for transfers in the first Standard Juvenile Court Act that was published in 1925 by the National Probation and Parole Association. The Act was intended to provide direction for the fledgling courts of the era (Paxman 1959). The only guidelines for transfers to adult courts were that they be used for youths aged 16 years and over charged with felonies. The Advisory Council of Judges (1962, 4) noted that subsequent amendments to the Act incorporated more formal transfer guidelines, and the 1959 Standard Juvenile Court Act recommended that the following be carried out prior to transfer:

> The Standard Act stipulates the following preliminary steps: (a) a finding that the act would be a felony if committed by an adult; (b) a full investigation; (c) a hearing; (d) a finding that retention of jurisdiction would be contrary to the best interest of the child or the public.

The recommendations within the Standard Juvenile Court Act, however, were not binding on states or individual juvenile courts, and transfers were sometimes made with no clear guidelines. The Advisory Council of Judges (1962, 5) reported the results of a survey that confirmed that some adolescent traffic offenders were transferred to adult courts, while other youths were transferred because of administrative concerns (e.g., the hearing would be lengthy) or because the judges felt that the case was "hopeless" or the juvenile had a "poor attitude."

By the 1960s, the movement to extend more due process protections for juveniles had gained significant momentum, and the first juvenile case to be heard in the Supreme Court was that of Morris Kent. *Kent v. United States* (1966) established the requirements of (1) waiver hearings before juveniles can be judicially transferred to criminal courts, and (2) entitling juveniles to consult with counsel prior to and during such hearings.

These are the facts in the case, as reported within the Supreme Court's decision.[1] In 1959, Morris A. Kent, Jr., a 14-year-old in the District of Columbia, was arrested as the result of several break-ins and attempted purse snatchings. He was placed on probation in the custody of his mother. In 1961, an intruder entered a woman's apartment, took her wallet, and raped her. Fingerprints at the crime scene were later identified as those of Kent, who was fingerprinted when he was arrested for housebreaking in 1959. On September 5, 1961, Kent, then 16, was taken into police custody, interrogated for seven hours, and admitted his involvement in the offense as well as volunteering information about other burglaries, robberies, and rapes.

Although the records are unclear about when Kent's mother became aware of his arrest, she obtained counsel for him shortly after 2:00 p.m. the following day. She and the attorney conferred with the juvenile court's social service director and learned there was a possibility Kent would be waived to criminal court. Kent's attorney advised the director of his intention to oppose the waiver.

Kent was detained in a receiving home (a secure facility in the District of Columbia) for one week. During that period, there was no arraignment and no judicial determination of probable cause for Kent's arrest. His attorney filed a motion with the juvenile court opposing the waiver as well as a request to inspect records relating to Kent's previous offenses. A psychiatric examination of Kent also was arranged. Kent's attorney argued that because his client was "a victim of severe psychopathology," it would be in his best interests to remain within juvenile court jurisdiction where he could receive adequate treatment in a hospital and would be a suitable subject for rehabilitation.

Typical of juvenile courts at the time, the judge failed to rule on any of Kent's attorney's motions, nor did he confer with his attorney or parents. In an arbitrary manner, the juvenile court judge declared that "after full investigation, I do hereby waive" jurisdiction of Kent and direct that he be "held for trial for [the alleged] offenses under the regular procedure of the U.S. District Court for the District of Columbia." He offered no findings, nor did he recite any reason for the waiver or make mention of Kent's attorney's motions. Paulsen (1966, 177) noted that the "action that he took probably satisfied the standards then set by the Court of Appeals for the District of Columbia . . . [as] no formal hearing was required under the District statute's waiver provision" and that "The full investigation by the Juvenile Court of which the statute speaks need only be whatever is needed to satisfy that court as to what action should be taken on the question of waiver."

Kent was later found guilty of six counts of housebreaking by a federal jury, although the jury found him "not guilty by reason of insanity" on the rape charge. Because of District of Columbia law, it was mandatory that Kent be transferred to a mental institution until he was deemed sane. On each of the housebreaking counts, Kent's sentence was 5 to 15 years, or a total of 30 to 90 years in prison. The time served during his commitment to a psychiatric facility would be counted as time served against the prison sentence.

Although Kent was originally taken into custody in September 1961, the case was not heard by the Supreme Court until January 19, 1966, and the Justices rendered their written decision about two months later. The time between his arrest and the appearance before the Court was the result of resolving a number of appeals to lower courts that had been dismissed. On March 21, 1966, the Supreme Court reversed Kent's conviction by a vote of 5 to 4. This case signified a shift in Supreme Court sentiment relating to juvenile rights.

The majority held that Kent's rights to due process and to the effective assistance of counsel were violated when he was denied a formal waiver hearing and his attorney's motions were ignored. Justice Fortas, writing for the majority, observed that:

We do not consider whether, on the merits, Kent should have been transferred; but there is no place in our system of law for reaching a result of such tremendous consequences without ceremony—without hearing, without effective assistance of counsel, without a statement of reasons. It is inconceivable that a court of justice dealing with adults with respect to a similar issue would proceed in this manner.

In a much-cited comment, Justice Fortas observed that this case demonstrated "that the child receives the worst of both worlds: that he gets neither the protections accorded to adults nor the solicitous care and regenerative treatment postulated for children."

It was significant that the Supreme Court stressed the phrase "critically important" when referring to the absence of counsel and waiver hearing. In adult cases, critical stages are those that relate to the defendant's potential incarceration. Because of the *Kent* decision, waiver hearings are now considered critical stages. The Court also regarded counsel's assistance as a "critically important" decision. The majority observed that "the right to representation by counsel is not a formality. It is not a grudging gesture to a ritualistic requirement. It is of the essence of justice. . . . Appointment of counsel without affording an opportunity for a hearing on a critically important decision is tantamount to a denial of counsel."

In their decision, the Court identified a number of criteria that juvenile court judges could consider in order to determine suitability for transfer, and Feld (1999a, 214) summarized them as follows:

1. The seriousness of the alleged offense
2. Whether the alleged offense was committed in an aggressive, violent, premeditated, or willful manner
3. Whether the alleged offense was against persons or against property
4. The prosecutive merit of the complaint
5. The desirability of trial and disposition of the entire offense in one court when the juvenile's associates in the alleged offense are adults
6. The sophistication and maturity of the juvenile as determined by consideration of his or her home, environmental situation, emotional attitude, and pattern of living
7. The record and previous history of the juvenile
8. The prospects for adequate protection of the public and the likelihood of reasonable rehabilitation of the juvenile

These criteria extended the guidelines laid out in the 1959 Standard Juvenile Court Act. Moreover, this decision meant that in all subsequent waiver proceedings juveniles and their attorneys now had access to reports and social histories that had previously been unavailable to them, further increasing the transparency of the process and enhancing the ability of advocates to challenge these transfers.

Kent was important because it signified the Court's intent to establish legal rights for juveniles as well as defining the limits of *parens patriae*. In doing so, there were immediate repercussions throughout the juvenile justice and legal communities. Paulsen (1966) wrote that this ruling was well received by lawyers and law professors who had expressed concern about the lack of due process protections for youths, although practitioners reacted differently. Weinstein and Goodman (1967) noted that many thought that *Kent* represented a death blow to the juvenile justice system and that a number of meetings and conferences were quickly convened to discuss this decision's impact. Having formalized transfers to criminal courts, the justices now looked at broader questions of the limits of due process for juveniles in four subsequent cases that were heard between 1966 and 1975.

THE DUE PROCESS REVOLUTION

Kent raised awareness that juveniles were in fact getting the worst of both worlds: a lack of due process protections as well as few opportunities to rehabilitate themselves once they entered the juvenile justice system. Norman Dorsen (2007, 2), the attorney who argued the *In re Gault* case before the Supreme Court, wrote that, "People in the field—lawyers in criminal defense, the few lawyers in juvenile justice, social workers, a few ministers—all felt that something was wrong and something had to be done about the system, but the public was generally unaware."

The lack of public awareness came from the fact that juvenile court activities were occurring behind closed doors to protect youths' confidentiality. Yet, during this time, status offenders as well as youths who were engaging in minor delinquency were being sent to secure training schools, sometimes for years. If their parents complained about these sanctions, the courts used these complaints as further evidence that the family was unfit. Paulsen (1966, 175) observed that "A parent who complained that his right to his child's custody had been violated when the child was sent to training school as the result of an act of delinquency was met with the argument that the delinquent act of the child substantially established the parents' unfitness for custody."

The case of *In re Gault* (1967) is perhaps the most noteworthy of all juvenile rights cases. Certainly it is the most far reaching. In a 7-to-2 vote, the U.S. Supreme Court granted the following rights for all juveniles: (1) the right to a notice of charges, (2) the right to counsel, (3) the right to confront and cross-examine witnesses, and (4) the protection against self-incrimination. Gault's attorneys requested that the Court rule on two additional rights: (1) the right to a transcript of the proceedings and (2) the right to appellate review, but the Court elected *not* to rule on either of these issues. Moreover, the Court was silent on the questions of using hearsay and the civil court standard of "a preponderance of the evidence" for juvenile cases rather than the stricter criminal court standard of "beyond a reasonable doubt" (Dorsen 2007). Although the court did not rule on all of these issues, granting these rights would change the nature of juvenile proceedings. Nevertheless, there is still concern whether juvenile courts have resisted some of these reforms, especially around the issue of providing counsel for all juvenile defendants (Birckhead 2012; Feld and Schaefer 2010).

In re Gault

The facts in the case are that Gerald Francis Gault, a 15-year-old, and a friend, Ronald Lewis, were taken into custody by the sheriff of Gila County, Arizona, on the morning of June 8, 1964. At the time, Gault was on probation as the result of "being in the company of another who had stolen a wallet from a lady's purse," a judgment entered on February 25, 1964. A verbal complaint had been filed by a neighbor, Mrs. Cook, alleging that Gerald had called her and made lewd and indecent remarks. When Gault was picked up, his mother and father were at work. Indeed, they did not learn that their son was being held at the Children's Detention Home until much later that evening.

Gault's parents proceeded to the Home. Officer Flagg, the deputy probation officer and superintendent of the facility where Gault was being detained, advised his parents that a hearing would be held in juvenile court at 3:00 p.m. the following day. Flagg filed a petition with the court on the hearing day, June 9, 1964. This petition stated only that "said minor is under the age of 18 years, and is in need of the protection of this Honorable Court; [and that] said minor is a delinquent minor." It asked for a hearing and an order regarding the "care and custody of said minor." No factual basis was provided for the petition, and Gault's parents were not provided with a copy in advance of the hearing.

On June 9 there was a hearing, with only Gault, his mother and older brother, probation officers Flagg and Henderson, and the juvenile judge present. The original complainant, Mrs. Cook, was not there. No one was sworn at the hearing, no transcript was made of it, and no memorandum of the proceedings was prepared. The testimony consisted largely of allegations by Officer Flagg about Gault's behavior and prior juvenile record. On June 15, there was another hearing, with all above present, plus Ronald Lewis, his father, and Gault's father. What actually transpired is unknown, although there are conflicting recollections from all parties who were there. Mrs. Gault asked why Mrs. Cook was not present. Judge

McGhee said, "She didn't have to be present at that hearing." In fact, the judge did not speak to Mrs. Cook or communicate with her at any time, and Flagg had spoken with her only once by telephone on June 9. Officially, the charge against Gault was "lewd phone calls." When the hearing was concluded, the judge committed Gault as a juvenile delinquent to the Arizona State Industrial School "for a period of his minority," at that point until age 21. Interestingly, if an adult had made obscene telephone calls, he or she would have received a maximum fine of $50 and no more than 60 days in jail. Gault was facing nearly six years in a juvenile prison for the same offense.

There was a *habeas corpus* hearing on August 17, and Judge McGhee was cross-examined regarding his actions. After hemming and hawing, the judge declared that Gault had "disturbed the peace" and was "habitually involved in immoral matters." Regarding the judge's reference to Gault's alleged habitual immoral behavior, the judge made vague references to an incident two years earlier when Gault had been accused of stealing someone's baseball glove and had lied to police by denying that he had taken it. The judge again vaguely recalled that Gault had testified some months earlier about making "silly calls, or funny calls, or something like that."

After exhausting their appeals in Arizona state courts, the Gaults appealed to the U.S. Supreme Court, and the case was heard on December 6, 1966. The Court was appalled that Gault's case had been handled in such a cavalier manner, and Justice Fortas, who wrote the majority opinion, called the proceedings a "kangaroo court." They reversed the Arizona Supreme Court, holding that Gault did have the right to an attorney, the right to confront his accuser and to cross-examine her, protection against self-incrimination, and the right to have notice of the charges filed against him. Perhaps Justice Hugo L. Black summed up the current juvenile court situation in the United States when he said, "This holding strikes a well-nigh fatal blow to much that is *unique* [emphasis added] about the juvenile courts in this Nation."

While Gerald Gault did receive justice, it took almost three years from the time he was taken into custody until his release from the Arizona training school, which was a very severe outcome for making one obscene phone call. In addition to freeing Gault, this case had significant implications for juvenile courts, and the decision was both acclaimed and criticized. Consistent with the outcome in *Kent* that formalized the process by which transfers could occur, *Gault* placed numerous restrictions on the activities of juvenile court judges and probation staff by reducing their flexibility and increasing their accountability (Kaye 2011).

Perhaps the core issue in *Gault* was that children would now be represented by counsel, and these attorneys would ensure that the procedural safeguards, now constitutionally guaranteed, would be followed (Dorsen 2007). Yet some scholars have observed that juvenile courts have resisted these reforms. Feld and Schaefer (2010, 736) noted that in 1995 the Minnesota legislature "creatively redefined most misdemeanors as status offenses, barred out-of-home placements, and thereby eliminated juveniles' constitutional right to counsel." Consequently, *Gault* has failed to live up the advocates' expectations for extending due process protections for children.

In re Winship

Winship was a relatively simple case compared with *Gault*. However, it set an important precedent for juvenile courts relating to the standard of proof used in establishing delinquency as well as civil proceedings today (Ball 2011). Up to this point, the standard of proof was based on a preponderance of the evidence, which is the norm in civil proceedings such as juvenile and family courts. Guilt based on a preponderance of the evidence means that the allegation is more likely to be true than not, or more than a 50 percent likelihood. As the purpose of the juvenile court was to aid children, and they were not seen as being punished, the lower standard of proof was not disconcerting. As *Gault* demonstrated, however, some youths were in jeopardy of serious sanctions in juvenile courts. The U.S. Supreme Court held in *Winship* that the "beyond a reasonable doubt" standard ordinarily used in adult criminal courts was to be used by juvenile court judges in establishing a youth's delinquency.

The facts relating to this case are that Samuel Winship was a 12-year-old charged with larceny in New York City. He purportedly entered a locker and stole $112 from a woman's purse. Under Section 712 of the New York Family Court Act, a juvenile delinquent was defined as "a person over seven and less than sixteen years of age who does any act, which, if done by an adult, would constitute a crime." In this case, the juvenile court judge acknowledged that the proof to be presented by the prosecution might be insufficient to establish Winship's guilt beyond a reasonable doubt. Nevertheless, he indicated that the Family Court Act provided that "any determination at the conclusion [of an adjudicatory hearing] that a [juvenile] did an act or acts must be based on a preponderance of the evidence" standard. Winship was found to be delinquent and ordered to a training school for 18 months, subject to annual extensions of his commitment until his 18th birthday. Appeals to the New York courts were unsuccessful.

The U.S. Supreme Court eventually heard Winship's case and in a 6-to-3 vote reversed the New York Family Court ruling. A comment by Justice Brennan stated the case for the beyond a reasonable doubt standard:

> In sum, the constitutional safeguard of proof beyond a reasonable doubt is as much required during the adjudicatory stage of a delinquency proceeding as are those constitutional safeguards applied in *Gault*—notice of charges, right to counsel, the rights of confrontation and examination, and the privilege against self-incrimination. We therefore hold, in agreement with Chief Justice Fuld in dissent in the Court of Appeals, that where a 12-year-old child is charged with an act of stealing which renders him liable to confinement for as long as six years, then, as a matter of due process . . . the case against him must be proved beyond a reasonable doubt.

Extending a higher standard of proof for youths in jeopardy of incarceration was of key importance to the court, and Bernard (1992) noted that the justices took the unexpected step of making the ruling retroactive two years later in the *Ivan V. v. City of New York* case. This meant that youths who had been sentenced using the lower standard of proof would have to be released from institutions unless they had a new proceeding and were adjudicated delinquent using the higher standard.

Loewy (2010, 65) observed that the Supreme Court had three concerns about establishing the guilt of defendants:

> (1) the interest of the defendant in not being convicted unless we are substantially sure of his guilt; (2) the interest of society in knowing that those imprisoned are in fact guilty of the crime with which they were charged; and finally, (3) the interest of each individual member of society, knowing that if he is ever charged with a crime, he cannot be convicted unless the State proves him guilty beyond a reasonable doubt.

Even though the standard of beyond a reasonable doubt is used today, Streib (2010) claimed that some youths are still wrongfully convicted, and in some cases those convictions are intentionally committed in order to provide rehabilitative opportunities for them.

By 1970 there was growing resistance on the part of the Supreme Court Justices to further extending constitutional protections for juveniles. By this time the Court had a new Chief Justice, Warren Burger, who felt that the addition of rights for juveniles "was turning back the clock back to the nineteenth century, pre-juvenile court era" (Kaye 2011, 73). One of the Court's challenges was defining the juvenile courts' boundaries without eliminating them altogether.

McKeiver v. Pennsylvania

In *McKeiver*, the Supreme Court held that juveniles are not entitled to a jury trial as a matter of right—signifying the limits to due process protections that they were willing to extend to juvenile defendants. The facts are that in May 1968, 16-year-old Joseph McKeiver was charged with robbery, larceny, and receiving stolen goods. Despite the serious charges, Bernard (1992: 123–124) noted that this offense involved several dozen youths who robbed three teenagers, from whom they took less than a dollar. In terms of mitigating factors, this was McKeiver's first arrest, and he was considered to be a good student who was also employed.

The Court noted that the "testimony of two of the victims was described by the court as somewhat inconsistent and as weak." As a result, McKeiver's counsel requested a trial by jury to demonstrate his guilt. Judge Gutowicz of the Philadelphia juvenile court denied the request, and McKeiver was subsequently found to be delinquent. On appeal to the U.S. Supreme Court, McKeiver's adjudication was upheld. The remarks of Justice Blackmun are insightful: "If the formalities of the criminal adjudicative process are to be superimposed upon the juvenile court system, there is little need for its separate existence. Perhaps that ultimate disillusionment will come one day, but for the moment, we are disinclined to give impetus to it."

The *McKeiver* opinion acknowledged that the Court was sensitive to the limitations in juvenile court procedures. Since criminal courts were already bogged down with formalities and lengthy procedures that frequently led to excessive court delays, it was not unreasonable for the Court to rule against subjecting juvenile courts to the same formalities. The Court was also hesitant to extend all of the protections that adult defendants had in order to preserve the juvenile court's unique rehabilitative aspects. Moreover the Court wanted to preserve what remained of the informal nature of juvenile proceedings and believed that the judge could satisfy the requirement of accurate fact finding to ensure due process and fundamental fairness (Feld 1999a). Wizner (1972, 391) analyzed the language in the *Gault, Winship*, and *McKeiver* decisions and concluded that the Court was reluctant to turn juvenile courts into fully adversarial bodies because of a fear of destroying the system entirely.

We must recognize that in this instance the Court merely ruled that it is not a *constitutional* right of juveniles to have a jury trial upon their request. This proclamation had no effect on individual states that wished to enact or preserve such a method of adjudicating delinquent juveniles. Szymanski (2008a, 1) reported that at the end of the 2007 legislative session, nine states allowed jury trials as a matter of right while in 11 states juveniles have access to jury trials under certain circumstances, such as in the case of a serious offender or a youth who is in jeopardy of placement in an adult correctional facility.[7] In the remaining 30 states and the District of Columbia, juveniles have no right to juvenile court jury trials, although Szymanski (2008a) speculated that, as the sanctions for juveniles become stricter, more states will extend this protection.

Breed v. Jones

In *Breed v. Jones* the constitutional issue of double jeopardy was raised, and the Supreme Court concluded that after a juvenile has been found to be delinquent the same charges may not be alleged subsequently in criminal courts through transfers or waivers.

The facts of the case are that on February 8, 1971, in Los Angeles, California, 17-year-old Gary Steven Jones was armed with a deadly weapon and allegedly committed robbery. Jones was apprehended, and an adjudicatory hearing was held on March 1. After testimony was taken from Jones and witnesses, the juvenile court found that the allegations were true and sustained the petition. A dispositional hearing date was set for March 15. At that time Jones was declared "not . . . amenable to the care, treatment and training program available through the facilities of the juvenile court." He then was transferred by judicial waiver to a California criminal court to be tried as an adult. In a later criminal trial, Jones was convicted of robbery and committed for an indeterminate period to the California Youth Authority. The California Supreme Court upheld the conviction.

When Jones appealed the decision, the Supreme Court reversed the robbery conviction. Chief Justice Warren Burger delivered the Court's opinion: "We hold that the prosecution of [Jones] in Superior Court, after an adjudicatory proceeding in Juvenile Court, violated the Double Jeopardy Clause of the Fifth Amendment, as applied to the States through the Fourteenth Amendment." The Court ordered Jones's release outright or a remand to juvenile court for disposition. In a lengthy opinion, Chief Justice Burger defined *double jeopardy* in this case as (1) being adjudicated delinquent in a juvenile court, and (2) subsequently being tried and convicted on the same charges in criminal court. Within the context of fundamental fairness, such action could not be tolerated.

Breed v. Jones was a rare unanimous decision of the Court, and Bernard (1992) noted that the ruling appealed to both liberals and conservatives. The liberals were happy to receive one additional protection for youths, while conservatives again prevailed in preserving the juvenile court's remaining rehabilitative and informal aspects. Bernard (1992, 129) observed that:

> In the original juvenile court, the juvenile could be trusting and open with the judge because the disposition of the case would be made on the basis of the juvenile's "best interests." But a juvenile could not be trusting and open if the judge might turn around and waive jurisdiction to criminal court. The Supreme Court argued that the juvenile court judge's actions had placed Gary Jones in a dilemma that undermined the very trust that the original juvenile court tried to nurture.

Kaye (2011) suggested that despite the Court's acknowledgement in *Breed v. Jones* that juvenile courts had failed to live up to reformers' expectations, the justices reiterated that the juvenile justice system offered broad social benefits to youths that they did not want jeopardized.

Feld (1999a, 214) observed that "*Kent* and *Breed* provide the formal procedural framework within which judges make waiver decisions." Yet it is unlikely that the Supreme Court anticipated that legislative amendments to juvenile codes would result in statutorily excluding many youthful offenders from juvenile courts altogether. Moreover, when prosecutors were granted the ability—and in states such as Florida the mandate in certain cases—to directly file juvenile cases in criminal courts, the juvenile court judge's place in the system becomes moot. The legislators and prosecutors gained power, and the juvenile court's boundaries shrank, along with the influence of juvenile court judges.

The *parens patriae* orientation provided juvenile court judges with considerable discretion in adjudicating cases, but this sometimes resulted in unjust outcomes. By the 1960s there was growing concern about what occurred behind the courts' closed doors. Despite this concern, at least 40 state appellate courts had upheld the lack of due process protections for youths (Paulsen 1966). Although the Supreme Court had traditionally held a "hands off" orientation when it came to juvenile court operations, they issued decisions on four landmark cases that shifted the boundaries of juvenile justice. Each of these cases represented attempts by juveniles to secure due process protections ordinarily extended to adults in criminal courts and juveniles generally fared well in these decisions.

The dilemma for the Supreme Court Justices was that they saw the importance of extending due process protections for youngsters but at the same time did not want to dismantle the juvenile court entirely, as they could see its potential, albeit unfulfilled. Instead, the Court stopped short of providing youths with all of the protections that adults received in return for the rehabilitative benefits of the juvenile justice system. In doing so, they established the juvenile court's boundaries. There is some commentary that suggests that the due process protections put in place have not lived up to the Court's expectations (Buss 2011; Dorsen 2007; Marrus 2008), and some states have used legislation to thwart providing counsel to some juvenile defendants (Feld and Schaefer 2010).

Having defined the legal boundaries of juvenile courts, the next challenge of the Supreme Court was to establish the limits of punishment for serious and violent offenses committed by juveniles. Once transferred to adult courts, youths were in jeopardy of adult sanctions, such as lengthy prison terms or the death penalty. Drawing a clear "line in the sand" on the upper limits of punishment, however, would take three decades.

DEFINING THE LIMITS OF PUNISHMENT

The death penalty is the most severe sanction criminal courts can impose. Throughout much of our nation's history, youngsters were eligible for the death penalty when they were tried as adults for capital crimes. While the Stubborn Child Law of 1646 specified death as a potential sanction for incorrigible youth, Rosenberg and Rosenberg (1976) claimed that no children were actually put to death for that behavior. But many individuals were executed for crimes that they committed as juveniles: Streib (2005) estimated that at least 366 were executed between 1642 and 2005. The first recorded U.S. execution of a juvenile occurred in 1642 and involved 16-year-old Thomas Granger, who had been convicted of bestiality. The youngest American ever executed was James Arcene, who at age 10 had been involved in a robbery-homicide and was put to death in 1885 (Scott 2005).

Despite the fact that hundreds of persons who committed crimes as juveniles had been executed, there was a reluctance to use this sanction (Forst 1995). Putting people to death who were not able to legally drink, sign a contract, purchase tobacco, or vote at the time of their offenses forces us to question the limits of punishment. Moreover, executing juveniles makes us confront our views about serious youthful offenders—whether immaturity should be a mitigating factor in punishment—as well as notions of retribution. Our tolerance for severe sanctions might be aggravated by the involvement of juveniles in serious crimes: by the late 1980s there was an epidemic of youth violence, and in Chapter 3 we highlighted the increased number of juvenile arrests for serious and violent crimes.

In a series of cases beginning in the early 1980s, the U.S. Supreme Court defined the circumstances under which the death penalty could be imposed for crimes committed before the defendant's 18th birthday (*Eddings v. Oklahoma* 1982; *Stanford v. Kentucky* 1989; *Thompson v. Oklahoma* 1988). During this time the Court never held that the death penalty for youthful offenders was unconstitutional, it merely required age to be considered as a mitigating factor and limited the ages and offenses for which capital punishment could be imposed. However, the U.S. Supreme Court removed this option for juvenile offenders transferred to adult courts in the case of *Roper v. Simmons* (2005). Citing principles such as evolving standards of decency and other nations' prohibitions against such executions, the Court established 18 as the minimum age at which the death penalty could be imposed.

As a result, a number of states have considered other options to this ultimate penalty. One alternative to the death penalty is life without parole (LWOP). In 2008, all 50 states and the federal government had either life sentences or LWOP provisions for their most serious offenders. Forty-three states had both life and LWOP sentences, and only Alaska provided parole eligibility for all life sentences. Six states—Illinois, Iowa, Louisiana, Maine, Pennsylvania, and South Dakota—along with the federal government had only life sentences without the possibility of parole (Nellis and King 2009, 5–9).

Having established the minimum age of 18 for the death penalty's imposition, the Court soon after considered the question of life without the possibility of parole for juveniles in the *Graham v. Florida* (2010) case. They decided that nonhomicide offenders could not be sentenced to terms of life without the possibility of parole. The following section describes these two cases; our analysis includes how these decisions were reached and some of the issues considered by the Court. Both *Roper* and *Graham* are important in better understanding the potential outcomes for juveniles who are transferred to adult courts, and *Graham* might serve as the foundation for future litigation that challenges existing transfer laws (Arya 2010).

Roper v. Simmons

The peak of arrests for juvenile homicide in the United States occurred in 1993, with nearly 3,800 youths arrested for murder (Snyder 2000). One of those arrestees was a Missouri youth named Christopher Simmons, a high school junior who at age 17 was convicted of murdering Shirley Crook while committing a home invasion. Like many other homicides committed by juveniles, this was a group offense as two other youths were involved, Charles Benjamin and John Tessmer, aged 15 and 16 respectively. A number of factors distinguish this case from most juvenile murders: prior to the offense, Simmons had allegedly told the two other youths that they could get away with the offense because they were minors. Moreover, unlike many juvenile homicides that are a product of impulse and poor decision making, this offense was premeditated. The facts of the case are reported in the following paragraphs.

Simmons, who was the leader in this offense, proposed to commit burglary and murder by breaking and entering, tying up their victim(s), and throwing them from a bridge. The three juveniles met at about 2:00 a.m. on the night of the offense but Tessmer left before the crimes occurred. Simmons and Benjamin entered the victim's home and bedroom; Simmons recognized Mrs. Crook from a car accident that had involved both of them, and he later admitted that this confirmed his resolve to murder her. The two youths bound their victim with duct tape, placed Mrs. Crook in her vehicle, drove to a state park, then threw her from a trestle into the Meramec River, where she drowned.

According to the case summary, Simmons showed little remorse and boasted about the killing to his friends, telling them that he murdered her because she could have identified him. Shortly thereafter he was arrested and, after less than two hours of interrogation, confessed to the murder, and he reenacted the homicide on video for the police. Simmons was charged with burglary, kidnapping, stealing, and first-degree murder. Missouri youths older than 17 years were outside of the juvenile court's jurisdiction, so he was charged, tried, and convicted of murder as an adult.

Prosecutors had sought the death penalty for Simmons, and in the penalty phase of his trial they noted a number of aggravating factors, including "the murder was committed for the purpose of receiving money; was committed for the purpose of avoiding, interfering with, or preventing lawful arrest of the defendant; and involved depravity of mind and was outrageously and wantonly vile, horrible and inhuman."[3] Moreover, the prosecutor used Simmons' status as a youth as an *aggravating* factor. Mrs. Crook's husband and her relatives provided victim impact statements that highlighted the devastation they experienced from the crime. Simmons' attorney countered the prosecution's position by showing that he had no prior juvenile or criminal record. In addition, family members as well as a neighbor and friend spoke of his good qualities, including being a caregiver to his younger siblings and grandmother.

Despite the fact that the defense had used Simmons' age as a mitigating factor, the jury recommended the death penalty, which was imposed by the trial judge. Simmons subsequently obtained a new attorney, who claimed that the youth's counsel had been ineffective as he had failed to introduce evidence that might have mitigated the severity of Simmons' sentence. The court, however, did not find any constitutional violation due to the alleged ineffective assistance of counsel, and further appeals to the Missouri Supreme Court, as well as federal courts, did not result in any changes to his sentence.

The Supreme Court's decision in *Atkins v. Virginia* in 2002, however, provided a legal rationale for Simmons to challenge his death sentence. In *Atkins*, the Court ruled that it was unconstitutional to execute a person who was mentally retarded using the Eighth Amendment's prohibition of cruel and unusual treatment. The Court found that being mentally retarded diminished the individual's culpability. If, the Court reasoned, the rationale for the death penalty was deterrence and retribution, then mentally retarded individuals, who had a diminished capacity, would not be deterred by this sanction. As a result, executing them would cause needless suffering. Furthermore, the Court based its decision on a national consensus that executing the mentally retarded was wrong—since a majority of states had abolished executions for the mentally retarded—and therefore the practice was considered to be inconsistent with evolving standards of decency.

The *Atkins* decision provided Simmons' attorneys with the legal rationale for challenging his death sentence. Since there was a national consensus that executing persons with a diminished capacity was wrong, juveniles might logically fit into that category as well, given their immaturity. Moreover, the *Eddings*, *Stanford*, and *Thompson* cases had been decided in the 1980s, and almost two decades later there was growing opposition to executing juveniles. Simmons filed a petition for postconviction relief with the Missouri Supreme Court, and in 2003 the Court agreed with his attorney's arguments and set aside his death sentence in favor of serving the rest of his life in prison without the possibility of release.

The Supreme Court heard the case in October 2004, and decided on March 1, 2005, that the Eighth and Fourteenth Amendments forbid the capital punishment of persons under the age of 18 years when their offenses were committed. The Court's 5-to-4 decision was controversial, but to understand the rationale of the justices who wrote the opinion, as well as those who dissented, it is important to see how the limits of punishment were established. One key question in both the *Roper* and *Graham* cases is who should decide how juveniles should be punished: the voters and state legislatures or the courts?

Justice Kennedy wrote the Court's opinion, and he articulated four arguments in favor of abolishment. First, the Court found that the juvenile death penalty violated society's evolving standards of decency as evidenced by 30 states' ban of juvenile executions demonstrating a national consensus against this sanction. Second, the Court applied its independent judgment on the issue by determining that persons under 18 were less culpable for their actions than adults due to biological reasons (their incomplete brain development) as well as their susceptibility to negative influences and underdeveloped sense of responsibility. Third, in determining whether a national consensus existed for executing juvenile offenders, Justice Kennedy counted non–death penalty states, whereas in the *Stanford* decision only the states that used the death penalty were counted. Last, the Court was also informed by international law, in that they considered that juvenile executions were abolished in all first-world nations—and that juvenile executions violated the United Nations Convention on the Rights of the Child and the International Covenant on Civil and Political Rights.

In concurring with Justice Kennedy, Justice Stevens highlighted the importance of observing the evolving standards of decency in terms of the Eighth Amendment's prohibition against cruel and unusual punishments and stated that, "If the meaning of that Amendment had been frozen when it was originally drafted, it would impose no impediment to the execution of 7-year-old children today."

The Justices who dissented, however, provided their rationale for not abolishing juvenile executions, and this reasoning is also instructive in helping us understand how the limits to punishment were decided. Justice O'Connor, for example, was not convinced that there was a national consensus against juvenile executions as eight state legislatures had upheld the practice. In Scott's (2005, 551) analysis of O'Connor's dissent, he also drew our attention to her assessment that chronological age was an imperfect measure of culpability and her concern that 17-year-olds were qualitatively and materially different from persons who were mentally retarded. While O'Connor was convinced that 17-year-olds were less mature than adults, she observed that there were some 17-year-olds who were mature enough to deserve the death penalty, and that juries should make the determination of their punishment (e.g., in the sentencing phase of a trial). Justice O'Connor's preference was to let the state legislatures establish the limits of punishment rather than setting a national standard.

Justice Scalia also dissented, and he criticized the majority's use of in-dependent judgment to determine whether the juvenile death penalty was a cruel and unusual punishment. Like O'Connor, he believed that the legislatures, which reflect the will of the people, should define society's evolving standards of decency. Moreover, he argued that the method of assessing the national consensus against the juvenile death penalty used by the majority was flawed and that "Our previous cases have required overwhelming opposition to a challenged practice, generally over a long period of time," and he referred to the execution of the mentally ill—which no state allowed. Last, Scalia and the other dissenting justices were critical of the majority for considering international standards, treaties, and law, and they observed that "Though the views of our own citizens are essentially irrelevant to the Court's decision today, the views of other countries and the so-called international community take center stage."

Having eliminated the death penalty for juveniles, the search for alternatives for serious juvenile offenders narrowed very quickly to life without parole. As previously mentioned, in 2008, 49 states had some LWOP provision although few jurisdictions actually used this option (Nellis and King 2009). One fear of the persons who want to hold youth accountable for their offenses is that authorities with the power to pardon will commute many of these life sentences to relatively short terms and that these serious offenders will once again be free. While the imposition of the death penalty on a person who was a juvenile at the time of his or her offense was a relatively rare event even prior to *Roper v. Simmons*, transfers to adult courts that have resulted in lengthy prison sentences are commonly used today (Human Rights Watch 2008).

Graham v. Florida

In Chapter 1 we reported that the issue of sentencing youths to terms of life without the possibility of parole has become quite controversial. Human Rights Watch (2008) estimated that 2,484 offenders under the age of 18 had been sentenced to LWOP. Some of these offenders were quite young: The Equal Justice Initiative (2007) reported that 73 persons who were 13 or 14 years of age at the time of their offense had received these sentences. In the case of *Graham v. Florida*, a six-member majority decided that the state may not impose the life without parole penalty on juvenile offenders who have been convicted of crimes other than homicide. Therefore, youthful offenders other than murderers may be sentenced as adults to lengthy prison terms including life sentences, but not to life with-out parole regardless of their offense history.

The facts of the case, as taken directly from the Supreme Court decision, were that in July 2003, 16-year-old Terrance Graham and three other juvenile accomplices attempted to rob a Jacksonville, Florida, restaurant. One of the youths had worked at the restaurant and had left the back door open, and Graham and another youth—both wearing masks—entered through the open door, where Graham's accomplice hit the restaurant's manager with a metal bar. The manager yelled at the two assailants, who fled the restaurant and drove away in a vehicle operated by a fourth youth. Graham was arrested, and the prosecutor charged him as an adult for armed burglary with assault and attempted armed robbery. Both of these offenses were felonies, and the first carried with it a maximum life sentence.

In December 2003, Graham pled guilty to both charges and was sentenced to two concurrent three-year terms of probation in a plea agreement under which he was required to serve the first 12 months of his probation in the county jail. He was subsequently released from custody in June 2004.

Graham was arrested on December 2, 2004, for his involvement in two home invasions and fleeing from the police. Graham, along with two adults, engaged in a home invasion where the male victim was threatened with a handgun, the home ransacked, and the victim barricaded in a closet. Later that evening, the trio engaged in another home invasion, during which one of the adult accomplices was shot. Graham, who was driving his father's car, drove the wounded man to a hospital, where he and the other accomplice were dropped off. While driving away from the hospital a police officer signaled Graham to stop, but he fled at high speed and later crashed into a tree. The police recovered three handguns from the vehicle. The Court noted that on the night that these offenses were committed Graham was 34 days short of his 18th birthday.

On December 13, 2004, an affidavit was filed by Graham's probation officer asserting that he had violated his probation conditions by possessing a firearm, committing crimes, and associating with offenders. In December 2005 a Florida court heard the case and found that he had violated his probation. A presentence report was prepared by the Florida Department of Corrections, and while the maximum sentence was life imprisonment, they recommended, at most, a four-year term of imprisonment (which would have required a downward departure by the judge as the minimum sentence was five years). The prosecutor, by contrast, recommended a 30-year sentence for the armed burglary and 15 years for the attempted robbery.

The judge sentenced Graham to the maximum sentence: life imprisonment for the armed burglary and 15 years for the attempted armed
robbery. As Florida did not have the option for parole, the imposition
of a life imprisonment sentence meant that Graham would die in
prison unless his sentence was commuted. The judge's comments at sentencing on Graham's conduct are instructive, expressing concern that
the severity of Graham's criminal behavior was escalating, that Graham
did not take advantage of his probationary sentence to rehabilitate
himself, and that the court could do nothing to deter him. In terms of
Graham's status as a 17-year-old at the time of the offense, Judge Day
remarked:

> I don't see where any youthful offenders sanctions would be app-
> ropriate. Given your escalating pattern of criminal conduct, it is
> apparent to the Court that you have decided that this is the way you
> are going to live your life and the only thing I can do now is to try
> and protect the community from your actions.

Thus, the judge sided with public safety through incapacitation. Graham
subsequently challenged his sentence under the Eighth Amendment,
which was denied, and the First District Court of Appeal of Florida
affirmed the sentence, finding that his sentence was not "grossly disproportionate to his crimes." The Supreme Court of Florida denied review,
but *certiorari* was granted by the U.S. Supreme Court; the case was
heard on November 9, 2009, and the decision rendered on May 17,
2010.

Justice Kennedy, who had also written the *Roper* opinion four years
earlier, wrote the *Graham* majority opinion. At the heart of the matter
was the question of whether a person of less than 18 years of age could
be sentenced to LWOP for a nonhomicide offense. In deciding the case,
the majority used the rationale that was established by *Atkins* and *Roper*
and applied their decision to an entire class of offenders (what is called a
categorical ruling). This was the first time that such a challenge was successful with nonhomicide cases.

A *Harvard Law Review* (2010, 210–11) analysis of the case identified
two parts to the categorical test in Graham. First, the justices weighed
objective criteria to determine whether there was a national consensus
against the juvenile LWOP sentence for nonhomicide crimes. Similar to
the analysis they used in *Roper* five years earlier, the justices found that
a relatively small number of states actually used the sanction, and the
Harvard Law Review (2010, 211) reported that "Only twelve jurisdictions

actually imposed nonhomicide JLWOP—and Florida was responsible for almost sixty percent of such sentences."

Similar to *Roper*, the second part of the test was based on the independent judgment of the Court, and the justices considered three issues in their analysis: (1) the culpability of juveniles, (2) the sanction's severity, and the (3) penological justifications for terms of life imprisonment without the possibility of parole (*Harvard Law Review* 2010). The Court found that juveniles were less culpable or blameworthy than adults, using some of the same reasons cited in *Roper* (e.g., a youth's immaturity and receptiveness to negative influences) as well as the fact that these offenders had not committed murder (making them less blameworthy). The majority also found that the sanction imposed on these youths was very severe— what Johnson and Tabriz (2011) have called death by incarceration— and, given their youth, they would serve a longer prison term than an adult with the same sentence. Last, the justices considered the penological justifications of retribution, deterrence, incapacitation, and rehabilitation for imposing life terms on juveniles who had not committed homicide (*Harvard Law Review* 2010). Smith and Cohen (2010) reported that the Court sided with redemption and a youth's potential to reform.

Some of the justices saw the issue of LWOP sentences from another perspective. As with the *Roper* case, the dissenting justices questioned whether the majority should impose their notions of proportionality and evolving standards of decency upon state legislatures. Justice Thomas' dissent noted that 37 states and the District of Columbia had the LWOP sanction for nonhomicide juvenile offenders and only five states specifically prohibited this sanction. Moreover, Thomas argued that terms of life imprisonment were not a cruel and unusual punishment as intended by the framers of the Constitution and that the majority had erred in their analysis. The result of this and prior decisions, Thomas claimed, is that entire classes of offenders are now categorically removed from certain punishments—primarily capital punishment as in the cases of *Atkins* and *Roper*—and that the Court had established a precedent for nonhomicide offenders in *Graham*. In addition, Thomas also criticized the majority citing examples of "foreign laws and sentencing practices" as he felt that international practices should not be considered.

In terms of the decision's impact, there were only 129 offenders who had been sentenced to these terms of imprisonment, and some had been incarcerated since the 1970s. These offenders, however, were not guaranteed an eventual release from prison, as the Court only ordered that they be provided with an opportunity for release and did not specify when such an opportunity would take place or the criteria by which the offender would be evaluated. Consequently, Birckhead (2010, 79) observed that "the long term significance of *Graham* may be found in its precedential effect rather than its direct impact." St. Vincent (2010, 13) suggested that legislatures could thwart this decision by enacting laws that imposed lengthy prison terms without the possibility of parole (e.g., 100 years) which would effectively be a life sentence—an issue addressed in Chapter 8.

SUMMARY

Birckhead (2012) observed that the Supreme Court has ushered in two separate series of juvenile justice reforms: the *Kent, Gault,* and *Winship* decisions and the *Roper, Graham,* and *J.D.B. v. North Carolina* decisions. The first three cases provided juvenile defendants with a series of due process protections. *Roper* and *Graham,* by contrast, have set precedent by limiting the punishment of juvenile offenders. *J.D.B.,* decided in June 2011, by contrast, extends *Miranda* rights to juvenile suspects beyond those required for adults.

Singer (2011, 971) noted "that there are disparities between the law in theory and action" and, consistent with that observation, the outcomes of these Supreme Court decisions have been mixed. While *Kent, Gault,* and *Winship* were important in providing youth with due process protections, a more critical examination of their impact suggests that, four decades after *Gault,* reformers' promises have been unfulfilled (Dorsen 2007; Feld and Schaefer 2010; Kaye 2011; Marrus 2008). For instance, youths still appear before juvenile courts without counsel, and Feld and Schaefer (2010) reported that this occurs because some state legislatures have redefined delinquency to reduce the due process protections that some youths receive. Similarly, in response to formalizing proceedings, most legislatures have either given prosecutors the ability to directly file juvenile cases in criminal courts or have excluded serious offenders from the juvenile courts altogether, effectively sidestepping the juvenile justice system's protections and traditional leniency.

Both the *Roper* and *Graham* decisions had very little real direct impact upon the punishment of actual offenders. Death sentences for juvenile offenders in the decades prior to *Roper* were rare, and their actual executions were uncommon. Streib (2005, 3) noted that from 1973 to 2005 a total of 226 juvenile death sentences were imposed, and of those 22 executions had been carried out (all after 1985) while 71 remained in force in 2005 (the rest had been reversed or commuted). In terms of juveniles sentenced to LWOP for nonhomicide offenses, 129 persons were impacted by the *Graham* decision. There were, by contrast, an estimated 1,536,550 arrests of persons under the age of 18 years for murder, robbery, forcible rape, and aggravated assaults between 1994 and 2007, and of those arrests, 25,910 were for homicide (Puzzanchera, Adams, and Kang 2009). As a result, the proportion of juveniles who received the death penalty or LWOP was very small.

Although the overall proportion of offenders sentenced to these tough sentences was small, they were almost all minority youths. Of the 22 juveniles executed between 1985 and 2003, Streib (2005, 4) reported that 11 were black and one was Latino, while 10 were white. In terms of the juveniles sentenced to LWOP for nonhomicide offenses, Agyepong (2010, 98) reported that *all* were minority youths and that 71 percent of juveniles serving LWOP sentences were members of minority groups, while minority youths represented about one-third of all U.S. youths. Such findings reinforce the belief that the juvenile justice system is discriminatory.

Despite the fact that the numbers of youths affected by *Roper* and *Graham* is relatively small, these decisions have an important symbolic impact in establishing the upper limits of punishment. They also speak to the larger issue of redemption and hope for juvenile offenders: that there is some potential for rehabilitation. Sentencing youths to die in prison is a commentary on American cultural values and beliefs. In addition to the symbolic value of these decisions, it is likely that *Roper* and *Graham* will establish the precedent for the further categorical exclusion of other groups of juveniles from lengthy sentences. Liptak and Petak (2011, A13) observed that "The Supreme Court has been methodically whittling away at severe sentences" and that the next possible step for reformers is to challenge the constitutionality of 13- and 14-year-olds sentenced to terms of LWOP for their involvement in homicides.

NOTES

1. In the summaries of the Supreme Court cases cited in this chapter the actual page numbers are not referenced, and some of our summaries, as well as the comments of the Justices, are taken verbatim from the Court's opinion.

2. The nine states that allowed jury trials were AK, MA, MI, MT, NM, OK, TX, WV, and WY, and the 11 states that authorized jury trials in specific circumstances were AR, CO, CT, ID, IL, KS, MN, NH, OH, RI, and VA.

3. Aggravating circumstances include a victim's death or the infliction of serious injuries, commission of a crime while on bail for another offense (or on probation or parole), use of extreme cruelty in the commission of the crime, use of a weapon in the commission of a crime, and a prior record or leadership in the commission of the alleged offenses. Mitigating circumstances—those factors that lessen the severity of sentencing—include duress or extreme provocation, assisting law enforcement with an investigation, mental incapacitation, motivation to provide necessities, youthfulness, and being a first-time offender.

SIX

Public Opinion, Public Policy, and Juvenile Justice

INTRODUCTION

During the last several decades, a gradual disenchantment with the criminal and juvenile justice systems has occurred. The public is increasingly cynical about law enforcement, the courts, and corrections and their respective abilities to process, punish, and manage offenders. Much of this disenchantment toward the justice system is shaped by the media's portrayal of the justice system's operations. The types of news reports that draw our attention typically focus upon the justice system's failures such as wrongful convictions and the inability to mete out justice to celebrity or high-profile defendants such as O. J. Simpson, Lindsay Lohan, or Casey Anthony. Furthermore, the Internet has allowed us to witness miscarriages of justice. Citizens with their cellular phones have placed law enforcement officials under significant scrutiny. While acts of brutality that occurred in the past were apt to be hidden, an officer's actions today are more likely to be posted on the Internet for millions of viewers.

Gamson, Croteau, Hoynes, and Sasson (1992, 373) observed that "we walk around with media-generated images of the world, using them to construct meaning about political and social issues." Our perceptions of the justice system are also shaped by the fictionalized accounts of cases in the entertainment media. Violent crime is presented as pervasive and increasing. Criminals are portrayed as vicious and sophisticated. By contrast, the officials working within justice systems are often presented as being at a disadvantage because of liberal judges and policies that "handcuff" the police, thereby preventing them from doing their duty. Researchers who have examined the relationships between popular culture and citizen perceptions have found that individuals who watch more television often are more fearful of crime (Goidel, Freeman, and Procopio 2006).

Some scholars have observed that news organizations are responsible for the construction of myths about crime or justice issues (Beckett and Sasson 2004; Feld 2003b; Kappeler and Potter 2005). Perrone and Chesney-Lind (1997) argued that media accounts of youth violence, weaponry, and gangs are greatly exaggerated. Indeed, they noted the tendency of the media and public policy groups to overreport levels of youth crime.

The public's perceptions of the justice system's failures have a basis in reality. Those who believe that we should be tough-on-crime, for example, point to the U.S. Supreme Court's obligation of law enforcement officers to adhere to more rigid standards in conducting arrests as well as in their procedures for seizing evidence as proof that we are soft on crime. A relatively modest percentage of the defendants who were arraigned in court are actually punished very severely. In their research for the Bureau of Justice Statistics, Cohen and Kyckelhahn (2010, 1) reported that for every 100 defendants appearing before the courts in large counties, 24 ultimately go to prison, 24 are jailed for a year or less, and 17 receive a probationary sentence.

In terms of actual punishments, while probation used to be reserved for relatively minor offenders, 51 percent of probationers on December 31, 2009, were felons (Glaze and Bonczar 2010, 4), and about 19 percent of all probationers had been convicted of a violent offense (Glaze and Bonczar 2010, 26). In some jurisdictions jails are so crowded that most offenders serve only part of their sentences. Most jail inmates in Los Angeles, for example, served about one-tenth of their sentence in 2006 (Ruddell and Mays 2006). Last, most state prisons have some form of parole, and this is used as a safety valve to reduce correctional crowding and to reward good behavior. While national-level statistics on time served in prison have not been published recently, the California Department of Corrections and Rehabilitation (2011, 2) reported that prisoners convicted of violent, drug, or property crimes served, on average, sentences of 48.0, 21.2, and 19.0 months respectively in 2010.[1]

Many citizens have also lost trust in justice systems to treat suspects in a just and fair manner. Reiman and Leighton (2010) observed that officials focus on the crimes of the poor while ignoring white-collar crime. Moreover, they argue that poor defendants are disadvantaged in their interactions with justice agencies. Since many of the poor are also minority group members, these individuals may be doubly disadvantaged. We saw in Chapter 3, for instance, that a disproportionate number of the juveniles transferred to adult courts were nonwhite, and those findings reinforce the beliefs of many people that the justice system discriminates against youths of color.

Those who believe that justice systems are rigged against poor defendants point out that most never go to trial. Cohen and Kyckelhahn (2010, 1) reported that 95 percent of all criminal convictions in large urban counties in 2006 were the result of plea bargaining and that trials are relatively rare events. In addition, legal aid resources in many jurisdictions are stretched thin, and the quality of some public defenders is questionable due to their inexperience and high workloads. In a study conducted on behalf of the American Bar Association, Stevens, Sheppard, Spangenberg, Wickman, and Gould (2010) reported that indigent defense in some jurisdictions was hampered by large caseloads and a chronic lack of funding for legal aid. A lack of resources is a factor contributing to many wrongful convictions (Gould and Leo 2010). For example, by November 2011 a total of 280 prisoners had been exonerated for crimes they had not committed, including 17 who had served part of their sentence on death row (Innocence Project 2011).

Punitive policies, such as adult imprisonment for juvenile offenders, may increase mistrust in criminal and juvenile justice systems and reduce their legitimacy among the groups most affected by these practices. Tyler and Huo (2002) observed that trust in justice systems is declining. This mistrust is not spread evenly among the general public, and there is a pronounced disconnect between the perceptions of whites and blacks. In a 2011 Gallup Poll, for example, 27 percent of whites reported very little or no confidence in the criminal justice system, while 37 percent of blacks had the same response (Maguire 2011, Table 2.11).

The transfers of juveniles to adult courts fits in with this disenchantment. Starting in the 1970s, the public became increasingly intolerant toward what it perceived as a growing leniency toward both adult and juvenile offenders. One reaction to this real or imaginary laxity was the emergence of the get-tough movement, which included a return to using the death penalty in some jurisdictions, longer prison terms, mandatory minimum sentences, three-strikes legislation, truth-in-sentencing initiatives, increased monetary penalties, and the civil forfeiture of possessions together with an increased number of community-based restrictions or sanctions for parolees.

There was a noticeable spillover effect of this get-tough movement into the juvenile justice system as well. Throughout the 1980s there was a significant increase in the number of juveniles arrested for homicide, especially for gang-involved, inner city youths. Moreover, there was a series of high-profile and heinous offenses committed by juveniles that drew an inordinate amount of media attention. Last, there were a number of very high-profile school shootings throughout the American heartland. Altogether, these rare but well-publicized events created a political climate that made it easy for politicians to enact legislation that increased the severity of sanctions for juvenile offenders.

Get-tough juvenile justice policies have been introduced in all U.S. jurisdictions. In order to send a message to youths that their delinquent behaviors would not be tolerated, Americans sent more of them to out-of-home placements. One of the problems with incarcerating youths was that it sometimes had a criminogenic effect: it essentially made the offender worse. Holman and Ziedenberg (2009) argued that detention increases the likelihood of recidivism by congregating delinquents together as well as disrupting their family lives, school, and employment. These investigators also reported that many detained youths had emotional and mental health problems and argued that detention was an inappropriate place for them.

Boot camps also appealed to our desire to hold youngsters accountable. Television documentaries and news accounts depicted the tough treatment that these offenders received, including military drill and hard physical labor. The images of camp staff yelling at these youths resonated with the public, but research into these programs' effectiveness demonstrated that they did not reduce recidivism, correctional budgets, or crowding (Armstrong and Kim 2009). Most of the boot camps disappeared as fast as they emerged, and very few county or state jurisdictions operate these facilities, although there are a number of privately operated boot camps still in operation.

Juveniles adjudicated on serious offenses and repeat offenders were placed in training schools or other secure facilities. Conditions in some of these institutions were found to be unconstitutional as they lacked appropriate levels of educational and health care services, especially for residents with mental health problems or disabilities (Ruddell 2009). Advocacy organizations such as the Youth Law Center successfully initiated a number of class action lawsuits to force juvenile correctional systems into complying with state and federal standards. In addition, by 2011 the U.S. Department of Justice (2011b) had investigated over 100 juvenile facilities in 16 state systems to ensure that they were in compliance with the Civil Rights for Institutionalized Persons Act.

Despite the fact that out-of-home placements such as detention, boot camps, and training schools existed, they were not seen as punitive enough for some youths. In addition, the juvenile justice system's jurisdiction was also seen as inadequate for holding serious youth offenders accountable. For example, 16- and 17-year-olds might only have been placed in these facilities until their 18th or 21st birthdays, and many policymakers were not convinced that older youths could be rehabilitated in a year or two. As a result, transfers to adult court were a logical alternative. More importantly for the advocates of the get-tough movement, these transfers opened up a new range of severe punishments such as the death penalty (prior to 2005) and life sentences, which appealed to both politicians and the public. This get-tough movement did not emerge overnight, but instead it was the product of a number of political, cultural, and social forces. In the pages that follow we examine some of the factors that influenced the use of transfers, starting with public perceptions of the youth crime problem.

PERCEPTIONS OF JUVENILE OFFENDERS

The public holds mixed feelings toward youths who have committed criminal acts. On the one hand, many of us engaged in youthful misconduct such as experimenting with drugs or alcohol, shoplifting, vandalism, fighting, or driving recklessly. A Gallup poll, for instance, revealed that 9 percent of respondents admitted having been arrested between the ages of 13 and 18, and that number increased to 17 percent for older respondents (Moore 1999, 1). Most of these acts are relatively minor offenses, and we tend not to stigmatize these youths because most of us committed similar acts but were never arrested.

On the other hand, the public is much less tolerant of juveniles who have committed serious and violent offenses or who are repeat offenders. As most of us have little direct experience with serious juvenile crime, many of these perceptions are shaped by the media (Soler 2001). Ruddell and Decker (2005) studied public perceptions toward youths and found that a number of individuals and groups benefitted from their portrayal as being dangerous, including news and entertainment organizations (whose goal was higher ratings), the police (who could advocate for expanding their organizations based on these sophisticated juvenile offenders), as well as research and interest groups that categorized offenders up to 24 years of age as "youths." Last, juveniles might exaggerate their own experiences with crime to impress researchers.

In his study of the relationships between the media and public opinion, Soler (2001, 7) found that while the public is less fearful of crime than in the past, they believe that juvenile crime—especially serious violence committed by young teenagers—is on the increase. One important question is how these misconceptions about juvenile crime are formed. Krisberg, Hartney, Wolf, and Silva (2009, iii) reported that a number of factors are responsible for our ideas about youngsters:

> Public perception of violent crime is largely a function of media coverage of crime, especially youth crime. Many adults have little contact with youth and most never directly experience youth crime. This leaves them to base their impressions of youth and youth crime on external sources such as word of mouth, public officials, and in particular, the media . . . [and]
>
> Media coverage does not reflect a sufficiently thorough or, in many cases, accurate understanding of youth crime. Most stories about young people depict them as troubled or, more likely, as trouble for society; stories about youth typically associate youth with violence, whether as victim or instigator. Far too much coverage focuses on infrequent but heinous cases, without any context.

The findings by Soler (2001) as well as those by Krisberg, Hartney, Wolf, and Silva (2009) support Bernard and Kurlycheck's (2010) observations that juvenile justice policy is driven by a number of myths.

Misleading perceptions toward juvenile crime have been present for almost a century. As far back as the Great Depression, the U.S. government had identified a disconnection between the public's perceptions of delinquency and the actual amount of youth crime that occurred. According to the Children's Bureau (1932, 5):

> No one can state with certainty whether juvenile delinquency as known to police and courts is increasing or decreasing, because of the absence of reliable and comprehensive data over a period of years. Clearly, however, such statistics as are available show no uniform and alarming tendency to increased juvenile delinquency and youthful crime. Agitation about "youth and the crime wave" is perennial but for the most part is without factual foundation.

Thus, the U.S. government was concerned in the 1930s that youth crime was being portrayed as a more significant problem than it actually was.

Juveniles do commit an inordinate amount of crime, but as we noted in Chapter 3, most of it is relatively minor. Yet politicians and advocates for the tough-on-crime perspective do not always distinguish between minor and serious offenses. Reed (1941, 114–15) noted that "juvenile delinquency has increased faster than adult crime and misdemeanor. This is reported as general throughout the country and would seem to fit the hypothesis that the increase of juvenile delinquency has been due to bad economic and social conditions." Bernard and Kurlychek (2010) noted that such observations may lead to a public demand that something be done about reducing youth crime.

In 1954, the U.S. Senate held hearings that examined the relationships between negative social influences, such as the characters and stories depicted in comic books, and delinquency. The Subcommittee to Investigate Juvenile Delinquency (1954, 28) heard the following testimony:

> Every parent, every responsible adult, should be shocked by the prediction of 400,000 juveniles in court as delinquents during 1954. This represents a 33 percent increase over 1948, just as 350,000 in court during last year was 19 percent higher than prior years. Delinquency is on the march, ever increasing, ever destroying our youth.

By the 1950s, the 1932 message from the Children's Bureau (that delinquency was under control) had been forgotten, and policymakers were focusing on the negative aspects of youth crime without fully understanding if it was actually increasing and whether this perceived increase was a result of status offenses, misdemeanors, or felonies.

Most of us have strong opinions about government social policies. The Gallup organization, for example, has asked Americans about the "most important problem" facing the nation since the 1930s. For most of that time, Americans reported that foreign affairs or economic issues (e.g., unemployment or inflation) were the most pressing problems (Erskine 1974; Newport 2010). Even at the height of the violent crime wave that ended in the early 1990s, crime was never at the top of the list. Yet, when asked specifically about crime levels, the public's responses are rarely accurate. Figure 6.1 shows the results from Gallup polls from 1989 to 2010, and in most of these years respondents reported that crime was increasing, when it was actually stable or decreasing (although there will be a lag as the Federal Bureau of Investigation's crime statistics are reported one or two years after they occur).

Krisberg and colleagues (2009) observed that the public believes that juveniles are responsible for a significant amount of serious crime. Table 6.1 shows the results from a number of national- and state-level polls where respondents were asked questions regarding youth crime. While the Steinhart (1988) and Schwartz (1992) results were consistent with the actual increases in juvenile crime that started in the late 1980s, the

Figure 6.1 Percentage of Respondents to Gallup Polls Stating That Crime Had Increased

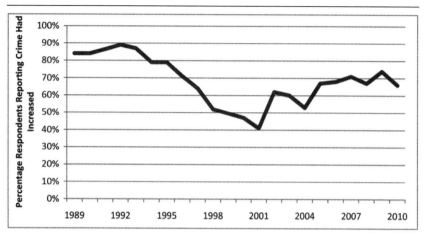

results afterwards do not reflect arrest or court data that showed decreasing youth crime. A review of the six studies conducted during or after 1995, for example, shows that an average of 75.5 percent of the respondents believed that crime was increasing, when youth crime rates were actually decreasing.

Race and Public Opinion

One of the long-standing concerns confronting juvenile justice systems is disproportionate minority contact (DMC) and the belief that youth of

Table 6.1   Perceptions of Juvenile Crime

Source	Poll Year	Percentage of Respondents Believing Crime Rates Have Increased Significantly	
Yoon and Wilson (2008)	2007	National Survey	70
Soler (2001)	1999	National Survey	62
Dorfman and Schiraldi (2001)	1998	National Survey	62
Soler (2001)	1995	National Survey	84
Doble Research Assoc. (1995a)	1995	North Carolina	85
Doble Research Assoc. (1995b)	1995	Oklahoma	90
Schwartz (1992)	1991	National Survey	62
Steinhart (1998)	1988	California	82
Krisberg and Austin (1993)	1982	National Survey	87

Source: Adapted from Roberts (2004).

color are treated in a discriminatory manner. Feld (2003b) argued that we cannot fully understand the movement toward punitive juvenile justice without acknowledging the issue of race and the role of politicians who use the issues of race and crime to advance their interests. In particular, Feld (2003b, 766) observed that:

> Republican politicians pursued a "southern strategy," used *crime* as a code word for race for electoral advantage, and advocated harsher policies that have affected juvenile justice throughout the nation. Media coverage increasingly put a black face on youth crime that was exploited for political advantage. This increased punitiveness in juvenile justice, which began in the 1970s, continued into the 1990s as a surge in homicides among black youths provided further political incentive to toughen responses to youth crime.

While Republicans may have first articulated tough-on-crime policies, no politician wants to be seen as soft on crime, and as a result Democrats are often just as punitive as their Republican counterparts (Tonry 2009).

Dorfman and Schiraldi (2001, 8–17) examined 77 different studies to determine how the media portrayed juveniles. They summarized their findings in the following manner: (1) that the media reports crime out of proportion, overreporting violent and rare or unusual crimes, and that crime reporting actually increased during times of decreasing crime; (2) that the media often neglects the economic, political, and social contexts in which crimes occur; (3) that television news programs disproportionately connect race and violent crime; and (4) that, of the news accounts that featured juveniles, most were connected with violence.

In terms of our attitudes toward race, Soler (2001, 8) observed that the public is uncertain whether justice systems treat minority group members in an unbiased manner and that they are concerned over the justice system's fairness. That concern is also matched with a willingness to support initiatives that work toward the fair treatment of minorities—in both the economic and justice systems. These results suggest that the public understands the complexities of issues such as DMC but has less knowledge about how to solve these long-entrenched problems.

Public Opinion on Transfers to Adult Court

Transferring juveniles to criminal courts for adult punishments is one aspect of the get-tough movement. Table 6.2 summarizes the results of 16 studies that examined public opinion on juvenile justice policies that were conducted between 1991 and 2007. These results show that the public overwhelmingly supports transferring youths from juvenile to adult courts. Of the 14 studies that specifically asked about transferring youths, an average of 72.8 percent of respondents supported transfers. Two studies were excluded from this analysis as respondents were asked about eliminating the juvenile justice system altogether and trying juveniles as adults in federal courts.

Table 6.2   Support for Transfers to Adult Courts

Source	Poll Year	Percentage of Respondents Supporting Transfer	
Steinberg and Piquero (2010)	2007	Some 17-year-old recidivists convicted of rape	85.0
Applegate, King-Davis, and Cullen (2009)	2002	Violent crimes	73.1
Krisberg and Marchionna (2007)	2007	Prosecuting more youth in the adult criminal justice system (effective or highly effective)	72.0
Mears, Hay, Gertz, and Mancini (2007)	2006	Eliminate juvenile justice system	19.6
Gallup (2003)	2003	Violent crimes	59.0
Bouley and Wells (2001)	1999	Property offense	64.8
		Selling illegal drugs	90.0
		Serious violent crime	71.3
Mears (2001)	1995	Property offense	64.0
		Selling illegal drugs	70.0
		Violent offense	87.0
Gallup (2000)	2000	Violent crimes	65.0
Wu (2000)	1995	Property offense	68.3
		Drug offense	73.5
		Violent offense	90.8
NBC News/*Wall Street Journal* (1999)	1999	Favor of laws trying juvenile offenders 13 years and younger as adults	50.0
PEW Research Center (1999)	1999	Favor of laws trying violent juveniles 14 years and older as adults	73.0

Table 6.2   *(continued)*

Source	Poll Year	Percentage of Respondents Supporting Transfer	
CBS (1999)	1998	Favor of 13 year olds charged with violent crimes being tried as adults	58.0
Schiraldi and Soler (1998)	1998	Prosecutor's discretion to try juveniles in adult courts (agree/strongly agree)	41.0
Pew Research Center (1998)	1997	Favor of laws trying juvenile offenders (14 years and older) as adults	66.0
Gallup Youth Survey (1995)	1995	Murderers	95.0
		Rapists	94.0
		Robbery	90.0
		Selling drugs	82.0
Schwartz et al. (1993)	1991	Property	49.6
		Drug offense	62.3
		Violent offense	67.5

What is surprising about the results in Table 6.2 is that 15 of the 16 studies occurred *after* the decrease in serious youth violence occurred in 1994. For the respondents in the three studies that were conducted in 1995, information about the crime decrease was either not well reported or was unavailable. As a result, respondents might have believed that youth violence rates remained high. Regardless of the reason, however, this shows that the public's perceptions about juvenile crime are often incorrect.

Concern over crime, whether it was committed by adults or juveniles, influences our political behavior, including our preferences for different policy responses. Figure 6.2 shows the results of questions from the General Social Survey (GSS) from 1973 to 2010 (Smith 2011). In this study respondents were asked a number of questions about national social spending and were specifically asked about whether too little was spent to halt the rising crime rate. Over these four decades an average of 67.2 percent of respondents said that too little was being spent, with the highest proportion of respondents occurring in 1994 (77.6%) which coincided with the peak of youth violence. In 2002, the lowest proportion of respondents (57.5%) said that too little was being spent to halt the rising crime rate.[2]

Figure 6.2 Respondents Stating Government Was Spending Too Little on Crime Control

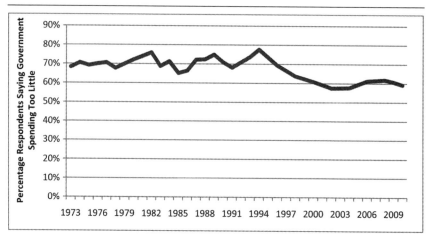

The findings reported above must be carefully interpreted. A significant issue in the validity of survey research is the manner in which a question is presented to a participant and how that influences possible responses. In the case of the GSS, respondents were asked about spending to halt the rising crime rate. Placing an emphasis on rising crime, especially in years when it was actually decreasing, might influence a participant's responses. The Gallup organization, for instance, has conducted polls on the use of the death penalty since the 1930s, and they have reported that the manner in which a question is asked (e.g., whether the option of life without the possibility of parole is presented in the question) influences the results that they received (Gallup 2008).

A number of investigators have examined how different factors have influenced the responses that they received in their research on youth justice. Hart (1998), for instance, found that the order in which questions about youth justice were asked influenced the responses that he received. More specifically, Hart (1998, 139) found that "respondents are significantly more likely to agree that growth of youth gangs explains the cause of increased juvenile crime and violence if it precedes statements about the consequences of juvenile crime and violence."

Steinberg and Piquero (2010) conducted research on public opinion toward transferring juveniles to adult courts. Participants were presented with a number of different options based on the demographic and offense-related characteristics of fictional delinquents, including whether they were 14 or 17 years of age at the time of the offense—either theft or rape—and whether the youth was a first-time or repeat offender. Not surprisingly, respondents were more likely to support the transfer of older, repeat, and violent offenders. Applegate, King-Davis, and Cullen (2009), and Feiler and Sheley (1999) used vignettes to show participants the offender's demographic characteristics (including age and race) and the nature of the offense. Scott, Reppucci, Antonishak, and De Gennaro (2006), incorporated photographs that depicted white and black juvenile offenders (at ages 12, 15, and 20 years) and a short video to illustrate the offense characteristics. Taken together, these investigators found that opinions about juvenile crime can be swayed according to the type of information provided.

These findings suggest that researchers examining punitive values must carefully design their surveys and ensure that all respondents have the same information when making a decision about the appropriateness of different sanctions, including transfers to adult courts. A secondary consideration is that many of these national-level polls were conducted by phone and had approximately 1,000 respondents. While that number is based on well-established survey research principles, there is increasing concern that some groups—such as young persons who only have cellular phones—are not considered in the survey samples that rely on random calls to homes with landlines (Ansolabehere and Schaffner 2010).

Politicians and policymakers are active consumers of public opinion research, and therefore it becomes more important that research be conducted in a manner that increases the usefulness of the results. Steinberg and Piquero (2010, 500) observed that "In some instances, the survey item wording is vague, which renders the public's real opinion completely unknowable because it is impossible to ascertain what respondents had in mind when answering the survey." For example, asking about transferring a violent juvenile to adult court could refer to a 13-year-old first-time offender involved in a schoolyard fistfight or a 17-year-old gangster charged with shooting a rival gang member. As Applegate, King-Davis, and Cullen (2009, 70) noted, however, "When few details are provided, the public appears to base responses on worst-case scenarios."

Support for Juvenile Rehabilitation

Earlier we observed that the public has mixed feelings toward youthful offenders. While we want delinquents held accountable, most poll results show that the public also supports their rehabilitation. Table 6.3 presents the results from 13 questions in seven studies that examined public perceptions toward rehabilitating juveniles. What is striking about these findings is the consistency of the results: respondents overwhelmingly indicated their support for rehabilitation and a juvenile's potential for rehabilitation. Regardless of the way in which the questions were posed, the average support for rehabilitation in these 13 questions was 80.74 percent. Within these studies, almost two-thirds had an optimistic view of rehabilitating violent juveniles (Mears, Hay, Gertz, and Mancini 2007), opted for community-based dispositions compared to placements outside the home (Moon, Sundt, Cullen, and Wright 2000), and expressed a willingness to pay additional taxes for preventative or rehabilitative interventions (Nagin, Piquero, Scott, and Steinberg 2006).

Table 6.3   Support for Juvenile Rehabilitation

Source	Poll Year	Percentage of Respondents Supporting Juvenile Rehabilitation	
GBA Strategies (2011)	2011	When it comes to youth who have committed crimes, the best thing for society is to rehabilitate them so they can become productive members of society (% agreeing)	77
Piquero, Cullen, Unnever, Piquero, and Gordon (2010)	2005	Juvenile offenders can benefit more from rehabilitative treatment than adult offenders (% agreeing)	77.2
		Juvenile offenders are more likely to become adult criminals if they are sent to a jail than if they get rehabilitation in juvenile facilities (% agreeing)	74.2
Applegate, King-Davis and Cullen (2009)	2002	Importance of juvenile sentencing goal of rehabilitation (Respondents selecting important and extremely important)	94.7
Krisberg and Marchionna (2007)	2007	Rehabilitative services and treatment for incarcerated youth can help prevent future crimes	89.0
		Considering taxpayer resources, spending on enhanced rehabilitation services for youth in the JJ system will save tax dollars in the long run	81.0

Table 6.3   (*continued*)

Source	Poll Year	Percentage of Respondents Supporting Juvenile Rehabilitation	
Mears, Hay, Gertz, and Mancini (2007)	2006	Violent juveniles can be rehabilitated	64.0
Nagin, Piquero, Scott and Steinberg (2006)	2005	Willingness to pay at least $50 in additional taxes for juvenile rehabilitation	72.3
		Willingness to pay $75 for a home visitation program (to reduce delinquency)	65.0
Moon, Sundt, Cullen, and Wright (2000)	1998	It is a good idea to provide treatment for juvenile offenders who are supervised by the courts and live in the community (% agreeing)	89.0
		It is a good idea to provide treatment for juvenile offenders who are in prison (% agreeing)	94.8
		It is important to try and rehabilitate juvenile offenders who have committed crimes and are now in the correctional system (% agreeing)	94.6
		Rehabilitative programs should be available even for juvenile offenders who have been involved in a lot of crime (% agreeing)	76.4

It is important to acknowledge that survey questions soliciting a respondent's opinion toward juvenile rehabilitation might also be asked in a manner that influences responses. In addition, the persons who participated in these studies will also shape the results. It is difficult to briefly summarize these studies as a number of dependent variables were used and the outcomes are often different for each question that was posed. The general findings, however, are that men tend to be more punitive than women (Applegate et al. 2009; Feiler and Sheley 1999; Jan, Ball, and Walsh 2008; Mears et al. 2007; Schwartz, Guo, and Kerbs 1993). Individuals with lower incomes (Bouley and Wells 2001) and less education

(Mears 2001; Schwartz et al. 1993) are also more punitive. Some investigators also collected information about the values or beliefs of the participants in their studies. Applegate, King-Davis, and Cullen (2009) reported that respondents who adhered to a literal interpretation of the Bible were more punitive. Mears and colleagues (2007) found that respondents with a conservative ideology and retributive philosophy were also more likely to support more punitive sanctions for youths. Last, Schwartz, Guo, and Kerbs (1993) found a relationship between an individual's fear of victimization and support for tough juvenile sanctions.

Altogether, we find that the public's attitudes toward juvenile offenders are mixed. Most of us tend to support the rehabilitation of juveniles, including those who have committed violent crimes. Yet the studies reported above revealed that these perceptions are also balanced by an equally high percentage of respondents who believed that delinquents should be held accountable for their offenses. These notions are influenced by the messages that we receive in the news and entertainment media. For the most part these messages focus upon rare and sensational or heinous crimes. While our attitudes toward juvenile offenders reflect the tension between punishment and rehabilitation, the United States has adopted tough-on-crime strategies for the control of juveniles while other nations have invested in rehabilitative approaches. Explaining why this occurred requires an examination of the political and social contexts that led to a war on adult and juvenile crime.

THE SOCIAL AND POLITICAL CONTEXTS
FOR TOUGH-ON-CRIME POLICIES

The growth in American tough-on-crime policies was the result of a complex interplay of social, cultural, and political conditions, and it cannot easily be explained by a single factor (Garland 1990). For example, the media alone could not have convinced the public that harsh sanctions policies for juveniles, including moving more of them to adult courts, were necessary. These notions had to be supported by the public as well as politicians, had to be funded by governments at all levels, and needed the approval of the electorate for almost four decades. Our preoccupation with crime and delinquency has created a climate where Americans are fearful about being victimized, even after almost two decades of decreasing crime rates.

In the pages that follow we examine how punitive crime control policies emerged at the same time as high levels of political upheaval, rapid social change, as well as increasing public disenchantment and political alienation. This environment created a demand to do something tangible to restore stability and order and to reassure the electorate that the country was headed in the right direction. In order to demonstrate policy success, politicians waged a war on drugs and crime. Being tough-on-crime and offenders was one of the few policy platforms that were supported by nearly every voter. The hazard is that some crime control strategies have proven to be very expensive and they may actually contribute to *higher* rates of crime.

The Social Context for Tough-on-Crime Policies

The get-tough-on-crime movement that started in the 1970s has to be understood within the context of changing social conditions that threatened long-standing social, political, and economic relationships. Specific examples include the growing prominence of the civil rights movement, an unpopular war in Vietnam, and changes in the political and economic roles of the young, women, and minority group members. Additionally, people became less socially connected to each other, the number of female-headed households increased as did the population of young people and persons of color, and whites fled the cities for the suburbs. The public also became more critical of their leaders. The Gallup organization, for example, had been asking Americans about the most important problem facing the nation since the 1950s, and for most of those years the public identified foreign policy issues as the most important. By the 1970s, however, domestic issues were the foremost concerns.

At about the same time as these social changes, there were a number of significant economic challenges as well. Throughout the 1970s there was increasing economic stress in the forms of inflation, rising consumer and corporate debt and bankruptcies, increasing numbers of strikes, unstable levels of employment, higher income inequality, and the transition to a service economy that eroded the number of blue collar union jobs that did not require a postsecondary education.

Parallel with these economic, social, and cultural changes, there was growing political disenchantment, and protests and riots increased. Respondents in national surveys expressed increased pessimism about the future (Putnam 2000). Despite the fact that the vote had been extended to 18- to 20-year-olds in 1971, voter turnout decreased, suggesting alienation and disaffection. For instance, 43 percent of respondents in the 1958 American National Election Studies (ANES) survey reported that "a lot" of the people in government waste tax money; by 2008 this proportion had increased to 72 percent. When the ANES questioned individuals

Figure 6.3 The Harris Alienation Index and Imprisonment Rates

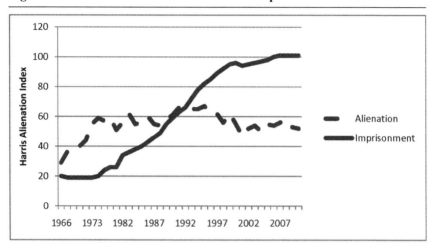

whether governments were run for the benefit of all in 1964, 29 percent of respondents reported that government was run for the benefit of a "few big interests"; by 2008, that had increased to 69 percent. These sentiments have also been captured in the Harris Alienation Index, which was first calculated in 1966. Interestingly, the highest rates of self-reported alienation occurred from 1991 to 1995, which also corresponds with the highest homicide rates. Figure 6.3 shows the Alienation Index from 1966 to 2010 (Harris Interactive 2010, 1)[3] and the combined U.S. federal and state imprisonment rate. This figure shows that adult imprisonment increased along with alienation but continued to grow after alienation peaked in 1995.[4]

Throughout the 1970s and 1980s politicians had an increasingly difficult time showing much policy success, and this might have contributed to higher levels of political disaffection.[5] A combination of growing alienation and disaffection created an environment where politicians needed to latch onto a policy issue where they could demonstrate some success. Parenti (2000, 3) argued that politicians used the issue of crime to demonstrate social policy success during a time when many thought that very few things were going right within the nation:

How bleak the world must have been for those with political and economic power during the late sixties and early seventies. Order seemed to be unraveling: massive anti-war protests on the Mall; a war effort bogged down and hemorrhaging in the mud of Southeast Asia; economic stagnation and declining profit rates; and, in the cities, skyrocketing crime coupled with some of the most violent riots since the Civil War.

Not only did the public see offenders as unsympathetic, they were also presented as dangerous. Kane (2003, 269) noted that offenders were labeled as social junk, social dynamite, and the underclass, while juveniles were portrayed as superpredators (Bennett, DiIulio, and Walters 1996) or the young and the ruthless (Fox 1992). Reduced sympathy for all offenders, and juveniles in particular, made it easier to sentence them to terms of life without the possibility of parole or put them on death row (see also Titus 2005).

The Political Context for Punitive Justice Policies

The subject of crime and punishment was a relatively unimportant electoral issue prior to Barry Goldwater's presidential run in 1964 (Western and Wildeman 2009). Legislators discovered that crime and the punishment of offenders was an ideal campaign issue: after all, who would oppose being tough on offenders? A number of scholars have speculated that the crime issue was part of a Republican strategy to lure white Democratic voters to their party in the 1970s (Feld 2003b; Gottschalk 2009).

Investigators who examined the relationships between political party control and tough-on-crime policies, however, have reported mixed findings. Nicholson-Crotty and Meier (2003) found that Democratic Party governance was associated with the growth in federal imprisonment. Both Jacobs and Carmichael (2001) and Smith (2004), by contrast, reported that Republican Party governance was positively associated with state prison population increases. Furthermore, Stucky, Heimer, and Lang (2007) found a positive relationship between Republican Party governance and state correctional spending. Spelman's (2009) comprehensive study of imprisonment trends, however, did not find an association between public opinion, partisan politics, electoral cycles, or theories that maintain that increases in minority populations led to a greater use of imprisonment.

Such contradictory findings in regards to the issue of political party governance might be caused by the eras being examined and the indicators of governance used (e.g., whether party affiliation includes both federal and state level politicians). Nicholson-Crotty, Peterson, and Ramirez (2009, 649) found that:

The political measures provide mixed results in regards to the punitiveness of federal crime policy. Having more Democrats in Congress leads to an increase in punitive policies inconsistent with our expectation that having more Republicans in Congress will lead to more punitive policies. However, the result is consist[ent] with accounts suggesting Democrats have tried to co-opt the crime issue by becoming just as, if not more, punitive, as Republicans.

The politicization of crime and punishment has led to a reluctance of being labeled soft on crime, and as a result it is politically dangerous to criticize any crime-control policy—including juvenile justice—regardless of one's party affiliation.

While acknowledging the contributions of Republicans in advancing a tough-on-crime agenda, Tonry (2009) explained that punitive policies are driven by four factors: paranoia based on a rigid black-and-white interpretation of good and evil, intolerance shaped by fundamentalist religious views, a weakened constitutional structure, and U.S. race relations. Tonry (2009, 389) observed that "Once the politics got rolling, American constitutional arrangements presented few impediments, and insensitivity to the interests of black Americans made their formidable human costs both tolerable and ignorable."

Altogether, there is widespread agreement that American politicians used the tough-on-crime issue to their own advantage. Gottschalk (2009, 104) noted that "Because of a variety of exceptional institutional and political factors, which include the absence of an insulated, highly skilled, widely respected professional civil service, U.S. public policy is more vulnerable to the vagaries of partisan politics." In European countries, where crime levels are similar to those in the United States, incarceration is used at about one-fifth of the U.S. rate.[6] In those nations, crime control is rarely used as a campaign issue, and punitive values are countered by long-established bureaucratic traditions (Jacobs and Kleban 2003). As a result, bureaucrats with expert knowledge are more likely to develop crime control strategies than are politicians.

SUMMARY

Tough-on-crime policies emerged in the 1970s and have become a uniquely American approach to crime control that have resulted in very strict sanctions meted out to juvenile offenders. Johnson and Tabriz (2011) noted that the United States is the only developed nation that still sentences juveniles to life without the possibility of parole, or what they have called death by incarceration. Moreover, until 2005, offenders who were juveniles at the time of their offense could be sentenced to death. These policies emerged during an era of political and social uncertainty. These practices, however, could only be sustained with public support. In the first part of this chapter we examined attitudes toward juvenile offenders, using poll data collected since the early 1980s. We found that about three-quarters of respondents supported the transfer of youths to adult courts and about the same proportion approved of rehabilitative interventions for these offenders. Such contradictory results demonstrate the often conflicting attitudes that Americans express in terms of youthful offenders and how to respond to their delinquency.

Much of our knowledge about juvenile offenders comes from the news media and their presentation of violent youth crime as a common feature of modern life. The entertainment media also glorifies youth violence (Ruddell and Decker 2005). This focus on juvenile crime—both real and fictional—has made the public fearful of youngsters. As a result, the public believes that juvenile crime is increasing, even when it is decreasing. An average of 75.5 percent of respondents in polls conducted between 1995 and 2007 believed that the juvenile crime rate was worse than in the past, despite the fact that the juvenile crime decline started in 1995 (see Puzzanchera, Adams, and Sickmund 2010).

We also examined the contexts from which these tough-on-crime policies emerged. Levels of social and economic uncertainty, political alienation, and distrust in government increased throughout the 1970s, along with the changing economic and political roles of minority groups and women. Altogether these challenges created a national crisis in confidence, and to respond to that crisis politicians used the issue of crime and its control to further their own interests. While Feld (2003b) and Gottschalk (2009) attributed tough-on-crime strategies to the Republicans, the Democrats have also seized this strategy, and together politicians have created an environment where being soft on crime is political suicide.

Merlo and Benekos (2010) noted that there has been a recent softening of attitudes toward the punishment of juveniles. This change has been reflected in a reduction in juvenile incarceration rates as well as the use of transfers to adult courts, although rates of serious juvenile crime have also decreased. The public opinion research cited in this chapter suggests that positive feelings toward the potential for juveniles to save themselves from a life of crime through rehabilitation are both long-standing and well entrenched, although Bernard and Kurlychek (2010) caution us that this part of the historical cycle of juvenile justice might be short lived.

NOTES

1. According to the California Department of Corrections and Rehabilitation (2011, 2), the median time served for violent, drug, or property offenses was 26.4, 15.6, and 13.0 months respectively. These totals included the time served in jail and prison.

2. Data were missing for 11 years (1979, 1981, 1992, 1995, 1997, 1999, 2001, 2003, 2005, 2007, and 2009), so averages of the prior and subsequent years were used to replace the missing data. When the missing data were not substituted, the average was 68 percent.

3. The Alienation Index is comprised of responses to the following statements: "The rich get richer and the poor get poorer"; "What you think doesn't count very much anymore"; "Most people with power try to take advantage of people like yourself"; "The people running the country don't really care what happens to you"; and "You're left out of things going on around you."

4. In order to test the relationships between alienation and imprisonment, we conducted a correlation analyses and found that the relationship between the two variables was $r = .621$ for the years 1966 to 2001 and $r = .365$ from 1966 to 2010.

5. Torcal (2003, 2) defined *disaffection* as "the subjective feeling of powerlessness, cynicism and lack of confidence in the political process, politicians and democratic institutions, but with no questioning of the political regime."

6. Lynch and Pridemore (2011: 5) noted that with the exception of serious violence, rates of minor violent and property crime in many developed nations are similar to those reported in the United States.

SEVEN

Implications of Transfers for Juvenile Offenders

INTRODUCTION

When youths are processed by the juvenile justice system, they are exposed to a variety of sanctions if they are found to be delinquent. These range from placement on informal probation to incarceration in a state training school. In most jurisdictions, these sanctions are limited by the upper age limit of a state's juvenile court jurisdiction. As a result, the youths' release will be required, whether they have rehabilitated themselves or not—a situation that the judge who sentenced Nathaniel Abraham (discussed in Chapter 1) had to confront. In most states, this jurisdiction ends at the youth's 21st birthday, although there is some variation in the upper limits (Szymanski 2008a).

Earlier we described the juvenile justice system's boundaries and the options available to juvenile court judges when imposing a sanction. This chapter expands on those themes and examines the implications of remaining within the juvenile system compared with transfer to criminal courts. There are both advantages and disadvantages for youthful offenders in remaining in the juvenile court, based on the course chosen. If they remain in juvenile court they do not necessarily enjoy the full range of constitutional protections associated with adult criminal court processing. Juvenile hearings in some jurisdictions continue to be governed by civil rules of procedure, and that has both advantages and disadvantages. When these youths reach the age of majority, their court records may be either sealed or expunged, effectively isolating their previous misdeeds (Snyder and Sickmund 2006, 108–9; Szymanski 2010c).

In Chapter 3 we reported that most youths transferred to adult courts between 1985 and 2008 were nonviolent offenders. If transfers are uncontested, they enter a criminal court where their offense may be considered to be a common, low-risk crime. Judges and juries may even take into account their youthfulness as a mitigating factor, and these youths may be sentenced to probation, have their cases dismissed, or have their sentences suspended.

This chapter examines some of the possible outcomes for juveniles if they (1) remain in juvenile courts or (2) enter criminal courts to have their alleged offenses tried. The right to a jury trial is optional for juvenile offenders, depending upon the jurisdiction (Szymanski 2008a). In criminal courts, however, jury trials are a matter of right for anyone charged with an offense where the possible punishment involves incarceration of six months or longer (*Baldwin v. New York* 1970; *Duncan v. Louisiana* 1968). Thus, juveniles have legal rights in criminal courts that are denied them in most juvenile court jurisdictions.

Nevertheless, harsh penalties are available for transferred juveniles. Therefore, we will examine questions such as: Are juvenile transfers to criminal courts desirable? and Is there a get-tough policy applicable to juvenile courts as well as criminal courts? Our analyses end with a review of the recent literature on the outcomes of transferring youths to criminal courts. One of the most significant gaps in our understanding of transfers is whether the youths who are transferred have lower involvement in later crimes. If transfers result in reduced recidivism, then this is a sound justice practice. By contrast, if juveniles who are transferred are involved in crime at higher rates, then the practice should be scrutinized more closely if public safety is truly the goal of transfers.

OUTCOMES OF JUVENILE COURT PROCESSING

Although juvenile court jurisdiction is limited, it should not be underestimated. It is a mistake to assume that having a case processed by a juvenile court is better than having a criminal court trial. By the same token, criminal court handling of an offense may not be better than juvenile court processing in any absolute sense. There are advantages and disadvantages associated with both systems, and each must be considered in order to understand the possible outcomes for affected juveniles.

Among the positive benefits of having one's case heard in juvenile court are:

1. Juvenile court proceedings may be considered civil, not criminal; thus, juveniles do not acquire criminal records.

2. Juveniles are less likely to be incarcerated.

3. Extremely harsh punishments generally lie beyond the jurisdiction of juvenile judges.

4. Juvenile courts are traditionally more lenient than criminal courts.

5. Considerably more public sympathy is extended to youngsters processed in the juvenile justice system, despite the general call for more get-tough policies.

6. Compared with criminal courts, juvenile courts do not have elaborate information-exchange systems to determine whether certain juveniles previously have been found delinquent by juvenile courts in other jurisdictions.

7. Compared with criminal court judges, juvenile court judges have considerably more discretion in influencing a youth's life chances prior to, or at the time of, adjudication.

First, since the juvenile court is treated as a civil court in some jurisdictions, juvenile hearing records are suppressed, expunged, or otherwise deleted whenever juveniles in those jurisdictions reach the age of majority. The sealing of juvenile records is a controversial issue, and those who believe in rehabilitation support this practice because it reduces the stigma of a criminal conviction to education, access to federal housing, and employment (Mauer and Chesney-Lind 2003). By contrast, proponents of public safety are apt to argue that the public is better protected if the criminal histories of offenders are more accessible (Sullivan 1998).

Szymanski (2010c, 1) reported that at the end of the 2009 legislative session all states except for Rhode Island had a procedure for sealing juvenile records, although most jurisdictions (31) can unseal these records if the individual has reoffended (e.g., is involved in a felony as an adult), while in 19 states there is no procedure for unsealing these records. Of special concern are youths who have committed sexual offenses as they are thought to be at higher risk of recidivism. While Megan's Law requires adults convicted of sexual offenses to register as sex offenders with law enforcement, Szymanski (2009b, 1) found that juveniles adjudicated as delinquent for a sex offense were required to register in 39 jurisdictions, while in four states juveniles convicted as adults had to register, and in eight states juveniles were not required to register. Sex offender registration has long-term implications for offenders, and Szymanski (2009b) noted that registration could be maintained as long as 25 years. Moreover, once posted on the Internet, it is possible that the information might be accessible forever.

One of the original juvenile court's cornerstones was protecting the confidentiality of the youths and their families. The increased access to juvenile records and sex offender registration are inconsistent with that goal. Moreover, juvenile proceedings were historically held "behind closed doors." Szymanski (2010a) reported, however, that an increasing number of states have made juvenile hearings more publicly accessible. Juvenile hearings in 35 jurisdictions in 2010, for instance, were open to the public (although there were some restrictions, and judges could close the proceedings); in three jurisdictions there were no restrictions; and in the remaining 13 jurisdictions proceedings were closed, although the judge could open them.

Second, juvenile judges often act compassionately by sentencing youthful offenders to probation, by issuing verbal warnings or reprimands, or by imposing some other nonincarcerative, nonfine alternative (Livsey 2009; Mays and Winfree 2006). A third advantage, related closely to the second, that juveniles may receive is that juvenile judges typically do not impose very harsh sentences. Thus, the juvenile judge's options are limited for offenders who have committed especially violent or heinous offenses. There are, however, some exceptions. Szymanski (2008a, 1) reported that Oregon enacted a law in 2007 that "extended the court's jurisdiction to life for a young person who was found to have committed an act that, if committed by an adult would have been murder or aggravated murder." Moreover, in Colorado, Hawaii, New Jersey, and Oregon, the juvenile court retains jurisdiction of a case for the full term of the order (Szymanski 2008a).

If a waiver to a criminal court is successful, the path is cleared for lengthy long prison terms including life without the possibility of parole (LWOP) for homicide offenders (see the discussion of *Graham v. Florida* in Chapter 5). Judges can no longer sentence nonhomicide offenders who were less than 18 years of age at the time of their offense to life imprisonment, but they still could be sentenced to decades of imprisonment that extend beyond their life expectancy (Arya 2010). While we have noted that juvenile homicide offenders are frequently transferred to adult courts, juvenile court statistics also show that approximately 41,200 cases of homicide were heard in juvenile courts between 1985 and 2008 (Sickmund, Sladky, and Kang 2011).

A fourth advantage is that juvenile courts historically have been noted for their lenient treatment of youthful offenders (Krisberg 2005, 3–4). A 2007 survey of juvenile justice practitioners from the largest U.S. counties conducted by Mears, Shollenberger, Willison, Owens, and Butts (2010) showed that there was significant support for the rehabilitation of juveniles. Mears and colleagues (2010, 556–57) noted that the following rehabilitative strategies were thought to be particularly effective:

> Mental health treatment, substance abuse treatment, reentry services and planning, sex offender treatment, coordination of juvenile justice with social services, restorative justice programs and policies, community-based alternatives to secure detention, graduated sanctions, specialized courts, and use of risk and needs assessment to aid in decision making . . . five policies and practices are not effective: reduced confidentiality of court records, transfer to criminal or adult court, juvenile curfew laws, parental accountability laws, and statutes and rules setting time limits in courts.

This support for juvenile rehabilitation is not universal, and these researchers found that prosecutors were more likely to support punitive sanctions such as transfers to adult courts.

While there is practitioner support for rehabilitation, there is also a need for residential placements for some youths, and these are increasingly used in some jurisdictions (Snyder and Sickmund 2006, 174–75). Sedlak and Bruce (2010, 4), for example, estimated that there were 101,040 youths in residential placements in 2003, representing a youth custody rate of 224 residents for every 100,000 youths in the population. One of the challenges of justice systems is trying to determine which youths should be placed outside-the-home as it is a very disruptive process. It can also be dangerous, whether one confines youths in local detention facilities or in state training schools (Fagan 2010; Holman and Ziedenberg 2009).

Moreover, juvenile incarceration is an expensive proposition. The Justice Policy Institute (2009, 4) reported that the average cost of housing a juvenile in a state-funded residential placement is $240.99 per day, or about $88,000 per year, and in California it was almost three times that amount ($224,712) in 2011 (Center on Criminal and Juvenile Justice 2011). As a result of the high individual risks as well as fiscal costs, such sanctions should be used prudently and should target the most violent and high-risk offenders. Sedlack and Bruce (2010, 5), however, found that only 43 percent of incarcerated youths were held on violent offenses in 2003.

A fifth advantage of juvenile court processing is that the public supports youthful offenders' rehabilitation (Piquero, Cullen, Unnever, Piquero, and Gordon 2010; Steinberg and Piquero 2010). Many believe that social, economic, or cultural factors that are beyond the control of youths contribute to their delinquency. Moreover, there is growing acknowledgement of the biological causes of juvenile impulsivity and immaturity. This means that individualized treatment is desirable, perhaps administered in community-based settings, in order to promote greater respect for the law and to offer the needed services. This belief has lead to a growing interest in treating youths in the least restrictive setting, although Kott (2010, 20) cautions that this approach "is based on sound principles, but when budgets are being cut and 'least restrictive' is also the least expensive alternative, placement selection may be made with greater attention to the bottom line than to the welfare of the child."

The last advantage of juvenile court processing is that these courts do not ordinarily exchange information with other juvenile courts in a national communication network. Local control over youthful offenders accomplishes precisely this limited objective—local control. Therefore, juveniles could move to other jurisdictions and reoffend, although being taken into custody in another jurisdiction would not be the equivalent of recidivism in one's home jurisdiction. This is of strategic value to juveniles who might commit numerous offenses in adjacent jurisdictions. The probability that their delinquent acts in another jurisdiction would come to the attention of juvenile officials in their own community is smaller compared to the likelihood for an adult.

On the negative side, juvenile judges may impose short- or long-term incarceration on offenders regardless of the seriousness of their offenses. Schwartz and Levick (2010, 365–366) described the 2007 case of a 15-year-old Pennsylvania high school student who was sentenced to three months in custody:

> Hillary Transue posted a MySpace parody of a school administrator. The posting included Hillary's unrealized hope that the administrator had a sense of humor. The administrator complained to the police, who charged Hillary with "harassment." Hillary and her mother appeared in the Luzerne County juvenile court before Judge Mark Ciavarella. They signed a document that turned out to be a waiver of Hillary's right to counsel. In a hearing eerily reminiscent of Gerald Gault's—except Hillary's was shorter and lasted only a couple of minutes—Hillary was adjudicated delinquent, shackled, dragged from the courtroom, and sent to a delinquency facility. Hillary had no lawyer, and neither the public defender who was in the room nor the district attorney who prosecuted the case uttered a word of protest.

Judge Ciavarella and his colleague Judge Michael T. Conahan later pled guilty to taking more than $2.6 million in kickbacks to send thousands of youths adjudicated as delinquent on relatively minor offenses to two privately operated detention facilities (see also Streib 2010).

While the case reported above is an egregious example, we still incarcerate minor juvenile offenders. There is still considerable concern, for example, that status offenders are being incarcerated, and a review of the latest *Census of Juveniles in Residential Placements* showed that there were 3,412 status offenders incarcerated in 2007 (Sickmund, Sladky, Kang, and Puzzanchera 2011b). Moreover, of those status offenders, almost two-thirds (64%) had been incarcerated for more than a month at the time of the census. Thousands of other status and minor offenders are placed in privately operated wilderness and boot camps, psychiatric facilities, and other residential placements (U.S. Government Accountability Office 2007).

Another disadvantage of juvenile courts is that granting any juvenile a jury trial may involve a great deal of discretion by prosecutors and juvenile judges. As mentioned in Chapter 5, at the end of the 2007 legislative session, only nine states allowed jury trials as a matter of right, while in 11 states juveniles had access to jury trials under certain circumstances (e.g., those accused of serious crimes), and in the remaining 31 jurisdictions juveniles had no right to a jury trial (Szymanski 2008a, 1). The question of whether all juveniles should have the right to a jury trial was decided by the Supreme Court in the 1971 *McKeiver v. Pennsylvania* case and remains controversial four decades latter. Many advocates for children, for example, believe that the consequences of a juvenile conviction are so serious that a juvenile's due process rights, including jury trials, should be guaranteed by the equal protection clause of the Fourteenth Amendment (Ko 2004; Rosenberg 2009).

A third limitation of juvenile proceedings is that the wide discretion enjoyed by most juvenile courts can be abused. This abuse of judicial discretion may come in the form of excessive leniency, such as in the matter of *In the Interest of R.W.* This case was heard before the Pennsylvania Supreme Court in 2004, and the court found that judges were abusing their discretion when they developed blanket practices of dismissing all cases of a certain type—in this matter, the possession of small amounts of marijuana. Because juvenile court proceedings had historically been held behind closed doors and many youths appeared without the assistance of counsel, these types of cases could continue with little outside scrutiny. These abuses of discretion do not occur exclusively at the adjudicatory stage of juvenile proceedings. Earlier, during intake, many cases are resolved, diverted, or dismissed without a formal petition being filed for a subsequent adjudication.

Because of this leniency and wide discretion, real or imagined, many juvenile courts have been criticized by the public and professionals alike. The usual allegation is that juvenile courts neglect accountability through the excessive use of probation or diversion (see, generally, Fagan and Zimring 2000). As there is little oversight of these informal actions—especially at the intake stage—it is possible that the rights of some youths are violated in these low-visibility practices (e.g., if a juvenile probation officer pressures a youth into a guilty plea in return for informal probation).

Another major criticism of these courts is that juveniles do not enjoy the full range of constitutional rights that apply in adult criminal courts (Feld 1999d, 2003a). In some jurisdictions, there are no transcripts of proceedings against juveniles where serious charges are alleged unless special arrangements are made. Thus, when juveniles in these jurisdictions appeal their convictions, they may not have the written record to rely upon while attempting to challenge a juvenile judge's sentence.

One of the arguments for extending the rights of juveniles to those guaranteed to adults is that the consequences of a juvenile adjudication have increased. Earlier we noted that a conviction might result in lifelong restrictions on education and employment. A conviction as a juvenile can also result in a number of other long-term negative outcomes including sex offender registration (Syzmanski 2009b), juvenile records that can be "unsealed" in 31 jurisdictions (Szymanski 2010c), and DNA registration (Szymanski 2009a). Moreover, a single conviction as a juvenile can result in one's family being evicted from federal housing (Kaplan and Rossman 2011). Juvenile convictions can also be counted as a "strike" in states with habitual offender or three-strikes legislation (Wood 2009). Altogether, the short- and long-term consequences of being adjudicated delinquent have increased over the past few decades.

Juveniles in Residential Placements

Earlier we observed that it is difficult to make generalizations about transfers using incomplete information. In some respects, the information about persons less than 18 years in jail or prison populations is more complete than the reporting of information on juvenile correctional populations. While the numbers of youths in secure placements are reported in a census and survey carried out by the OJJDP every two years, we do not know how many youths are held in privately operated facilities, such as group homes, psychiatric facilities, drug and alcohol treatment centers, as well as facilities that conduct assessments and behavioral treatment of youths (U.S. Government Accountability Office 2007). Moreover, since

Figure 7.1 Male and Female Juveniles in Residential Placements, 1975 to 2007

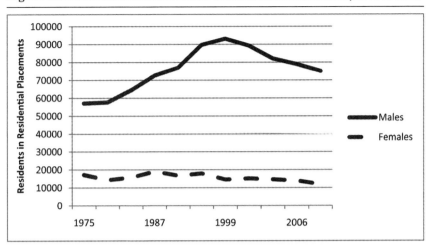

many of these organizations are not publically funded, there is little oversight of their operations (Ruddell 2009).

Figure 7.1 shows the number of incarcerated males and females between 1975 and 2007 using data from the biennial census of juvenile facilities carried out by the OJJDP (Sickmund, Sladky, Kang, and Puzzanchera 2011b). This figure reveals that the overall population peaked in 1999 with 107,667 juveniles, but that total has decreased to 86,927 youths in 2007. During this 32-year era, the female population fluctuated less than the male, peaking in 1987 with 19,035 incarcerated and decreasing to 11,826 in 2007. The number of incarcerated males, by contrast, grew significantly throughout the series and only started decreasing in the 2001 census.

It is important to acknowledge that while arrests of juveniles have decreased by almost one-half, the use of juvenile incarceration has remained relatively steady. From 1995 to 2007, for instance, there was a 19.2 percent decrease in incarcerated youths (107,667 to 86,927 residents). During that same time, however, Federal Bureau of Investigation (2010) data showed that the rate of juvenile arrests for index offenses (homicide, rape, robbery, aggravated assault, burglary, auto theft, larceny, and arson) dropped from 2,980.5 to 1526.8 arrests per 100,000 residents in the population, a 47.3 percent decline. If arrests for serious offenses dropped by almost one-half, we have to question why the number of youths incarcerated has decreased by less than one-fifth.

Figure 7.2 shows youth incarceration by race and reveals that a majority of the incarcerated population is nonwhite and that the proportion of nonwhite juveniles has increased substantially over time. The *Children in*

Figure 7.2 Incarcerated Juveniles by Race

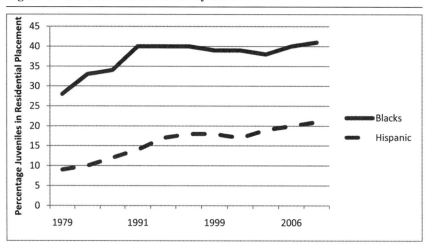

Custody Reports, summarized by Smith (1998) indicated that in 1979, 37 percent of the residential population was comprised of blacks and Latinos, but this had increased to 61.6 percent by 2007 according to the *Census of Juveniles in Residential Placement* (Sickmund, Sladky, Kang, and Puzzanchera 2011b). While the proportion of blacks increased by approximately 30 percent, the percentage of Latinos increased by over 100 percent. Some caution has to be used in interpreting statistics from the 1970s, as sometimes Latinos were counted with white populations, but regardless of that limitation, the recent statistics show that there is a significant overrepresentation of nonwhites in the incarcerated juvenile population.[1] These numbers are troubling to youth advocates (Krisberg 2005). Among the arguments opposing juvenile incarceration is that youthful misbehavior and crime are transient, and that with proper guidance most youths mature out of delinquency over a relatively short time period (Lawrence and Hemmens 2008; Mays and Winfree 2006; Snyder and Sickmund 2006).

IMPLICATIONS OF CRIMINAL COURT PROCESSING

When juveniles are transferred to criminal court, they receive all the constitutional protections possessed by adults. We have already examined the advantages of permitting the juvenile court to retain jurisdiction in certain cases. If the juvenile has a choice, the absence of a formal criminal record, limited punishments, and a greater variety of discretionary options on the part of juvenile judges make juvenile courts an attractive forum for adjudication. Of course, even if the crimes alleged are serious, leniency may result in a dismissal of charges, charge reductions, warnings, and other nonadjudicatory sanctions.

There are two primary outcomes for juveniles of being processed through the criminal justice system, and they are quite important. First, depending upon the seriousness of the offenses alleged, a jury trial may be a matter of right. Second, lengthy incarceration periods in secure correctional facilities with adults become a real possibility.

Jury Trials as a Matter of Right for Serious Crimes

A primary benefit of a transfer to criminal court is the right to a jury trial. When juveniles reach criminal courts certain constitutional provisions apply to them as well as to adults. First, any defendant who *may be* subject to six months or more in jail or prison on the basis of the prescribed statutory punishment associated with the criminal offenses alleged shall receive a jury trial, in either state or federal courts (*Baldwin v. New York* 1970; *Duncan v. Louisiana* 1968). Therefore, it is not a matter resting solely with the judge's discretion.

Juveniles charged with particularly serious crimes, and where several aggravating circumstances are apparent, still stand a chance of favorable treatment from judges and juries. While youthfulness historically has been regarded as a mitigating factor at sentencing, there are some exceptions. In the *Roper v. Simmons* case, described in Chapter 5, the prosecutor used Simmons' youth as an *aggravating* factor in presenting his case to the jury. The following quote from the prosecutor is repeated from the Supreme Court's opinion:

> Let's look at the mitigating circumstances . . . Age, he says. Think about age. Seventeen years old. Isn't that scary? Doesn't that scare you? Mitigating? Quite the contrary I submit. Quite the contrary

Dobbs (2004) observed that prosecutors have used the youthfulness argument as an aggravating factor in at least seven other juvenile death penalty cases, and one can only guess how many times such sentiments are repeated by prosecutors in juvenile proceedings that are less visible. Emens (2005, 101) speculated that such opinions feed into the negative stereotypes and attitudes of jurors toward juveniles and that "they may treat youth as aggravating, thus creating a peculiarly troubling type of error: treating an individual *less favorably* on the basis of the trait, youth, that should prompt *more favorable* treatment."

Inconsistent with the intent of *Gault*, Feld and Schaefer (2010) also make the argument that the presence of defense counsel in juvenile courts can be an aggravating factor. This is not a new observation: Burruss and Kempf-Leonard (2002) also found that juveniles who appeared in court with attorneys received more punitive dispositions (see also Kempf-Leonard 2010). Feld and Schaefer (2010, 714) attributed these outcomes to a number of factors, including that "lawyers who appear in juvenile court are incompetent and prejudice their clients' cases; judges pre-determine sentences and appoint counsel when they anticipate out-of-home placements; or judges punish delinquents who exercise procedural rights."

No one can predict accurately how juries will decide cases. Although some evidence exists to show the influence of age, race, and gender on jury decision making, the results tend to be inconsistent and inconclusive. One of the limitations to understanding what occurs in jury deliberations is that it is almost ethically impossible to conduct research on juries. Thus, much of our knowledge comes from asking individuals how they would behave if they were sitting on a jury. Warling and Peterson-Badali (2003) reported that mock jurors did not take age into account when deliberating a verdict, but they did recommend shorter sentences for younger offenders, suggesting that age was a mitigating factor at sentencing. Tang and Nunez (2003, 37) found that mock jurors who had a prosecution bias (who were more likely to side with the prosecution) "found the defendant guilty more often, had higher confidence in the defendant's guilt, and set a lower standard of proof." Nunez, Dahl, Tang, and Jensen (2007) observed that mock jurors were more likely to recommend keeping younger offenders in the juvenile court. Furthermore, Nunez and colleagues (2007) found that offenders who had been abused as children were apt to receive a less severe sanction, as were female juvenile defendants. Last, Walker and Woody (2011, 1) reported that jurors were more likely to convict defendants who were charged with violent crimes and that "jurors recommended longer sentences for an adult defendant, a defendant charged with a crime against a person, and a defendant charged with a crime with a severe outcome." Thus, the offense may play a more significant role in the finding of guilt or imposing severe sanctions than the offender's age.

Altogether, such comparative leniency may indicate how juries might view youthful defendants in homicide cases as well as those crimes associated with less serious punishments. Youthfulness may be a mitigating factor in almost every criminal courtroom—especially given the recent scientific evidence that shows a biological basis to teenage immaturity, as acknowledged in the *Roper v. Simmons* and *Graham v. Florida* cases (see also Maroney 2011; Walsh 2011).

It is also important to note that among the aggravating and mitigating circumstances, having a prior record becomes an important consideration. Youths transferred to criminal courts most likely do not have previous *criminal* records. This does not mean that they have not previously committed crimes but rather their records are juvenile court records. As such, technically they do not bring prior criminal records into the adult court. This is a favorable factor for juveniles to consider when deciding whether to challenge transfers or have their automatic waivers reversed. An absence of a prior criminal record, together with youthfulness, might be persuasive enough for juries to acquit certain defendants or find them guilty of lesser offenses (the exception is if a first-time offender has committed a serious crime). However, it is important to remember that in most jurisdictions juvenile records can be unsealed if the individual has been convicted of an offense (Szymanski 2010c). This may result in sentence enhancements and it is part of what has been called the "collateral consequences" of harsher punishment of juvenile offenders (Mauer and Chesney-Lind 2003).

Another important factor relative to having access to a jury trial is that prosecutors often seek to avoid them, favoring plea bargain arrangements instead (Mears 2008; Sanborn 2003). Plea bargaining involves negotiations between the state and the defendant where the defendant enters a guilty plea in exchange for leniency in the form of fewer counts, reduced charges, or less severe sentences. Plea bargaining accounts for over 95 percent of the adult felony convictions in large urban counties (Cohen and Kyckelhahn 2010, 1) and similar proportions of juveniles (Feld 2003a).

Jury trials are costly, and the results of jury deliberations are unpredictable. If prosecutors can obtain guilty pleas from transferred juveniles, they assist the state and themselves in terms of both the costs of trials and avoidance of jury whims in youthful offender cases. Also, plea bargaining in transferred juvenile cases may result in convictions on lesser charges, specifically charges that would not have prompted the transfer or waiver from juvenile courts initially (Sanborn 2003). This is ironic since it suggests that the criminal justice system undermines one of the primary purposes of juvenile transfers through plea bargaining arrangements that are commonplace for adult criminals.

Another important consideration is worth mentioning. When prosecutors make decisions, there should be sufficient evidence to increase the chances of a conviction. This means that the charges alleged should be serious ones. However, as revealed in Chapter 3, most transferred juveniles are not necessarily serious offenders, and the standard of evidence in juvenile courts may not be as rigorous as it is in criminal courts. Thus, many transferred cases "crumble" at the outset and are dismissed by the prosecutors.

Closely associated with prosecutorial reluctance to proceed against some transferred juveniles is the fact that most of those transferred are charged with property, drug, and public order crimes. While these cases may stand out from other cases coming before juvenile judges, prosecutors and criminal court judges might not regard them as significant. Thus, juveniles enter the adult system with "special tags" from juvenile courts, but they become one of many nonviolent offenders for criminal court processing. Their ages also work in their behalf—improving the chances of having their cases dismissed or of being acquitted by juries. Most prosecutors wish to reserve jury trials for only the most serious offenders. Therefore, their general inclination is to treat youthful property offenders with leniency, or they elect to *nolle prosequi* outright (see, for example, Kinder, Veneziano, Fichter, and Azuma 1995). This is consistent with Kupchik's (2006) observations of youths transferred to New Jersey and New York criminal courts. Kupchik found that adult courts at the sentencing stage often took into consideration the offender's youthfulness and mitigated sanctions accordingly, operating in a fashion that was often very similar to what he observed in juvenile courts.

The possibility of incarceration looms large for those juveniles who reach criminal courts. A number of states currently employ presumptive or determinate sentencing systems (or sentencing guidelines) that establish standard punishments for all criminal offenses. While judges in those jurisdictions have some latitude in varying the amount of incarceration, some imprisonment may be required, especially for those convicted of serious crimes.

Adult Time for Adult Crimes

Ernest van den Haag (1986) argued that it is cheaper to build more prisons than it is to tolerate a growing crime rate. He advocated blanket punishment in criminal courts for juveniles who have committed crimes. Many of us believe, for instance, that the punishment for juvenile offenders should match the severity of the crime and that if youths commit adult crimes, they should serve adult sentences. However, are those sentiments valid given that rates of both adult and juvenile crime and violence have decreased for almost two decades? Furthermore, does the placement of young offenders in adult jails or prisons serve as a "wake up call" that contributes to their rehabilitation, or does it push youths further into a life of crime?

A contrary sentiment is that there has been an overuse of out-of-home placements for juveniles, from detention to state training schools (see Howell 2008; Krisberg 2005). Many of those facilities are ill suited to provide a proper rehabilitative atmosphere (Fagan 2010), despite the fact that the cost of housing juveniles is much greater than adults (Justice Policy Institute 2009). Consequently, attorneys from the Youth Law Center, the Juvenile Law Center, and other public interest law firms have used litigation to improve the conditions for incarcerated youths. Moreover, the U.S. Department of Justice (2011a) has conducted investigations of juvenile correctional facilities and systems to ensure that these incarcerated youths receive constitutionally guaranteed treatment. Common elements in these lawsuits are improperly trained staff, a lack of services for residents with mental and physical health problems, a lack of gender-specific programs for girls, noncompliance with the Americans with Disabilities Act, institutional cultures that lead to violence, as well as inadequate opportunities for education and rehabilitation (Ruddell 2009).

Juveniles placed in adult jails or prisons are in further jeopardy of victimization from their adult counterparts, as well as being placed in an environment where they may be more susceptible to negative influences (Leigey et al. 2009). In order to reduce that risk, some state departments of corrections have separated youngsters from the regular prison population by holding them in different housing units. In addition, these youths receive an enhanced educational and rehabilitative program that targets their unmet needs. Yet once these inmates reach the age of majority they can be transferred to the general prison population.

Both Fagan (1996) and Singer (2003) reported that placing juveniles in adult facilities can increase recidivism. Redding's (2010) review of the research literature on juveniles transferred to criminal justice systems showed that they were more likely to reoffend than those who stayed in the juvenile justice system. In particular, Redding cited six different studies—with samples from diverse states as well as using different research strategies—that all produced similar findings. Moreover, even youths who were treated leniently in adult courts (e.g., received a probationary sentence) had higher recidivism rates than their juvenile counterparts.

There appears to be strong support for keeping juveniles away from adult jails and prisons not only because such facilities are less well-equipped to meet their needs but also because a greater range of community-based services exists for juveniles diverted or placed on probation (Davis 2003; Snyder and Sickmund 2006). An offsetting argument is made for preserving incarceration as a punishment, in part because of the fear of apprehension and punishment among juveniles.

As juveniles are less mature than adults and tend to act impulsively without fully considering the consequences of their actions, it has been argued that deterrence-based sanctions are ineffective strategies. A number of scholars have examined the issue of deterring juveniles using get-tough measures such as increasing the severity of sanctions or making it easier to send them to adult courts. Most of these studies evaluated the outcomes of legislation in a single state. Singer and McDowall (1988) examined the impact of New York's juvenile offender law that allowed 13 year olds to be prosecuted in criminal courts and enabled courts to impose severe sanctions on them, including terms of life imprisonment. At the time, these laws were considered to be among the toughest in the nation. These investigators analyzed monthly arrests for juveniles for serious offenses (homicide, rape, robbery, assault, and arson) four years prior to the 1978 introduction of the reform and for six years afterwards. Singer and McDowall did not find an overall deterrent effect of the legislation, although the results for robbery were mixed (e.g., arrests increased in some jurisdictions but decreased in others).

Jensen and Metsger (1994) examined the relationship between introducing legislative exclusion in Idaho and juvenile arrests for serious crimes (homicide, forcible rape, robbery, and aggravated assaults) and compared these findings with juvenile arrests in Montana and Wyoming (which did not enact similar legislation). Inconsistent with the deterrence perspective, Jensen and Metsger reported that juvenile arrest rates increased in Idaho after the introduction of the legislation but decreased in both Montana and Wyoming. Risler, Sweatman, and Nackerud (1998) conducted a similar study examining the effects on juvenile arrests for homicide, robbery, rape, aggravated assaults, and sexual offenses before and after the introduction of Georgia's legislative exclusion law in 1994. Like the results reported by Jensen and Metsger (1994), juvenile arrests increased slightly after the legislation was enacted.

Steiner and Wright (2006) extended these deterrence studies by evaluating the impact of legislation in 14 states using arrest statistics from 1975 to 2002. They examined the pre- and post-implementation periods of prosecutorial direct file legislation, arguing that introducing these policies would deter violent juvenile offending. If, they reasoned, deterrence was an effective approach, then arrest rates for violence should decrease. After examining the arrest trends five years pre- and post-implementation of the reforms, these investigators found a decrease in the number of arrests for violent offenses in only one state and no effect in the remaining 13 states. Steiner and Wright (2006, 1469) attributed the lack of a deterrent effect to the juveniles' abilities to "understand, envision, or focus on the long-term consequences of their actions," and concluded that "juvenile decisions, as opposed to adult decisions, are influenced more heavily by the potential rewards of their choices rather than by the potential risks involved."

Deterrence theories propose that sanctions for wrongdoing must be swift, certain, and severe. Jordan and Myers (2011) examined the transfers of 345 Pennsylvania youths legislatively waived to criminal courts and found that, while the punishments were more severe, the case processing time in adult courts was longer and that there was no difference in punishment certainty. Thus, transfers might not deter delinquent behavior. One limitation of deterrence-based sanctions is that adolescents are not always aware of laws that place them at greater jeopardy of adult sanctions—which is a cornerstone of this approach (i.e., offenders carefully weighing the costs and consequences of crime).

In order to test the awareness of punitive sanctions, Redding and Fuller (2004) interviewed 37 youths who had been transferred to criminal courts in Georgia. They found that these juveniles were generally unaware of the possibility of transfer and the implications for them once waived to a criminal court. Redding and Fuller reported that less than one-third (30.7%) were aware that they could be charged as adults and that none had known a juvenile who had been prosecuted as an adult. Most of these youths (60%) reported that they did not consider being caught while committing the offense but thought that if juveniles were aware of the possible sanctions they would be less inclined to commit a crime.

Juveniles in Adult Facilities

The number of incarcerated offenders under age 18 in adult facilities represents less than 1 percent of all inmates. Earlier we noted that the jail population of juveniles has fluctuated somewhat over time. Minton (2011: 7) reported that on June 30, 2010, there were 7,560 jail inmates under the age of 18 years and that 1,912 were held as juveniles while the rest were legally defined as adults. These inmates were either awaiting court appearances or serving sentences of less than one year. Figure 7.3 shows the changes in jail populations from 1993 to 2010 for inmates under the age of 18 years who were legally defined as adults. This figure shows that the jail incarceration rate spiked in 1999, with almost 8,600 inmates held as adults, and has decreased since then.

Figure 7.3 also shows the changes in the number of state prisoners who were younger than 18. West (2010, 24) reported that there were 2,778 of these state prisoners on June 30, 2009 (2,644 males and 134 females). The three states where youths became legally defined adults at 16 years

Figure 7.3 Jail and Prison Inmates under 18 Held as Adults

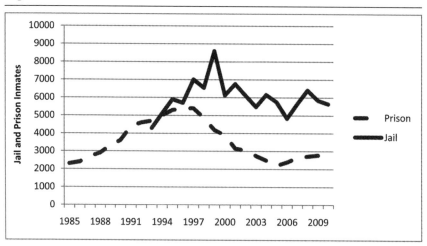

(CT, NY, and NC) held 26.5 percent of all the offenders less than 18 years of age on June 30, 2009.[2] Seven states (CA, ID, KY, ME, NH, ND, and WV), by contrast, held no juveniles in their prison systems.

There are a number of limitations to these data. First, in terms of the jail and prison populations, the numbers reported above will not reflect all of the arrestees or offenders sentenced prior to their 18th birthdays, as these data only count the inmates who were younger than 18 when the annual census took place. Second, the jail totals were based on estimates from a one-day snapshot. In 2010, for instance, Minton (2011, 14) reported that 930 jails, representing about one-third of all U.S. jails, participated in the census, and it is likely that small and rural jails (which may be more likely to hold juveniles) were underrepresented in the census. Third, since these jail totals are based on one-day snapshots, they do not capture the total number of individuals less than 18 years of age who are admitted and discharged each year, which could represent tens of thousands of inmates. Thus, while we have a good estimate from which to base our analyses, we are unsure of the true numbers admitted and discharged each year in jails and of the total number of youths sentenced to prison who were younger than 18 years.

Another limitation in our understanding of these correctional populations is that we do not know much about the demographic or offense-related characteristics of these youths. Since the state prison totals based on race were rounded to the nearest hundred, we could not develop an accurate estimate of the minority representation, although our analyses suggest that whites represented about 500 male and 100 female prisoners (see West, Sabol, and Greenman 2010, 27), or less than one-quarter of the total, suggesting that minority youths are overrepresented. This percentage is very similar to the white populations reported in juvenile corrections and suggests that our estimate approximates the true proportion.

Although somewhat dated, Strom (2000) produced a profile of state prisoners under age 18 from 1985 to 1997 for the Bureau of Justice Statistics. Strom (2000, 1) reported that in 1997 whites represented only 19 percent of these adolescent prisoners, with blacks accounting for 60 percent, Latinos representing 13 percent, and the remaining 8 percent classified as "other." Thus, the total nonwhite population in 1997 closely approximates our estimate of nonwhites in the 2009 state prison population. Strom (2000, 4) reported that in 1997 almost two-thirds of these state prisoners (61%) had been convicted of a violent offense, which was followed by property (22%), drug (11%), and public order offenses (5%). Similar to the transfer statistics reported earlier, Strom (2000, 6) found that in 1997 almost all (95%) of these inmates were admitted at age 16 (21%) or 17 years (66%), but that 4 percent were 15 and 1 percent were 14 years or younger.

Understanding sentence severity is important if we are going to base transfer policies on their costs and benefits. Strom (2000, 7) reported that while the average minimum sentence to be served for these offenses increased from 35 months in 1985 to 44 months in 1997, the maximum sentence length decreased somewhat, from 86 months in 1985 to 82 months in 1997. Strom (2000, 9) also found that of these offenders who were sentenced prior to their 18th birthday, and were released in 1997, on average, served about 37 months, or 50 percent of their sentences, with violent offenders serving the highest proportion of their sentences (53%), followed by public order offenders (51%), property offenders (50%), and drug offenders (37%). Given those statistics, most of the offenders sentenced at age 16 or 17 would be released on parole prior to their 21st birthdays—which is the upper jurisdiction limit in 33 states (Szymanski 2008a). This suggests that they could have been held and treated in the juvenile justice system without compromising public safety through early releases.

SUMMARY

Juveniles who are 16 or 17 years old and are charged with serious crimes have a good chance of being transferred to adult criminal courts. In some states, automatic transfers occur for specific kinds of serious offenses. Juveniles may challenge these waivers, although there are both advantages and disadvantages associated with such challenges.

Remaining in juvenile court can mean that records relating to a finding of delinquency will be sealed when juveniles reach the age of majority. Nevertheless, as Snyder and Sickmund (2006, 109) noted:

> Formerly confidential records are now being made available to a wide variety of individuals. Many states open records to schools and youth-serving agencies as well as individuals and agencies within the justice system. However, access is not necessarily unlimited or automatic. It may be restricted to certain parts of the record and may require a court order.

Szymanski (2010c) reported that in 31 jurisdictions these records can be unsealed. Furthermore, juvenile sex offenders are increasingly being placed on registries, and they could remain on those lists for decades (Szymanski 2009b).

Many juvenile courts still operate as civil proceedings; thus, it is not possible for juveniles to acquire criminal records if they are processed in these courts. However, being treated as juveniles means that they do not enjoy the full range of constitutional protections available to adults, which is troubling to youth advocates (Ko 2004; Rosenberg 2009). The trade-off is that juvenile courts traditionally have been noted for their leniency. Even in instances of repeat offenses, certain delinquents are supervised on probation rather than confined.[3] Yet our analysis also showed that despite the fact that juvenile arrest rates for serious offenses have decreased by nearly one-half, the number of confined juveniles has decreased by less than one-fifth. A large proportion of these youths— somewhere around two-thirds—are nonwhite, suggesting that DMC remains a significant challenge for juvenile justice systems.

For those youths who appear in criminal courts, juveniles are extended the full range of rights available to adults. But in such courts, convictions may place youths in jeopardy of serious sanctions, including imprisonment for the rest of their lives. One advantage for juveniles is that they may receive a jury trial, provided their possible punishment involves incarceration of six months or longer. In most juvenile courts, they enjoy no such option (Szymanski 2008a). Jury trials are regarded by some experts as an advantage to youths since jury members are likely to consider youthfulness as a mitigating factor. Furthermore, when juveniles appear before criminal court judges, their crimes do not seem to be as serious as they might have been regarded by juvenile judges. Crowded court dockets and overworked prosecutors often mean case dismissals, plea bargaining resulting in probation, and little if any time behind bars. Many juveniles are aware of this and take advantage of the system by not fighting waivers in juvenile court. More often than not, their patience is rewarded through diversion, probation, or case dismissal (Kinder et al. 1995).

We also reported that on any given day, there are about 10,000 jail inmates and state prisoners who are under the age of 18, and these young people will be exposed to all of the negative aspects of adult correctional life. Some will be victimized, while the experience of others will drive them further into a life of crime. While we do not have recent national-level research on the outcomes of prisoners who were sentenced prior to their 18th birthdays, Strom (2000) reported that most of these prisoners only serve a few years. This suggests that they could have received juvenile justice system dispositions and still served the same amount of time before their mandatory release at the end of the juvenile court's jurisdiction (typically when these youths reach their 21st birthday). Incarceration in a juvenile facility is far more costly than adult imprisonment (Justice Policy Institute 2009), but offering these offenders meaningful rehabilitative opportunities may result in less recidivism (Drake 2010). Recent research shows that offenders who remain in the juvenile justice system have higher rates of community success than those who are transferred, even if the transferred youths only receive a probationary sentence (Redding 2010).

Currently, the juvenile justice system is targeted for numerous reforms, including new sentencing systems, greater uniformity in the laws of diverse jurisdictions, and a more consistent concept of what constitutes delinquent conduct. Both public and political sentiment seem to favor the continuation of juvenile courts but with measured accountability through greater use of restitution, community service, and limited use of detention or incarceration. Furthermore, recent surveys show that the public supports juvenile rehabilitation compared to incarcerating youths (Piquero, Cullen, Unnever, Piquero, and Gordon 2010; Steinberg and Piquero 2010; see also Chapter 6). There is also a growing body of empirical research that shows that these rehabilitative interventions are effective, cost-efficient, and better able to reduce recidivism than some of our get-tough strategies. Practitioners, youth advocates, and juvenile justice scholars have known this for years, but the challenge is convincing the public and our legislators that it may be better to be "smart on crime" rather than being tough-on-crime.

NOTES

1. The *Survey of Youth in Residential Placement* (Sedlak and Bruce 2010), sponsored by the OJJDP, reported fewer black youths in custody in 2003 than the *Census of Juveniles in Residential Placements* (32% compared to 38%) and a higher Latino population (24% compared to 19%). By contrast, the white population for 2003 was reported as 35 percent in the Survey but 38.6 percent in the Census. Thus, there is some variation between the two measures, but both indicate a significant over-representation of minority youths.

2. Connecticut has subsequently increased the age of adult criminal responsibility to 18 years of age.

3. Livsey (2009, 1) reported that 63 percent of juveniles supervised on probation had been adjudicated delinquent on a violent offense.

EIGHT

Future of Transfers

INTRODUCTION

Throughout this book we have observed that transfers to adult court can be an important tool used by juvenile justice system officials to manage the risks posed by serious and repeat youthful offenders. In theory, these are the youths that pose the greatest potential public safety threats. But a closer look at the evidence suggests that most of these transferred youths are older, nonviolent offenders who pose little risk to public safety. More-over, while youth involvement in crime has decreased substantially, the number of transfers has stayed relatively stable over the past decade. This shows the divide between the intent of transfer and its actual application, and suggests that transfers might be used for reasons other than crime control. To put the use of transfer in context, the following paragraphs summarize current statistics on youth crime and the punishments that are meted out to these offenders. We find that while we have much to be grateful about in terms of reduced juvenile involvement in crime, our use of severe sanctions, such as incarceration, has not decreased at the same rate.

On July 1, 2009, there were almost 25 million persons aged 12 to 17 years in the United States (Puzzanchera, Sladky, and Kang 2010). Of that population, juveniles (persons younger than 18) accounted for 942 homicide arrests; 2,385 arrests for rape; 25,280 robbery arrests; and 39,467 arrests for aggravated assault (FBI 2010, Table 38). Altogether, these arrestees represented less than three out of every 1,000 juveniles in the population.[1] There were undoubtedly many more youths who were not arrested for their offenses, but comparisons of arrest, juvenile court, and victimization data suggest that juveniles today are less likely to engage in crime than the youths a generation ago: FBI (2010) data show that juvenile murder arrests in 2009 were less than one-quarter of those in 1993 (Snyder 2000).

Juvenile arrests for index offenses (homicide, rape, robbery, aggravated assaults, burglary, larceny, auto theft, and arson) decreased by over one-third (34.4%) between 1995 and 2007 and have remained more or less stable since then. The number of youths incarcerated during that time, however, has dropped by only 19.2 percent, suggesting that the use of the most severe sanctions available to juvenile courts is not closely related with youth involvement in crime. Almost two-thirds of these incarcerated juveniles are minority youths, and statistics from 1979 to 2007 showed that this proportion increased for almost 20 years and then stabilized in the past decade. This overrepresentation continues despite the fact that reducing the proportion of minority youths in custodial placements has been a federal government priority since the 1988 reauthorization of the JJDPA (Leiber, Bishop, and Chamlin 2011).

The use of juvenile detention and incarceration has decreased slightly in recent years, and data from the 2007 *Census of Juveniles in Residential Placement* revealed that there were 86,927 youths in custody including 24,958 in detention (Sickmund, Sladky, Kang, and Puzzanchera 2011b). The total number of juveniles, however, is a one-day count, and it is likely that many thousands of juveniles will be admitted to and discharged from detention facilities in any given year—given the short-term nature of those placements. The 2007 *Census* showed, for example, that slightly more than one-half (53.5%) of this population had served more than two weeks. Based on those numbers, it is possible that over 400,000 juvenile detainees pass through these facilities each year.[2]

The number of persons under age 18 placed in adult jails or state prisons since the peak of youth homicide arrests in 1993 has also decreased. Despite this reduction, on any given day there are about 10,000 persons under age 18 in these adult correctional facilities. Of the 7,560 jail inmates younger than 18, most were held as legally defined adults, including youngsters who were transferred to adult courts but have not yet been convicted (Minton 2011). Like the juvenile detention census, the jail population estimate is based on a one-day count, and it is possible that over 125,000 youths will be admitted to and discharged from American jails each year given the short-term nature of these placements.[3]

In addition to youths held in juvenile facilities or adult jails, there were 2,778 persons who were younger than 18 in state prisons in 2009 (West

2010). These youths had been convicted in adult courts and represent a group of offenders in jeopardy of serious sanctions, including life in prison without the possibility of parole (for homicide offenders). Juveniles can also be sentenced to terms of life imprisonment for nonhomicide offenses as long as there is some form of parole review. Other youths convicted of nonhomicide offenses can be sentenced to lengthy prison terms that basically ensure that they will die in prison (see *People v. Ramirez*).

Despite decades of research and hundreds of scholarly articles written about transfers to adult courts, we still do not have a complete national-level understanding of the age of admission of these offenders, the actual offenses (and prior convictions) that precipitated their transfers, the nature of their sentences (e.g., probation, jail, or prison) or sentence length, and how much time they actually served (Griffin, Addie, Adams, and Firestine 2011). There is also a gap in our understanding of the effects of transfer mechanism (e.g., whether youths who are transferred from juvenile courts are sentenced more severely than those who have been direct filed; see Verrecchia 2011). We also lack knowledge of whether these factors have changed over time. Thus, legislators, policymakers, and practitioners are making decisions about transfers with incomplete knowledge.

Investigators do have access to juvenile court statistics dating back to 1985, and these results show that most of the youths transferred to adult courts today are 16- or 17-year-old males who were nonviolent offenders (Sickmund, Sladky, and Kang 2011). This finding is troubling to many who believe that these youths do not represent the most serious offenders. Strom's (2000) research shows that once imprisoned, many are released prior to their 21st birthdays, which is the upper limit of juvenile court jurisdiction in most states (Szymanski 2008b). As a result, these youths could have been treated in juvenile justice systems without compromising public safety. The advantage of retaining these youths in juvenile justice systems is their access to a greater number of treatment or rehabilitative opportunities. Even if these youths were the most violent offenders, there is a growing body of research that shows that effective treatment can significantly reduce their recidivism (Drake 2010; Drake, Aos, and Miller 2009).

Our review of the data also produced some troubling findings, including the transfer of children 12 years and younger to adult courts. More disconcerting is the fact that many of these children were nonviolent offenders. A criticism of sending these young and nonviolent offenders to adult courts is that a transfer suggests that the system has given up on them and they are not amenable to treatment (Deitch, Barstow, Lukens, and Reyna 2009). In addition, these youngsters are also in jeopardy of once-waived, always-waived status in 33 jurisdictions (Szymanski 2011, 1), which means that most will remain in the adult system if they ever reoffend.[4]

Having outlined the context for waivers, we discuss the future of transfers by focusing on a number of key issues. First we examine the role of the prosecutors, with special attention placed on the power that they have gained in juvenile justice systems. Second, we analyze the use of transfers as public policy and describe how waivers have reconfigured the juvenile justice system's boundaries. Last, we examine the limits to punishment and interpret how recent U.S. Supreme Court decisions such as *Roper v. Simmons*, *Graham v. Florida*, and *J.D.B. v. North Carolina* may have a more significant influence on justice systems than the first wave of legal reforms ushered in by the Supreme Court in the 1960s (e.g., *Kent v. United States*, *In re Gault*, and *In re Winship*). Altogether, these factors will play a critical role in the future of transfers and the practice of juvenile justice.

POWER, POLITICS, AND PROSECUTORS

In Chapter 1 we described how state legislatures reduced the power of juvenile court judges to make waiver decisions in favor of prosecutorial discretion and statutory exclusion. Zimring (2010) analyzed these changes in power relationships and reported that prosecutors gained considerable power at the expense of judges in the 1990s. This change has implications for the future of transfers. For most of the history of the juvenile court, judges and probation staff wielded considerable power. As we noted in Chapter 4, probation staff, who are often employed by the juvenile courts, screened cases and acted as the court's gatekeepers. Consequently, many status and minor offenders were placed on informal probation and never actually appeared before a judge.

Although juvenile court judges often have less status in the legal community than their criminal court counterparts, their positions have some desirable perks. First, they traditionally were able to operate with little interference from prosecutors or defense attorneys due to the informal nature of the proceedings. Second, until recently most of the hearings were confidential, meaning that they were closed to the public. Even today, a juvenile court judge can close proceedings to the public, even in states with open courts (Szymanski 2010d). Third, while juvenile court judges in some jurisdictions are elected, these elections tend to be low-visibility events, and incumbents are seldom challenged and usually reelected (see, for example American Judicature Society 2008; Rottman and Strickland 2006). Fourth, juvenile court judges in a number of jurisdictions also oversee probation departments, which enhances their status and influence. Last, because of the informal nature of these proceedings and the lack of transcripts in some courts, these judges were rarely subject to appellate review. Altogether, these judges enjoy considerable autonomy, even compared to criminal court judges, whose primary role in many jurisdictions is to approve plea bargains made by the prosecutor and defense (Zimring 2010).

Throughout the 1980s and 1990s, most jurisdictions got tough on juvenile crime by enacting laws giving prosecutors the ability to directly file juvenile cases in adult courts, excluding certain offenders from the juvenile court's jurisdiction, and introducing blended sentencing schemes that straddled the adult and youth justice systems. In addition, several states lowered their ages of adult responsibility from 18 to 17, and many states reduced the juvenile court's traditional confidentiality by opening proceedings to the public, making juvenile criminal records accessible, and placing juvenile sex offenders on sex offender registries. Many scholars and practitioners saw these changes as an assault on the entire juvenile justice system.

Zimring (2010) challenged the proposition that the juvenile justice system was under attack and instead argued that the real intent of these changes was to enhance prosecutorial powers. Prosecutors gained influence in three ways. First, legislative changes resulted in direct filing in 15 jurisdictions. Second, statutory exclusion of certain types of crimes resulted in cases that again side-stepped the juvenile courts. Zimring (2010, 9) noted that in the case of statutory exclusion, "it is the prosecutor who determines what charges to file. If murder charges go directly to criminal court but manslaughter may be tried in juvenile court, the selection of the charge becomes the selection of the court." Third, prosecutors gained some control over youth detention. Zimring (2010) found support for these claims in his examination of California's Proposition 21 legislation. That law mandated the detention of youths charged with a large number of felony offenses—greatly expanding the number of juveniles who could be detained. Prior to the introduction of Proposition 21, juvenile court judges determined whether youths would be detained pending their court appearances, but once these decisions were mandated by the charge the prosecutor again gained power.

Over the past three decades there has been growing concern about the political role of American prosecutors and how they have used severe sanctions to bolster their political capital (see Bortner 1988). As prosecutors are elected officials, their motivation for pursuing a tough-on-crime agenda may be based on enhancing their political appeal rather than the best interests of a youth. Moreover, unlike judges, when prosecutors exercise their discretion in the transfer process, those decisions are practically without administrative or judicial review (see, for example, *Russell v. Parratt* 1976; *People v. Portland* 1979; *People v. Thorpe* 1982). Interestingly, appellate courts have recognized that prosecutors traditionally have exercised discretion not permissible for judges (see, for example, *Bordenkircher v. Hayes* 1978). Thus, prosecutors enjoy a great deal of unchecked decision-making authority and may play an even greater role in shaping the juvenile court's future.

PUBLIC POLICY, COSMETIC CHANGES, AND TRANSFERS

Throughout this book we have described how the juvenile justice system's boundaries have constricted in two important ways. A significant proportion of the juvenile court's traditional workload was handling status offenders, who were considered to be at risk of delinquency. McNamara (2008,12) observed that the prevailing public perception was that "status offenders were not that different from traditional delinquents." The enactment of the Juvenile Justice and Delinquency Prevention Act in 1974, however, led to fewer status offenders appearing before juvenile courts as social and human service agencies were tasked with handling these youths. These interventions were seen as less stigmatizing than using the court to process cases of incorrigible, truant, or runaway youngsters.

Scholars suggest that some of these status offenders were relabeled from "bad" to "mad" and placed into what Feld (1999c, 11) called "a hidden system of social control in the private sector mental health and chemical dependency industries." Some investigators have observed that the behaviors of other status offenders were criminalized if they violated orders of informal or formal probation (Arthur and Waugh 2009). Feld (2009) contends that the status offenses of girls (e.g., incorrigibility), in particular, have been criminalized, thus resulting in a smaller percentage of female status offenders but a larger number of delinquent girls appearing in juvenile justice systems. Altogether, however, the main result of these changes was to lower the juvenile justice system's limits and divert status offenders to other social or human service agencies.

Transfers to criminal courts, by contrast, helped to define the juvenile court's upper boundaries. A combination of transfers, statutory exclusion, and direct filing resulted in the redirection of tens of thousands of cases each year to adult justice systems. The result is that the core workload of the juvenile courts is now the processing of a large proportion of middle range delinquent youths—younger and minor violent offenders (e.g., those charged with simple assaults), property, drug, and public order offenders. These youths may be perceived by policymakers as more amenable to rehabilitation and less threatening if the courts impose lenient dispositions.

While arguing that juvenile courts now process a growing number of middle range delinquents, we also acknowledge that juvenile courts still deal with many tough cases including juveniles accused of murder. Sickmund, Sladky, and Kang (2011) reported that approximately 1,400 cases of criminal homicide were processed by juvenile courts in 2008. Moreover, there are many repeat property, drug, or public order offenders who have failed to benefit from the rehabilitative opportunities that were extended to them. These statistics demonstrate that juvenile court judges still have to make difficult decisions about many serious and repeat youthful offenders.

In addition to redefining the juvenile justice system's borders, some scholars have argued that the transfer of youths to criminal courts is a symbolic action intended to show the public that juvenile courts are tough-on-crime (Rubin 1986; Titus 2005). Titus (2005, 122), in particular, argued that there is a long tradition of using child scapegoats for "purifying the community" and that "the sacrificial victim protects the community from its own violence by uniting the community in their hatred for a common enemy." Throughout history, these scapegoats have typically lived at the margins of society or are of low status, children Titus (2005, 122) called, "imperfectly assimilated people, social outcasts or outsiders."

Our analyses of the youths transferred to adult courts suggests that Titus' (2005) assessment may be accurate given that most are minority youths, and it is likely that most of these offenders are drawn from the most impoverished social groups. Considered not amenable to rehabilitation, they are symbolically transferred to adult courts to show that the juvenile justice system is tough-on-crime. While we have no other evidence to support Titus' (2005) claims, her arguments are appealing because they help explain transfer policies that do not seem, on their face, to be rational—such as the transfer of 12-year-old, nonviolent children to adult courts.

In order to maintain public support, justice system officials need to be aware of the community's views about crime and justice. In describing the reasons for transfers, Caldwell (1961, 504) stated that, "Certainly no court can exist apart from the community in which it functions and to which it must look for support, and to hold that the court should try to ignore the deep feelings and strong desires of the people whose values it is called upon to enforce is a highly unrealistic and arbitrary attitude."

Such sentiments suggest that the juvenile court's operations are dependent upon the public's good will. As such, the symbolic sacrifice of some juvenile offenders to adult courts may be an expedient method of maintaining the public's support.

Transfers to adult courts are public policies, and we can assume four things about public policy initiatives regardless of the substantive area they might address:

1. Some policies will be effective and will work as they were envisioned.
2. Some policies will work, but not fully as they were intended to work.
3. Some policies will not work, even though attempted as originally designed.
4. Some policies do not work because they were not implemented as intended.

This section examines the outcomes of transfer decisions in terms of their effectiveness based on the reasons for employing this process. It is possible that transfers are accomplishing what they are intended to or that they may actually serve as "eyewash" or "whitewash."

To understand the effectiveness of transfers, we must ask: to what extent is public safety being enhanced or the delivery of treatment services being increased? The answers to these questions should tell us something about the general effectiveness of the waiver process. The option of a broader range of punishments that may be imposed is the logical basis for increasing the frequency with which juveniles are waived to criminal courts. In most states the juvenile court's jurisdiction does not include long periods of incarceration as an option, except in the four states that retain juvenile court jurisdiction until the end of the disposition (Szymanski 2008b). When compared with adult prison terms, however, the incarceration periods for juveniles are relatively short: Strom (2000, 9) reported that offenders who were admitted to state prisons prior to their 18th birthday and were released in 1997 served an average of 37 months prior to their first release.

In terms of sheer numbers, most juveniles transferred to adult courts in the past three decades have been property offenders. In 1985, for example, violent offenders represented about one-third of all youths transferred (Sickmund, Sladky, and Kang 2011). However, beginning in the mid-1990s the types of cases began to shift. According to Sickmund, Sladky, and Kang (2011), during 2008 there were about 8,900 delinquency cases transferred to adult courts in the United States. Of this number less than one-half (49.8%) were for personal offenses, 28.8 percent were for property crimes, 11.7 percent were drug offenses, and 9.7 percent were public order violations.

Nonviolent offenders tend to be persistent, and they may be deemed "not amenable to rehabilitation." Basing a transfer on a lack of amenability to rehabilitation, however, is becoming a controversial issue because it implies that the state has actually provided the youth with reasonable rehabilitation opportunities. Grisso (2010, 177) observed that amenability to rehabilitation "is not merely a characteristic of the youth. It is also necessary to take stock of the system's interventions, its prospects for rehabilitating youth, and the potential to 'match' youth with intervention methods." Thus, the amenability issue seems to be shifting from the youth to the system's ability to provide meaningful opportunities for youths to make positive changes in their lives.

While the public generally expresses little faith in the justice system's ability to reform offenders, studies of rehabilitative interventions show that they reduce recidivism (Lipsey 2009). The Supreme Court has cited the outcomes of empirical research on treatment and rehabilitation to question the degree to which states provide interventions that reduce recidivism. Arya (2010, 103), for example, interpreted the Court's opinion in the *Graham v. Florida* case to mean that "youth have a right to rehabilitation." Thus, the future of transfer, and juvenile justice, may be informed by a growing body of research showing the effectiveness of rehabilitative interventions in reducing juvenile offenders' recidivism.

When juvenile offenders are transferred to adult courts, they often do not receive the type of punishment originally envisioned. In fact, as we described in Chapter 7, transfer does not necessarily mean that they will be subjected to prosecution. It also does not automatically mean that more severe punishments will be handed out by criminal court judges, although this is the motive behind many transfers. While some of these offenders are relatively serious compared with other youngsters appearing before the juvenile court, their offenses are often minor in comparison to most of their adult counterparts.

If charges are not dismissed or reduced, then plea bargaining may occur, reducing sentence severity. For example, Sanborn (2003, 208) says that "Even if there is a guilt plea via a plea bargain in criminal court, prosecutors may be willing to sweeten the deal considerably by reducing charges significantly so as to avoid the uncertainties of a jury trial. This could lead to a sentence that would be both shorter and less intrusive than that which the offender would have received in juvenile court." Other youths who are sent to adult courts, however, are punished severely compared to those who remained in the youth justice system (Jordan and Myers 2011). This lack of consistency in the results reported by different investigators may be a result of the era when the research was conducted, the offense that led to the transfer, the jurisdiction where the transfer occurred, and the mechanism that was used to transfer the youths to criminal court (e.g., judicial waiver compared to statutory exclusion).

Violent offenders present a different case. These are the juveniles for whom the transfer process seems best suited, although they represent less than half of all transferred youths (Sickmund 2009; Snyder and Sickmund 2006). The question remains: are there appropriate treatment services in existence and available in the adult system for these offenders? The irony is that some of these youngsters will commit only one offense, even though it is a serious one. Therefore, transferring these youths to adult court is based on the assumption that there is no hope for their rehabilitation in the juvenile justice system and that future treatment will be provided by the adult system, no matter the type and seriousness of the offense.

In order to manage the risks that violent youthful offenders pose, there is a growing acceptance of the use of risk assessments to predict recidivism. These instruments are valuable in assessing dangerousness. Risk assessments are typically based upon a number of factors that are associated with criminal behavior, such as age at first arrest, number of previous offenses, and the types of victims. Implemented by clinicians, these instruments typically rank a youth as being of low, moderate, or high risk of future delinquency. Grisso (2010, 170) cautions, however, that "for many risk-of-aggression tools, 'high risk' groups of youth often have a 40 to 60% likelihood of future aggression." In other words, these tools tend to overpredict future risk, an outcome that social scientists call a false positive result. Even considering this limitation, these instruments represent a significant improvement over risk predictions made by clinicians using their judgment (Campbell, French, and Gendreau 2009; Grisso 2010). As a result, it is likely that risk assessments will play a more important role in future transfer decisions.

Altogether, when considering the factors mentioned in connection with the findings of other researchers, it does not appear that all juveniles receive harsher penalties when transferred to criminal courts. Almost three decades ago Rubin (1986, 26) suggested that waivers appeared to be cosmetic, primarily "escape valves" designed to appease the public by ridding juvenile courts of chronic repeat violators, largely property offenders. This means that many of the so-called "tough, new laws" are not as tough as they sometimes appear. Inconsistent with good public policy, however, some youngsters appear to be subjected to injustices—such as the transfer of preteens to adult courts or the use of LWOP sentences for 13- and 14-year-olds. In addition, the individual, social, and financial costs to society are high if we unnecessarily remove youths from the juvenile justice system (and their ability to access rehabilitative programs) by sending them to adult justice systems.

Shay Bilchik, a former Florida prosecutor who also headed the Office of Juvenile Justice and Delinquency Prevention in the 1990s, testified to Congress in 2008 about transfers to adult courts:

> This goes back to your question, Mr. Scott, about transfers, and the thought that somehow if we transferred enough kids who were the bad kids into the criminal justice system, we would reduce crime. And the research is clear—from the Centers for Disease Control and, a recent report issued by OJDDP itself, another thing for them to be commended about—that if you transfer young people into the criminal justice system, you will accelerate recidivism, it will happen with more serious crime and more frequent. This is the trifecta of bad criminal justice policy. That is strong research with clear findings.

If transfers do result in all these negative outcomes, and these consequences are supported by federal government–sponsored research (see Redding 2010), then it appears that we must rethink whether our transfer practices are sound.

The evidence suggests that waiver of jurisdiction is a policy without a substantial positive impact. The outcome of most transfers appears to be that policies are merely cosmetic rather than real crime control. The punishment envisioned for some transferred juveniles never materializes or it never is quite as severe as expected. In other cases, our punishments are severe, but they seem misdirected, especially when they result in 13- and 14-year-olds serving life terms without parole (Equal Justice Initiative 2007).

As previously mentioned, transfers can be viewed as eyewash or whitewash. Viewing policies as eyewash simply means that they have little actual impact but that they are intended to make the world look better. Whitewash gives the impression that circumstances are better than they really are or that they are different from what they have been. For some policymakers and politicians there is little concern for what these policies can achieve as long as they look good to the public or make the public think that something is being done about juvenile crime.

Transfers can have punishment effects for juvenile offenders, but most of this potential remains unrealized. The most serious, personal offenders do receive transfers to adult courts, and some receive severe sentences (Jordan and Myers 2011; Myers 2003; Redding 2010; Snyder and Sickmund 2006). Persistent nonviolent offenders represent most of the waiver recipients; however, these are the types of youngsters least likely to be incarcerated by adult criminal courts. Thus, the policy outcomes desired may not be the actual policy results realized when juveniles are transferred.

Mears (2003, 162–65) identified other unintended consequences of transferring youths. He observed, for instance, that waiver was inconsistently used between jurisdictions and that this might result in a failure to achieve consistent or coherent outcomes. Another negative outcome identified by Feld (1991) is justice by geography, meaning that the location where one is sentenced sometimes determines how severely a youth will be punished. This is a particular problem when comparing urban and rural courts. Sentencing disparities related to geography persist, and Macallair, McCracken, and Teji (2011) reported finding significant differences in the use of direct filing in California counties as some counties with high rates of juvenile crime had comparatively low levels of direct filings.

Another unintentional outcome identified by Mears (2003) is the disparity in the race of juveniles being transferred; this was confirmed in our analyses of the characteristics of youths waived between 1985 and 2008. Soler (2010), for example, identified several practices that resulted in a high percentage of minority youths appearing before criminal courts. In particular, he noted a 1980s Illinois law that mandated the automatic transfer of cases where drugs were sold within 1,000 feet of public schools or housing. When Chicago reporters studied the impact of this practice from 1995 to 1999, Soler (2010, 22–23) noted that they found "Slightly less than 95% were black, and just over 4% were Latino—more than 99% youth of color." A subsequent investigation by Cook County public defenders confirmed the accuracy of those findings in their examination of 1999–2000 transfer statistics (Soler 2010). Yet, as these cases were directly filed in adult courts, they do not appear in the OJJDP juvenile court statistics and are therefore unavailable to most researchers.

Because transfers can be used inconsistently, their use might reduce the justice system's legitimacy, especially from the groups most impacted by these practices. Thus, it is possible that the strategy of using transfers is a successful method of bolstering the juvenile court's status with mainstream America by getting tough, scapegoating or ritually sacrificing juveniles who are living at the economic and social margins of society.

The unanticipated outcome of this strategy might be a corresponding decrease in the justice system's perceived legitimacy by those living on the margins, which may in turn result in higher crime levels (Tyler 2006). As a result, the transfer of youths to a criminal court might result in a greater likelihood of their recidivism as well as increasing the likelihood of their peers, families, and community members committing crimes.

Mears (2003) also identified the risks of victimization when juveniles are placed in an adult jail or prison as unanticipated outcomes of transfers. The negative outcomes of mixing juveniles with adult offenders, however, have long been documented (see Fishman 1923). Some might argue that this victimization is part of the sacrificing process and that these youths are getting their just deserts. At the very least, Human Rights Watch (2001) described the sexual abuse of prisoners as deliberate indifference on the part of correctional officials. While this perspective seems cynical—and one that cannot be supported empirically—we question why juveniles continue to be placed in these high-risk situations when we have been aware of these negative outcomes for the past century.

One dimension of transfers that has received comparatively less attention in our analyses has been the development of blended-sentencing schemes. As highlighted in the Nathaniel Abraham case in Chapter 1, these models straddle both the juvenile and adult justice systems. This approach has been called a "middle road" between the justice systems or a "third justice system" and typically enables youths to remain in the juvenile justice system if they have complied with the conditions that the court has imposed. While there are no national-level studies that have examined the prevalence of blended sentencing or the outcomes of these cases, there have been several state-level studies, and these provide us with some insight into these models. Trulson, Caudill, Belshaw and DeLisi (2011, 269) examined 1,504 offenders sentenced under a state's Serious and Violent Offender Act (SVOA) and found that 40 percent had their juvenile sentences revoked and that these youths were comprised of "offenders who were committed for the most serious and violent offenses, were older at their SVOA commitment, and those who engaged in heightened levels of any misconduct while confined."

Zimring (2010) has questioned whether blended sentencing was an attempt to appease those who were critical of the traditional leniency of the juvenile court. As with the direct file provisions mentioned above, Zimring (2010) noted that prosecutors gained power as they could use the threat of an adult term of imprisonment to secure a guilty plea from a youth. Regardless of the intent of introducing blended sentencing, some form of this approach is present in more than one-half of all states (Griffin 2011). While this sentencing scheme gives youthful offenders a last chance to reform themselves, that is sometimes a tall order if there are few rehabilitative opportunities for these youths, as well as for those youngsters who cannot foresee the consequences of failing to abide by the judge's conditions, including terms of imprisonment that might last several decades.

Throughout the second half of this book we questioned whether waivers, as currently used, are an effective, rational, or sound public policy. While acknowledging that transfers have an important role in the juvenile justice system, their use often appears to be inconsistent with rational juvenile justice practices, especially given the growing body of evidence showing that transfers do not deter crime and that even high-risk juveniles can be reformed. As a result, we predict that youth advocates and public interest law firms will place increased pressure on juvenile justice officials to provide more meaningful rehabilitative interventions for youthful offenders. Cash-strapped governments, however, will resist these changes given the current budget shortfalls. As a result, the states' responsibility to provide higher levels of care for juveniles will likely be resolved in the courts.

DUE PROCESS PROTECTIONS AND THE LIMITS TO PUNISHMENT

The hazards of failing to address youths' due process protections have long been recognized (Lindsey 1914). In Chapter 2 we described how youths would trade these protections for treatment-oriented dispositions. Many of the people who worked within juvenile justice systems were "true believers" in their ability to reform youths. Van Waters (1922) compared fact-finding in California juvenile and criminal courts and observed that, "The Juvenile Court . . . can demand the whole truth because it has the power to save, to protect, and to remedy. Its orders, or judgments, are not penal, but parental." Sentiments of saving, protecting, and remedying youths in a parental manner speak to these youth advocates' good intentions.

It is likely that some of these well-intentioned reformers were blind to the abuses of authority that occurred in juvenile courts and the fact that status offenders and at-risk youths were placed in dangerous out-of-home placements (Bernard 1992). There was also growing recognition that some youths received neither treatment nor leniency, prompting Tappan (1946, 208) to ask, "Who is to save the child from his saviors?" Platt (1977) called these juvenile court supporters "child-savers," but

Diana (1957, 568) observed that "The point is not that the state should not step in to help 'save' a child, but does the child need to be 'saved,' and if so, does it need to be saved by the state?"

In Chapter 5 we described that there was growing recognition that the consequences of being adjudicated delinquent have increased over time and that juveniles required some form of protection from the juvenile court's informal, indeterminate, and confidential operations. The *Kent, Gault,* and *Winship* decisions in the 1960s and 1970s promised a number of changes in juvenile justice operations. A review of scholarship from that era suggested that juvenile justice practitioners were threatened by these reforms (see Weinstein and Goodman 1967).

Four decades later, however, youths still appear before juvenile courts without the assistance of counsel, and there is a consensus that the reforms promised by *Kent, Gault,* and *Winship* remain unfulfilled (Dorsen 2007; Kaye 2011). Berkheiser (2002) wrote that juvenile court judges have resisted and frustrated legislative and court-ordered reforms such as access to counsel. Perhaps more troubling is that some youths may actually be *punished* with harsher sanctions by exercising their due process rights (Feld and Schaefer 2010).

It is possible that the Supreme Court's reach in the administration of juvenile justice diminishes the closer one gets to the front lines, representing the divide between legal theory and what actually occurs. Birckhead (2012, 19–20) analyzed the early cases (*Kent, Gault,* and *Winship*) and the postmillennial reforms (*Simmons, Graham,* and *J.D.B.)* and argued that the Supreme Court's influences in the first reform wave were moderated by a number of factors, observing that:

> Very few of the key elements needed for institutional reform litigation to succeed were present. There were no incentives from outside actors that served to catalyze change within the juvenile court. Equally important, there were few incentives for the main participants *within* the system to change, as most were invested in maintaining the informal culture of the court. ... Likewise, there were no outside actors or parallel institutions imposing *costs* for noncompliance. Because hearings were either closed to or ignored by the public, there was little to no oversight of the proceedings.

Altogether, there is significant scholarly agreement about the lack of compliance with the promise of juvenile justice reforms of the 1960s (Arya 2010; Berkheiser 2002; Birckhead 2010; 2012; Dorsen 2007; Feld and Schaefer 2010; Kaye 2011). The question we consider is whether the post–*Roper v. Simmons* era of reforms will be more successful? The success or failure will directly impact both the limits to youth punishment as well as the future of transfers.

It is possible that the second reform wave may be more successful at altering the juvenile justice system's operations, establishing a legal foundation for juvenile rehabilitation, and challenging existing legislation. From 2005 to 2011, three Supreme Court decisions that specifically related to juvenile justice were delivered. *Roper v. Simmons*, *Graham v. Florida*, and *J.D.B. v. North Carolina* have already altered the boundaries of juvenile justice. *Simmons* and *Graham* limited the punishments of juveniles transferred to adult courts, while *J.D.B.* forced the police to take into account the age of a youth in their interrogations. The common element in these decisions is the recognition of the immaturity of youths and their diminished culpability. Moreover, *Graham* acknowledged a juvenile offender's need for rehabilitation. Last, both the *Simmons* and *Graham* decisions exempted entire categories of individuals from certain punishments.

Arya (2010) speculated that the *Graham* decision might be used by youth advocates to increase access to treatment for delinquent youths. The language of the majority in *Graham*, for instance, suggests that states reexamine their balances of rehabilitation, retribution, and incapacitation as they relate to juvenile offenders, with a strong emphasis on rehabilitation. Arya (2010, 103) also described three key issues raised in the *Graham* opinion and argued that these apply to all transferred juveniles:

> First, judges and experts have problems evaluating the culpability and maturity of youth. Second, adult perceptions of youth are biased by the severity and manner in which the crimes were conducted. Third, counsel have difficulty representing youth in the adult system.

In terms of using *Graham* to challenge transfer legislation, Arya (2010, 137–52) observed that two strategies could be used: (1) Eighth Amendment challenges of transfers based on the lifelong consequences of a criminal conviction; and (2) overruling existing transfer legislation by challenging the validity of juvenile waiver statutes. Arya (2010, 152) speculated that transfers often result in fewer rehabilitative opportunities for juveniles and that, "This element of *Graham* found in the Court's collateral holdings that youth have a right to rehabilitation and that dispositions which prospectively remove this option are therefore unconstitutional, also applies to juvenile transfer decisions."

The possibility of challenging existing transfer legislation must be balanced with the acknowledgment that apart from youth advocates, some practitioners, and academics there appears to be little public awareness of or support for change. Moreover, Berkheiser (2002) and Kaye (2011) have noted that juvenile courts have resisted reforms. Birckhead (2012) contended that courts have not abided by the spirit of the *Graham* decision and specifically cited that lengthy prison terms for juveniles have been upheld in appellate decisions. More specifically, on March 16, 2011, the California Court of Appeals decided that a 120-year sentence for a juvenile nonhomicide offender was constitutionally appropriate because "*Graham* did not apply to a juvenile offender who receives a term-of-years sentence that results in the functional equivalent of a life sentence without the possibility of parole" and that "We adhere to that view" (see *People v. Ramirez*).[5]

In a dissent, Justice Manella challenged the Court's opinion that upheld the lengthy sentence, noting that:

> Appellant's 120-year sentence is, for all intents and purposes, the same as that at issue in *Graham*. He has been sentenced to a term which deprives him of any meaningful opportunity for parole. The parties agree that the date on which he will first become eligible for parole—more than a century from now—is far beyond his life expectancy. ... He has thus effectively been sentenced to "life without parole"—a sentence *Graham* prohibits for juvenile nonhomicide offenders.

California's Supreme Court will be considering whether these lengthy sentences are the functional equivalent of a life without the possibility of parole sentence. In the meantime, however, this case serves as an example of how judges can act in a constitutionally valid way while circumventing the spirit and intent of the Supreme Court's decision.

SUMMARY

Scholars and practitioners trying to predict the future of juvenile justice are often thwarted by unforeseen social, economic, or political changes that disrupt our ability to make accurate forecasts. Ohlin (1983), for example, wrote about the growing influence of the conservative "law and order reaction" but did not predict increases in the use of juvenile imprisonment, the growth of transfers to adult court, and the public acceptance of placing youths in penitentiaries or on death row. These outcomes were associated with a crack cocaine epidemic that started in the mid-1980s. The abuse of that drug over the next decade, combined with the proliferation of well-armed and aggressive youth gangs, resulted in nearly 3,800 juvenile arrests for murder in 1993 (Snyder 2000). As a result, there was a legitimate need for getting tough on juvenile crime to respond to an unanticipated social and legal problem.

Bernard (1992), by contrast, speculated that the nation was at the tail end of the latest wave of tough-on-juvenile-crime practices and that this would result in a new cycle of support for leniency and rehabilitation. It turned out, however, that we were still almost two decades away from a softening of public opinion toward juvenile offenders, support for juvenile rehabilitation, and jurisdictions that moderated their tough-on-juvenile-crime sanctions (Merlo and Benekos 2010). Youth advocacy organizations are now reporting victories as state legislatures increase the age of adult responsibility, restrict the detention of juveniles in adult jails, and make it more difficult to send juveniles to adult courts (Campaign for Youth Justice 2011). Yet there is no guarantee that these legislative changes will continue or that officials in the juvenile justice system won't circumvent these policies.

Bernard and Kurlychek (2010) cautioned us that we should not forget the lessons of history when it comes to the administration of juvenile justice. They noted that juvenile justice operates in a cycle that is characterized by shifts in punitive and rehabilitative philosophies, legislation, and practices. It is important to acknowledge that historical events sometimes influence current organizational practices (King 2009). A review of the legal literature from the early 1900s, for example, shows that scholars of the era grappled with the same challenges that we do today: respecting juveniles' due process rights, debating the degree to which juveniles should be rehabilitated or punished, as well as dealing with the difficulty of community reentry and reducing recidivism. By failing to learn these lessons from the past, we are more likely to repeat the mistakes that were previously made.

Cohn (1994) observed that changes in the philosophy, operations, or processes of juvenile justice systems can either be revolutionary (e.g., the *Gault* decision) or incremental and evolutionary. The recent landmark Supreme Court decisions discussed in this chapter have already had a revolutionary impact in terms of defining the upper limits of punishing juvenile offenders transferred to criminal courts. Yet the actual number of youths directly impacted by the *Simmons* and *Graham* decisions is only a few hundred who had already been sentenced. Even this victory might be short lived as judges have already circumvented *Graham's* prohibition of LWOP sentences by sentencing nonhomicide offenders to terms of imprisonment that exceed their life expectancy (e.g., *People v. Ramirez*).

As a result, it is possible that these Supreme Court cases may have a more important evolutionary impact by setting the foundation for future court decisions. The Court's decision to exempt entire categories of juveniles (all offenders who committed a homicide prior to their 18th birthday can no longer be executed), for example, is unprecedented in juvenile justice (Arya 2010; Birckhead 2012; Singer 2011). The recent wave of juvenile justice reform may lead to further restrictions in how much punishment can be imposed on youths.

The outcomes of the three recent Supreme Court cases have energized youth advocates. Birckhead (2012) observed that the reforms of the first wave of Supreme Court decisions were unfulfilled. Yet the costs of noncompliance with these court mandates could be much higher today. Public interest law firms and advocacy groups are more skilled in using litigation to force changes on juvenile justice systems to ensure that they are complying with constitutional protections. Consequently, while these changes may be incremental, the long-term results may be revolutionary. Yet revolutionary change can also produce unanticipated outcomes.

California's juvenile correctional system, for example, has long been the target of advocacy organizations, such as the Prison Law Center, because of the failure of the California Youth Authority (now operating as the Division of Juvenile Justice) to provide a safe and rehabilitative environment for the youths in their care (see the *Farrell v. Allen* consent decree). The Prison Law Center initiated a class action lawsuit in 2004 that forced the juvenile correctional system into a series of reforms that were still being undertaken in 2011. In March 2011, however, California's Governor Jerry Brown announced his intention to close the state's training schools by 2014 and transfer the responsibility for sentenced juvenile offenders to the counties.

These changes may lead to an *increased* use of transfers. The cost of incarcerating a juvenile in California's Division of Juvenile Facilities was $175,616 in 2007, whereas it cost $49,000 to imprison an adult offender in 2008, or about 27.9 percent of the cost.[6] If counties are financially responsible for youth incarceration, there may be a powerful economic incentive to transfer a greater number of youths to adult courts: If they are sentenced to state prisons these offenders become the state government's responsibility. In his study of juvenile court practitioners, for instance, Urbina (2005, 164) reported that some judges perceived transfers as "cost effective because the state pays for incarceration if classified as an adult, and thus ... less expensive to the county." A prosecutor in Urbina's (2005, 168) study echoed that sentiment and stated that "human services in our county want to waive more juveniles because they do not want to spend the money on juvenile placements." Thus, youths could be exposed to all of the negative and lifelong consequences of an adult conviction because county officials want to shift the costs of incarceration to the state.

Macallair, McCracken, and Teji (2011, 1) examined the direct filing of juvenile cases into California's adult courts, finding that there was a disproportionate use of transfers in 2009 and that 13 counties "accounted for 37% of juvenile felony arrests but 61% of all direct adult criminal court filings," and more specifically "Kings County is the most State-dependent county, direct filing in adult criminal court 50 times more than Los Angeles, 39 times more than San Diego, and 36 times more than San Francisco in 2009." These investigators questioned whether state budget cutbacks that forced counties to pay a greater proportion of the youth incarceration costs would result in even higher numbers of transfers.

It is possible that economic conditions will play an increasingly important role in the operations of juvenile justice systems, especially given that rates of juvenile crime are at the lowest levels since the 1960s. While politicians may be reluctant to appear soft on crime, cash-strapped local governments cannot sustain high rates of youth detention, and many states cannot afford placing low-risk juvenile offenders in training schools at an average cost of $88,000 per year (Justice Policy Institute 2009: 4). Thus, politicians may be motivated to increase support for community-based treatments—which are sound juvenile justice practices that reduce recidivism (Armstrong, Armstrong, Webb, and Atkin 2011). Moreover, these community-based interventions are supported by cost-benefit analyses (Drake 2010, Drake, Aos and Miller 2009).

The future of transfers to adult court and juvenile justice are tightly coupled, meaning that changes in one field will influence what happens in the other. It is likely that empirical research will drive some of the future changes in juvenile justice, including the transfers of juveniles to adult courts. There is a growing body of studies that show that youths can be rehabilitated and that the costs of intervention are minimal compared to losing these youths to a life of crime (Cohen and Piquero 2009).

Crime is also tied to the use of transfers. We reported in Chapter 3 that when youth arrests and court appearances for serious crimes increase, so do the numbers of transfers. Thus, the future of waivers is also linked to crime trends. Juvenile crime rates today are similar to those of the 1960s, but increasing unemployment and inflation can contribute to higher crime levels. These changes may have a greater impact on those who already live at society's margins, such as minority youths living within

America's inner cities. Economic hardship may also exacerbate feelings of alienation, mistrust, and hostility toward the justice system.

Fagan and Meares (2008, 228) observed that mass incarceration policies "sustains a process that contributes to the marginalization of already isolated communities and individuals, further weakening informal controls and continuing the cycle of discontrol and punishment." Many of these communities have high populations of people of color, and our analyses showed that members of minority groups are disproportionately represented in transfers and that many of these youths have committed nonviolent offenses. While the issue of DMC has been a priority of the federal government since the 1992 reauthorization of the JJDPA, there has been comparatively little success in reducing the numbers of these youths coming into contact with juvenile justice systems. The fact that so little has been done in the two decades since the reauthorization of the JJDPA to identify and reduce the sources of DMC is troubling to many scholars (Cabaniss, Frabutt, Kendrick, and Arbuckle 2007; Leiber and Rodriguez 2011; Kempf-Leonard 2007).

The future of juvenile justice systems will be shaped by their history and organizational arrangements as well as by the social, political, and economic conditions we have identified throughout this book. Moreover, the media and politicians can inflame the public's feelings toward juvenile offenders (Feld 2003b; Soler 2001). Acting together, these factors can increase our support for tough-on-crime policies such as transferring youths to juvenile courts.

Throughout this book we have identified some key issues related to waivers, but in this process we also raised more questions than we answered. It is difficult to make sweeping generalizations about transfers, for example, if we don't know how many juveniles appear before criminal courts each year, and especially how many appear in courts as a result of legislative exclusion or direct filing. Mears (2003, 165) critiqued waiver research and reported that we need to have a "greater understanding and assessment of intended effects, including: (1) targeting of serious and violent offenders, (2) greater punishment, (3) preservation of the juvenile justice system and it capacity to rehabilitate youth, (4) reduced recidivism and (5) reduced delinquency." In addition, while the federally sponsored collection of data through the OJJDP is a good resource, we do not have an accurate accounting of race and ethnicity as Latino populations are grouped with white juveniles. Last, we need a better national-level understanding of the prior criminal histories and outcomes of youths who have been transferred.

We have also expressed concern about the unintended effects of waivers to adult courts and our lack of knowledge about outcomes of youths who have been transferred. Mears (2003, 165) also identified the need to examine these unintended effects, including:

(1) inconsistent meaning and use of waiver across jurisdictions, (2) plea bargaining to juvenile sanctions through the unofficial use of waiver, (3) net widening through plea bargaining and sanctioning of lesser offenders, (4) limited competency of juvenile defendants and thus unfair or harmful sanctions, (5) disparity in the use of waiver, (6) lengthy pretrial detention and victimization in adult jail facilities, (7) increased likelihood of victimization among youth incarcerated in adult prisons, and (8) perceptions and experiences of unfair processing and negative effects on recidivism.

It is important to understand unanticipated consequences of waivers, especially in light of recent research that finds that transfers result in higher rates of recidivism (Hahn et al. 2007; Redding 2010).

Transfers to adult courts represent the end of the line for many juvenile offenders, from nonviolent 12-year-old children to gang-involved homicide offenders. While everybody agrees that transfers are an important safety valve for the juvenile justice system, there is less consensus about the types of youths who ought to be transferred. When juvenile crime rates are low, the economy is strained, and the public is optimistic about rehabilitation, elected officials may support less harmful transfer practices. Yet the conditions that support such reforms are fragile and can quickly become derailed. Whatever the future of transfers will bring, politicians, policymakers, and practitioners should work toward evidence-based practices that enhance public safety.

NOTES

1. This statistic was developed by dividing the 68,074 arrests for homicide, rape, aggravated assault, and robbery into the estimated population of 24,751,425 youths aged 12 to 17 years, producing a ratio of 2.75 per 1,000 youths.

2. We estimated an annual youth detention population of 424,286 admissions using the same multiplier as the Bureau of Justice Statistics in its calculation of jail populations. Minton (2011) estimated that the annual number of jail inmates was 17 times the midyear census jail

population. This estimate reflects the number of admissions, not the actual number of juveniles, as some youths would be admitted more than once in a calendar year.

3. This estimate was developed using the same methodology as outlined in note 2 (multiplying the one-day census total of 7,560 by 17).

4. Szymanski (2011, 1) notes that "Maryland has a procedure that is close to, but is not quite once an adult/always an adult."

5. Ramirez was convicted of three attempted homicides in a shooting alleged to be gang-related.

6. The Center on Juvenile and Criminal Justice (2011) reported that the cost to keep a California juvenile in the Division of Juvenile Facilities was $224,712. The cost for adult imprisonment is from the California Department of Corrections and Rehabilitation (2009).

Cases Cited

Atkins v. Virginia, 536 U.S. 304 (2002)
Baldwin v. New York, 399 U.S. 66 (1970)
Bordenkircher v. Hayes, 434 U.S. 357 (1978)
Breed v. Jones, 421 U.S. 519 (1975)
Duncan v. Louisiana, 391 U.S. 145 (1968)
Eddings v. Oklahoma, 455 U.S. 104 (1982)
Ex Parte Crouse, 4 Wharton (PA.) 9 (1838)
Fare v. Michael C., 442 U.S. 707 (1979)
Farrell v. Allen, County of Alameda, Case No. RG 03079344
Gallegos v. Colorado, 370 U.S. 49 (1962)
Gideon v. Wainwright, 372 U.S. 335 (1963)
Graham v. Florida, 560 U.S. ___ (2010)
Haley v. Ohio, 332 U.S. 596 (1948)
In the Interest of R.W., 2004 PA Super 282
In re Gault, 387 U.S. 1 (1967)
In re Winship, 397 U.S. 358 (1970)
Ivan V. v. City of New York, 407 U.S. 203 (1972)
J.D.B. v. North Carolina, No. 09-11121
Kent v. United States, 383 U.S. 541 (1966)
McKeiver v. Pennsylvania, 403 U.S. 528 (1971)
Miranda v. Arizona, 384 U.S. 436 (1966)
People v. Portland, 423 N.Y.S. 2d 999 (Crim. Ct. 1979)
People v. Ramirez, (2011) 193 Cal. App. 4th 613

People v. Thorpe, 641 P. 2d 935 (Colo. 1982)
People v. Turner, 55 Ill. 280 (1870)
Roper v. Simmons, 543 U.S. 551 (2005)
Russell v. Parratt, 543 F. 2d 1214 (8th Circuit 1976)
Stanford v. Kentucky, 492 U.S. 361 (1989)
Thompson v. Oklahoma, 487 U.S. 815 (1988)

References

Adams, Benjamin, and Sean Addie. (2010). *Delinquency Cases Waived to Criminal Court, 2007*. Washington, DC: Office of Juvenile Justice and Delinquency Prevention.

Advisory Council of Judges. (1962). "Transfer of Cases between Juvenile and Criminal Courts: A Policy Statement, Advisory Council of Judges, National Council on Crime and Delinquency." *Crime & Delinquency* 8(1): 3–11.

Agyepong, Tera. (2010). "Children Left behind Bars: Sullivan, Graham, and Juvenile Life without Parole Sentences." *Northwestern Journal of International Human Rights* 9(1):83–102.

Ainsworth, Janet E. (1999). "Re-imagining Childhood and Reconstructing the Legal Order: The Case for Abolishing the Juvenile Court." In Barry C. Feld (Ed.), *Readings in Juvenile Justice Administration*, pp. 8–13. New York: Oxford University Press.

American Bar Association. (2004). *Adolescence, Brain Development and Legal Culpability*. Washington, DC: Author.

American Judicature Society. (2008). *Judicial Selection in the States: How It Works, Why It Matters*. Denver, CO: Institute for the Advancement of the American Legal System.

American National Election Studies. (2010). *The ANES Guide to Public Opinion and Electoral Behavior*. Retrieved Nov. 20, 2011, from http://electionstudies.org/nesguide/nesguide.htm.

Amnesty International. (1998). *Betraying the Young: Children in the US Justice System*. New York: Author.

Ansolabehere, Stephen, and Brian F. Schaffner. (2010). "Residential Mobility, Family Structure, and the Cell-Only Population." *Public Opinion Quarterly* 74(2): 244–59.

Applegate, Brandon K., Robin King-Davis, and Francis T. Cullen. (2009). "Reconsidering Child Saving: The Extent and Correlates of Public Support for Excluding Youths from the Juvenile Court." *Crime & Delinquency* 55(1): 51–77.

Armstrong, Gaylene S., Todd A. Armstrong, Vince J. Webb, and Cassandra A. Atkin. (2011). "Can Financial Incentives Reduce Juvenile Confinement Levels? An Evaluation of the Redeploy Illinois Program." *Journal of Criminal Justice* 39(2): 183–91.

Armstrong, Gaylene S., and Bitna Kim. (2009). "The Rise and Fall of Boot Camps in the United States." In Rick Ruddell and Matthew O. Thomas (Eds.), *Juvenile Corrections*, pp. 75–91. Richmond, KY: Newgate Press.

Arthur, Patricia J., and Regina Waugh. (2009). "Status Offenses and the Juvenile Justice and Delinquency Prevention Act: The Exception That Swallowed the Rule." *Seattle Journal for Social Justice* 7(2): 555–76.

Arya, Neelum. (2010). "Using *Graham v. Florida* to Challenge Juvenile Transfer Laws." *Louisiana Law Review* 71(1): 99–155.

Austin, James F., and Barry Krisberg. (1981). "Wider, Stronger, and Different Nets: The Dialectics of Criminal Justice Reform." *Journal of Research in Crime and Delinquency* 18(1): 165–96.

Ball, W. David. (2011). "The Civil Case at the Heart of Criminal Procedure: *In re Winship*, Stigma, and the Civil-Criminal Distinction." *American Journal of Criminal Law* 38(2): 101–62.

Baumer, Eric P., and Janet L. Lauritsen. (2010). "Reporting Crime to the Police, 1973-2005: A Multivariate Analysis of Long-Term Trends in the National Crime Survey (NCS) and National Crime Victimization Survey (NCVS)." *Criminology* 48(1): 131–85.

Beckett, Katherine A., and Theodore Sasson. (2004). *The Politics of Injustice: Crime and Punishment in America*. Thousand Oaks, CA: Sage.

Benekos, Peter. (2003). "Juvenile Courts: Current Status." In Marilyn D. McShane and Frank P. Williams III (Eds.), *Encyclopedia of Juvenile Justice*, pp. 83–87. Thousand Oaks, CA: Sage Publications.

Bennett, William J., John J. DiIulio, and John P. Walters. (1996). *Body Count: Moral Poverty and How to Win America's War against Crime and Drugs*. New York: Simon and Schuster.

Bergin, Tiffany. (2010). "How and Why Do Criminal Justice Public Policies Spread throughout U.S. States? A Critical Review of the

Diffusion Literature." *Criminal Justice Policy Review*. Retrieved Nov. 20, 2011, from http://cjp.sagepub.com/content/early/2010/08/ 16/0887403410381443.full.pdf+html.

Berkheiser, Mary. (2002). "The Fiction of Juvenile Right to Counsel: Waiver in the Juvenile Courts." *Florida Law Review* 54(4): 577–686.

Bernard, Thomas J. (1992). *The Cycle of Juvenile Justice*. New York: Oxford University Press.

Bernard, Thomas J., and Megan C. Kurlychek. (2010). *The Cycle of Juvenile Justice* (2nd ed.). New York: Oxford University Press.

Bilchik, Shay. (2008, Sept. 18). *Hearing Before the Subcommittee on Crime, Terrorism and Homeland Security, 110th Congress*. Retrieved Nov. 20, 2011, from http://judiciary.house.gov/hearings/ printers/110th/44494.PDF.

Birckhead, Tamar R. (2008). "North Carolina, Juvenile Court Jurisdiction, and the Resistance to Reform." *North Carolina Law Review* 86(6): 1443–1500.

Birckhead, Tamar R. (2010). "*Graham v. Florida*: Justice Kennedy's Vision of Childhood and the Role of Judges." *Duke Journal of Constitutional Law & Public Policy* 6(1): 66–80.

Birckhead, Tamar R. (2012). "Juvenile Justice Reform 2.0." *Brooklyn Journal of Law and Policy* Retrieved Nov. 20, 2011, from http:// papers.ssrn.com/sol3/papers.cfm?abstract_id=1856257.

Bishop, Donna M. (2000). "Juvenile Offenders in the Adult Criminal Justice System." *Crime and Justice* 27: 81–167.

Bishop, Donna M. (2006). "Public Opinion and Juvenile Justice Policy: Myths and Misconceptions." *Criminology & Public Policy* 5(4): 653–64.

Bishop, Donna M. (2009). "Juvenile Transfer in the United States." In Josine Junger-Tas and Frieder Dunkel (Eds.), *Reforming Juvenile Justice*, pp. 85–104. New York: Springer-Verlag.

Bishop, Donna M., Charles E. Frazier, and John C. Henretta. (1999). "Prosecutorial Waiver: Case Study of a Questionable Reform." In Barry C. Feld (Ed.), *Readings in Juvenile Justice Administration*, pp. 210–25. New York: Oxford University Press.

Bishop, Donna M., Michael Leiber, and Joseph Johnson. (2010). "Contexts of Decision Making in the Juvenile Justice System: An Organizational Approach to Understanding Minority Overrepresentation." *Youth Violence and Juvenile Justice* 8(3): 213–33.

Bortner, M. A. (1988). *Delinquency and Justice: An Age of Crisis*. New York: McGraw Hill.

Boswell, John (1988). *The Kindness of Strangers: The Abandonment of Children in Western Europe from Late Antiquity to the Renaissance.* Chicago: University of Chicago Press.

Bouley, Eugene E. Jr., and Terry L. Wells. (2001). "Attitudes of Citizens in a Southern Rural County toward Juvenile Crime and Justice Issues." *Journal of Contemporary Criminal Justice* 17(1): 60–70.

Burruss, George W. Jr., and Kimberly Kempf-Leonard. (2002). "The Questionable Advantage of Defense Counsel in Juvenile Court." *Justice Quarterly* 19(1): 37–68.

Buss, Emily. (2011). "Failing Juvenile Courts, and What Lawyers and Judges Can Do About It." *Northwestern Journal of Law and Social Policy* 6(2): 318–333.

Buzawa, Eve S., and David Hirschel. (2010). "Criminalizing Assault: Do Age and Gender Matter?" In Meda Chesney-Lind and Nikki Jones (Eds.), *Fighting for Girls: New Perspectives on Gender and Violence*, pp. 33–55, Albany: State University of New York Press.

Cabaniss, Emily R., James M. Frabutt, Mary H. Kendrick, and Margaret B. Arbuckle. (2007). "Reducing Disproportionate Minority Contact in the Juvenile Justice System: Promising Practices." *Aggression and Violent Behavior* 12(4): 393–401.

Caldwell, Robert G. (1961). "The Juvenile Court: Its Development and Some Major Problems." *The Journal of Criminal Law, Criminology and Police Science* 51(5): 493–511.

California Department of Corrections and Rehabilitation. (2009). *Fourth Quarter 2008 Facts and Figures.* Retrieved Nov. 20, 2011, from http://www.cdcr.ca.gov/Adult_Operations/docs/Fourth_Quarter_2009 _Facts_and_Figures.pdf.

California Department of Corrections and Rehabilitation. (2011). *Time Served on Prison Sentence.* Sacramento, CA: Author.

Campaign for Youth Justice. (2007). *Jailing Juveniles: The Dangers of Incarcerating Youth in Adult Jails in America.* Washington, DC: Author.

Campaign for Youth Justice. (2011). *State Trends: Legislative Victories from 2005 to 2010 Removing Youth from the Adult Criminal Justice System.* Washington, DC: Author.

Campbell, Mary Ann, Sheila French, and Paul Gendreau. (2009). "The Prediction of Violence in Adult Offenders: A Meta-analytic Comparison of Instruments and Methods of Assessment." *Criminal Justice and Behavior* 36(6): 567–90.

Catalano, Shannan M. (2006). *The Measurement of Crime: Victim Reporting and Police Recording.* El Paso, TX: LFB Scholarly Publishing.

Center on Criminal and Juvenile Justice. (2011). *The Cost of the State's Division of Juvenile Facilities: Is There Incentive for California Counties to Serve Youth Locally?* San Francisco: Author.

Champion, Dean J., and G. Larry Mays. (1991). *Transferring Juveniles to Criminal Courts: Trends and Implications for Criminal Justice.* New York: Praeger.

Chesney-Lind, Meda, and Randall G. Shelden. (2003). *Girls, Delinquency, and Juvenile Justice* (3rd ed.). Belmont, CA: Wadsworth.

Children's Bureau. (1932). *Facts about Juvenile Delinquency: Its Prevention and Treatment.* Washington DC: Author.

Citizens Crime Commission of New York City. (2010). *Juvenile Crime: Raise the Age to 18.* Retrieved Nov. 20, 2011, from http://www.nycrimecommission.org/initiative2-age18.php.

Cohen, Mark A., and Alex R. Piquero. (2009). "New Evidence on the Monetary Value of Saving a High Risk Youth." *Journal of Quantitative Criminology* 25(1): 25–49.

Cohen, Thomas H., and Tracey Kyckelhahn. (2010). *Felony Defendants in Large Urban Counties, 2006.* Washington, DC: Bureau of Justice Statistics.

Cohn, Alvin W. (1994). "Future of Juvenile Justice Administration: Evolution v. Revolution." *Juvenile and Family Court Journal* 45(3): 51–64.

Colgate Love, Margaret. (2011). "Paying Their Debt to Society: Forgiveness, Redemption, and the Uniform Collateral Consequences of Conviction Act." *Howard Law Journal* 54(3): 753–93.

Cooley, Valerie A. (2011). "Community-Based Sanctions for Juvenile Offenders: Issues in Policy Implementation." *Criminal Justice Policy Review* 22(1): 65–89.

Council of Juvenile Correctional Administrators. (2009). *Position Statement: Waiver and Transfer of Youths to Adult Systems.* Retrieved Nov. 20, 2011, from http://cjca.net/cjcaresources/20/CJCA-Waiver-Position-Paper.pdf.

Court TV. (2000). *13-Year-Old and Michigan Juvenile Law under Fire in Murder Trial.* Retrieved January 29, 2003, from www.courttv.com/trials/abraham/101999_ctv.html.

Curry, G. David, Cheryl L. Maxson, and James C. Howell. (2001). *Youth Gang Homicides in the 1990's.* Washington, DC: Office of Juvenile Justice and Delinquency Prevention.

Daleiden, Eric L., Dawn Pang, Deborah Roberts, Lesley A. Slavin, and Sarah L. Pestle. (2010). "Intensive Home Based Services within a Comprehensive System of Care for Youth." *Journal of Children and Family Studies* 19(3): 318–25.

Davis, Laura. (2003). "Juvenile Probation." In Marilyn D. McShane and Frank P. Williams III (Eds.), *Encyclopedia of Juvenile Justice*, pp. 301–4. Thousand Oaks, CA: Sage Publications.

Deitch, Michele, Amanda Barstow, Leslie Lukens, and Ryan Reyna. (2009). *From Time Out to Hard Time: Young Children in the Adult Criminal Justice System*. Austin, TX: Lyndon B. Johnson School of Public Affairs.

DeLisi, Matt, Andy Hochstetler, Gloria Jones-Johnson, Jonathan W. Caudill, and James W. Marquart. (2011). "The Road to Murder: The Enduring Criminogenic Effects of Juvenile Confinement among a Sample of Adult Career Criminals." *Youth Violence and Juvenile Justice* 9(3): 207–21.

Diana, Lewis. (1957). "The Rights of Juvenile Delinquents: An Appraisal of Juvenile Court Procedures." *The Journal of Criminal Law, Criminology, and Police Science* 47(5): 561–69.

DiIulio, John J. Jr. (1995, November 27). "The Coming of the Superpredator." *The Weekly Standard*, 23.

Dobbs, Ashley. (2004). "The Use of Youth as an Aggravating Factor in Death Penalty Cases Involving Minors." *Juvenile Justice Update* 10(3): 1–2, 13–16.

Doble Research Associates. (1995a). *Crime and Corrections: The Views of the People of North Carolina*. Englewood Cliffs, NJ: Author.

Doble Research Associates. (1995b). *Crime and Corrections: The Views of the People of Oklahoma*. Englewood Cliffs, NJ: Author.

Dorfman, Lori, and Vincent Schiraldi. (2001). *Off Balance: Youth, Race & Crime in the News*. Retrieved Nov. 20, 2011, from http://www.justicepolicy.org/uploads/justicepolicy/documents/pre/01-04_REP_OffBalanceNews_JJ-RD.pdf.

Dorsen, Norman. (2007). "Reflections on *In re Gault*." *Rutgers Law Review* 60(1): 1–10.

Drake, Elizabeth. (2007). *Evidence-Based Juvenile Offender Programs: Program Description, Quality Assurance, and Cost*. Olympia: Washington State Institute for Public Policy.

Drake, Elizabeth. (2010). *Washington State Juvenile Court Funding: Applying Research in a Public Policy Setting*. Olympia: Washington State Institute for Public Policy.

Drake, Elizabeth, Steve Aos, and Marna G. Miller. (2009). "Evidence-Based Public Policy Options to Reduce Crime and Criminal Justice Costs: Implications in Washington State." *Victims & Offenders* 4 (2): 170–96.

Duran, Robert J. (2009). "Legitimated Oppression: Inner-City Mexican American Experiences with Police Gang Enforcement." *Journal of Contemporary Ethnography* 38(2): 143–68.

Egley, Arlen Jr. (2005). *Highlights of the 2002–2003 National Youth Gang Surveys.* Washington, DC: Office of Juvenile Justice and Delinquency Prevention.

Egley, Arlen Jr., and James C. Howell. (2011). *Highlights of the 2009 National Youth Gang Survey.* Washington, DC: Office of Juvenile Justice and Delinquency Prevention.

Ella Baker Center. (2011). *Books Not Bars Campaign.* Retrieved Nov. 20, 2011, from http://www.ellabakercenter.org/page.php?pageid=2.

Emens, Elizabeth F. (2005). "Aggravating Youth: *Roper v. Simmons* and Age Discrimination." *2005 Supreme Court Review* 2005 (1): 51–102.

Equal Justice Initiative. (2007). *Cruel and Unusual: Sentencing 13- and 14-Year Old Children to Die in Prison.* Montgomery, AL: Author.

Erskine, Hazel. (1974). "The Polls: Fear of Violence and Crime." *Public Opinion Quarterly* 38(1): 131–35.

Fagan, Jeffrey. (1996). "The Comparative Advantage of Juvenile versus Criminal Court Sanctions on Recidivism among Adolescent Felony Offenders." *Law & Policy* 18(1–2): 77–144.

Fagan, Jeffrey. (2008). "Juvenile Crime and Criminal Justice: Resolving Border Disputes." *The Future of Children* 18(2): 81–118.

Fagan, Jeffrey. (2010). "The Contradictions of Juvenile Crime & Punishment." *Daedalus: Journal of the American Academy of Arts & Sciences* (Summer): 43–61.

Fagan, Jeffrey, and Tracey L. Meares. (2008). "Punishment, Deterrence and Social Control: The Paradox of Punishment in Minority Communities." *Ohio State Journal of Criminal Law* 6(1): 173–229.

Fagan, Jeffrey, and Franklin E. Zimring. (2000). *The Changing Borders of Juvenile Justice: Transfer of Adolescents to the Criminal Court.* Chicago: University of Chicago Press.

Federal Bureau of Investigation. (2003). *Age-Specific Arrest Rates and Race-Specific Arrest Rates for Selected Offenses, 1993 to 2001.* Washington, DC: Author.

Federal Bureau of Investigation. (2010). *Crime in the United States, 2009.* Washington, DC: Author.

Federal Register. (2011). "Office of Juvenile Justice and Delinquency Prevention Proposed Plan for Fiscal Year 2011." *Federal Register* 76 (8): 2135–42.

Feiler, Stephen M., and Joseph F. Sheley. (1999). "Legal and Racial Elements of Public Willingness to Transfer Juvenile Offenders to Adult Court." *Journal of Criminal Justice* 27(1): 55–64.

Feld, Barry C. (1991). "Justice by Geography: Urban, Suburban, and Rural Variations in Juvenile Justice Administration." *The Journal of Criminal Law and Criminology* 82(1): 156–210.

Feld, Barry C. (1997). "Abolish the Juvenile Court: Youthfulness, Criminal Responsibility, and Sentencing Policy." *Journal of Criminal Law and Criminology* 88(1): 68–136.

Feld, Barry C. (1998). "Juvenile and Criminal Justice Systems' Responses to Youth Violence." *Crime and Justice* 24: 189–261

Feld, Barry C. (1999a). *Bad Kids: Race and the Transformation of the Juvenile Court.* New York: Oxford University Press.

Feld, Barry C. (1999b). "Criminalizing the American Juvenile Court." In Barry C. Feld (Ed.), *Readings in Juvenile Justice Administration*, pp. 356–67. New York: Oxford University Press.

Feld, Barry C. (1999c). "The Honest Politician's Guide to Juvenile Justice in the Twenty-First Century." *The Annals of the American Academy of Political and Social Science* 564(1): 10–27.

Feld, Barry C. (1999d). "The Right to Counsel in Juvenile Court: An Empirical Study of When Lawyers Appear and the Difference They Make." In Barry C. Feld (Ed.), *Readings in Juvenile Justice Administration*, pp. 127–39. New York: Oxford University Press.

Feld, Barry C. (2003a). *Juvenile Justice Administration.* St. Paul, MN: West Group.

Feld, Barry C. (2003b). "The Politics of Race and Juvenile Justice: The 'Due Process Revolution' and the Conservative Reaction." *Justice Quarterly* 20(4): 765–800.

Feld, Barry C. (2009). "Violent Girls or Relabeled Status Offenders?: An Alternative Interpretation of the Data." *Crime & Delinquency* 55(2): 241–65.

Feld, Barry C., and Shelly Schaefer. (2010). "The Right to Counsel in Juvenile Court: The Conundrum of Attorneys as an Aggravating Factor at Disposition." *Justice Quarterly* 27(5): 713–41.

Felson, Marcus. (1994). *Crime and Everyday Life: Insight and Implications for Society.* Thousand Oaks, CA: Pine Forge Press.

Finley, Laura L. (2007). *Juvenile Justice.* Westport, CT: Greenwood Press.

Fishman, Joseph F. (1923). *Crucibles of Crime: The Shocking Story of the American Jail.* Montclair, NJ: Patterson Smith.

Flexner, Bernard, and Roger N. Baldwin. (1914). *Juvenile Courts and Probation*. New York: Century Company.

Florida Department of Juvenile Justice. (2002). *A DJJ Success Story: Trends in Transfer of Juveniles to Adult Criminal Court*. Retrieved Nov. 20, 2011, from http://www.pdmiami.com/DJJ_study_transfer_summary.pdf.

Florida Department of Juvenile Justice. (2008). *History of the Juvenile Justice System in Florida*. Retrieved Nov. 20, 2011, from http://www.djj.state.fl.us/AboutDJJ/history.html.

Florida Department of Juvenile Justice. (2010). *2009-2010 Comprehensive Accountability Report*. Retrieved Nov. 20, 2011, from http://www.djj.state.fl.us/Research/CAR/CAR_2010/(2009-10-CAR)-Full-CAR-Document.pdf.

Forst, Martin L. (1995). *The New Juvenile Justice*, Chicago: Nelson Hall.

Fox, James A. (1992, June 10). "The Young and the Ruthless." *The Chicago Tribune*, 23.

Fox, James A., and Marc L. Swatt. (2008). *The Recent Surge in Homicides Involving Young Black Males and Guns: Time to Reinvest in Prevention and Crime Control*. Retrieved Nov. 20, 2011, from: http://www.jfox.neu.edu/Documents/Fox%20Swatt%20Homicide%20Report%20Dec%2029%202008.pdf.

Gallup. (2008). *Americans Hold Firm to Support for Death Penalty*. Retrieved Nov. 20, 2011, from http://www.gallup.com/poll/111931/Americans-Hold-Firm-Support-Death-Penalty.aspx.

Gallup. (2010). *Americans Still Perceive Crime as on the Rise*. Retrieved Nov. 20, 2011, from http://www.gallup.com/poll/144827/americans-perceive-crime-rise.aspx.

Gamson, William A., David Croteau, William Hoynes, and Theodore Sasson. (1992). "Media Images and the Social Construction of Reality." *Annual Review of Sociology* 18: 373–93.

Gardner, Martin R. (2009). *Understanding Juvenile Law* (3rd ed.). San Francisco: Matthew Bender/LexisNexis.

Garland, David. (1990). *Punishment and Modern Society: A Study in Social Theory*. Chicago: University of Chicago Press.

GBA Strategies. (2011). *Campaign for Youth Justice Youth Justice System Survey*. Retrieved November 20, 2011, from http://www.gbastrategies.com/public_files/cfyj101111m1.pdf.

Glaze, Lauren E., and Thomas P. Bonczar. (2010). *Probation and Parole in the United States, 2009*. Washington, DC: Bureau of Justice Statistics.

Goidel, Robert K., Craig M. Freeman, and Steven T. Procopio. (2006). "The Impact of Television Viewing on Perceptions of Juvenile Crime." *Journal of Broadcasting & Electronic Media* 50(1): 119–39.

Gottschalk, Marie. (2009). "Money and Mass Incarceration: The Bad, the Mad, and Penal Reform." *Criminology & Public Policy* 8(1): 97–109.

Gould, Jon B., and Richard A. Leo. (2010). "One Hundred Years Later: Wrongful Convictions after a Century of Research." *The Journal of Criminal Law & Criminology* 100(3): 825–68.

Griffin, Patrick. (2011). *National Overviews: State Juvenile Justice Profiles*. Pittsburgh, PA: National Center for Juvenile Justice.

Griffin, Patrick, and Melanie King. (2006). *National Overviews: State Juvenile Justice Profiles*. Pittsburgh, PA: National Center for Juvenile Justice.

Griffin, Patrick, Patricia Torbet, and Linda Szymanski. (1998). *Trying Juveniles as Adults in Criminal Court: An Analysis of State Transfer Provisions*. Pittsburgh, PA: National Center for Juvenile Justice.

Griffin, Patrick, Sean Addie, Benjamin Adams, and Kathy Firestine. (2011). *Trying Juveniles as Adults: An Analysis of State Transfer Laws and Reporting*, Washington, DC: Office of Juvenile Justice and Delinquency Prevention.

Grisso, Thomas. (1980). "Juveniles' Capacities to Waive *Miranda* Rights: An Empirical Analysis." *California Law Review* 68(6): 1134–66.

Grisso, Thomas. (2010). "Clinicians' Transfer Evaluations: How Well Can They Assist Judicial Discretion?" *Louisiana Law Review* 71(1): 157–89.

Hahn, Robert, et al. (2007). "Effects on Violence of Laws and Policies Facilitating the Transfer of Youth from the Juvenile to the Adult Justice System." *Morbidity and Mortality Weekly Report* 56(RR09): 1–11.

Harris Interactive. (2010). *Harris Alienation Index Remains Lower Than It Was for Most of the Last 20 Years*. Retrieved Nov. 20, 2011, from http://www.harrisinteractive.com/NewsRoom/Harris Polls/tabid/447/ctl/ReadCustom%20Default/mid/1508/ArticleId/450/Default.aspx.

Harrison, Wayne, Alan Gathright, and Kim Nguyen (2011). *12-Year-Old Son Arrested in Parents' Deaths in Burlington*. Retrieved June 27, 2011, from http://www.thedenverchannel.com/news/27047659/detail.html.

Hart, Timothy C. (1998). "Causes and Consequences of Juvenile Crime and Violence: Public Attitudes and Question-Order Effect." *American Journal of Criminal Justice* 23(1): 129–43.

Harvard Law Review. (2010). "Eighth Amendment: Juvenile Life Without Parole Sentences." *Harvard Law Review* 124(179): 209–19.

Hechinger, Scott. (2011). "Juvenile Life without Parole (JLWOP): An Antidote to Congress's One-Way Criminal Law Ratchet?" *New York University Law & Social Change* 35(2): 409–95.

Heide, Kathleen M., and Jessica McCurdy (2010). "Juvenile Parricide Offenders Sentenced to Death." *Victims & Offenders* 5(1): 76–99.

Heide, Kathleen M., and Thomas A. Petee (2007). "Parricide: An Empirical Analysis of 24 Years of U.S. Data." *Journal of Interpersonal Violence* 22(11): 1382–99.

Hemmens, Craig, Benjamin Steiner, and David Mueller. (2004). *Significant Cases in Juvenile Justice*. Los Angeles: Roxbury Publishing Co.

Hockenberry, Sarah, Melissa Sickmund, and Anthony Sladky. (2009). *Juvenile Residential Facility Census, 2006: Selected Findings*. Washington, DC: Office of Juvenile Justice and Delinquency Prevention.

Holman, Barry, and Jason Ziedenberg. (2009). "The Dangers of Detention." In Rick Ruddell and Matthew O. Thomas (Eds.), *Juvenile Corrections*, pp. 93–111. Richmond, KY: Newgate Press.

Hornberger, Nancy G. (2010). "Improving Outcomes for Status Offenders in the JJDPA Reauthorization." *Juvenile and Family Justice Today* (Summer): 14–19.

Horwitz, Allan, and Michael Wasserman. (1980). "Formal Rationality, Substantive Justice, and Discrimination: A Study of a Juvenile Court." *Law and Human Behavior* 4(1/2): 103–15.

Howell, James C. (2007). "Menacing or Mimicking? Realities of Youth Gangs." *Juvenile and Family Court Journal* 58(2): 39–50.

Howell, James C. (2008). "The Comprehensive Strategy Framework." In Richard Lawrence and Craig Hemmens (Eds.), *Juvenile Justice*, pp. 551–80. Thousand Oaks, CA: Sage Publications.

Human Rights Watch. (2001). *No Escape: Male Rape in U.S. Prisons*. New York: Author.

Human Rights Watch. (2008). *The Rest of Their Lives: Life without Parole for Youth Offenders in the United States in 2008*. New York: Author.

Innocence Project. (2011). *Mission Statement*. Retrieved Nov. 20, 2011, from http://www.innocenceproject.org/about/Mission -Statement.php.

Jacobs, David, and Jason T. Carmichael. (2001). "The Politics of Punishment across Time and Space: A Pooled Time-Series Analyses of Imprisonment Rates." *Social Forces* 80(1): 61–91.

Jacobs, David, and Richard Kleban. (2003). "Political Institutions, Minorities, and Punishment: A Pooled Cross-National Analysis of Imprisonment Rates." *Social Forces* 82(2): 725–55.

Jan, I-Fang, Jeremy D. Ball, and Anthony Walsh. (2008). "Predicting Public Opinion about Juvenile Waivers." *Criminal Justice Policy Review* 19(3): 285–300.

Jensen, Eric L., and Linda K. Metsger. (1994). "A Test of the Deterrent Effect of Legislative Waiver on Violent Juvenile Crime." *Crime & Delinquency* 40(1): 96–104.

Johnson, Robert, and Sonia Tabriz. (2011). "Sentencing Children to Death by Incarceration: A Deadly Denial of Social Responsibility." *The Prison Journal* 91(2): 198–206.

Jordan, Kareem L., and David L. Myers. (2011). "Juvenile Transfer and Deterrence: Reexamining the Effectiveness of a 'Get-Tough' Policy." *Crime & Delinquency* 57(2): 247–70.

Justice Policy Institute. (2009). *The Costs of Confinement: Why Good Juvenile Justice Policies Make Good Fiscal Sense*. Washington, DC: Author.

Kane, Robert J. (2003). "Social Control in the Metropolis: A Community-Level Examination of the Minority Group-Threat Hypothesis." *Justice Quarterly* 20(2): 265–95.

Kaplan, Wendy J., and David Rossman. (2011). "Called 'Out' at Home: The One Strike Eviction Policy and Juvenile Court." *Duke Forum for Law and Social Change*. Retrieved Nov. 20, 2011, from: http://works.bepress.com/cgi/viewcontent.cgi?article=1002&context=david_rossman.

Kappeler, Victor E., and Gary W. Potter. (2005). *The Mythology of Crime and Criminal Justice*. Long Grove, IL: Waveland Press.

Kaye, Judith S. (2011). "The Supreme Court and Juvenile Justice." *Journal of Supreme Court History* 36(1): 62–80.

Kelly, John. (2011). *Senate Committee Approves Funding to OJJDP, With Cuts*. Retrieved November 20, 2011, from http://jjie.org/senate-committee-approves-funding-ojjdp-cuts/36302.

Kempf-Leonard, Kimberly. (2007). "Minority Youths and Juvenile Justice: Disproportionate Minority Contact after Nearly 20 Years of Reform Efforts." *Youth Violence and Juvenile Justice* 5(1): 71–87.

Kempf-Leonard, Kimberly. (2010). "Does Having an Attorney Provide a Better Outcome? The Right to Counsel Does Not Mean Attorneys Help Youths." *Criminology & Public Policy* 9(2): 357–63.

Kim, Julie J. (2010). "Left Behind: The Paternalistic Treatment of Status Offenders within the Juvenile Justice System." *Washington University Law Review* (87)4: 843–67.

Kinder, Kristine, Carol Veneziano, Michael Fichter, and Henry Azuma. (1995). "A Comparison of the Dispositions of Juvenile Offenders

Certified as Adults with Juvenile Offenders Not Certified." *Juvenile and Family Court Journal* 46(3): 37–42.

King, Melanie. (2006). *Guide to the State Juvenile Justice Profiles*. Pittsburgh, PA: National Center for Juvenile Justice.

King, William R. (2009). "Toward a Life-Course Perspective of Police Organizations." *Journal of Research in Crime and Delinquency* 46 (2): 213–44.

Knoll, Crystal, and Melissa Sickmund. (2010). *Delinquency Cases in Juvenile Court, 2007*. Washington, DC: Office of Juvenile Justice and Delinquency Prevention.

Ko, Sandra M. (2004). "Why Do They Continue to Get the Worst of Both Worlds? The Case for Providing Louisiana's Juveniles with the Right to a Jury in Delinquency Adjudications." *Journal of Gender, Social Policy & The Law* 12(1): 161–96.

Kott, Katherine. (2010). "Considering Residential Treatment for Youth in the Continuum of Care: A Systems Perspective." *Residential Treatment for Children & Youth* 27(1): 14–22.

Krisberg, Barry. (2005). *Juvenile Justice: Redeeming Our Children*. Thousand Oaks, CA: Sage Publications.

Krisberg, Barry, and James F. Austin. (1993). *Reinventing Juvenile Justice*. Newbury Park, CA: Sage Publications.

Krisberg, Barry, Christopher Hartney, Angela Wolf, and Fabiana Silva. (2009). *Youth Violence Myths and Realities: A Tale of Three Cities*. Oakland, CA: National Council on Crime and Delinquency.

Krisberg, Barry, and Susan Marchionna. (2007). *Attitudes of US Voters toward Youth Crime and the Justice System*. Oakland, CA: National Council on Crime and Delinquency.

Kupchik, Aaron. (2006). *Judging Juveniles: Prosecuting Adolescents in Adult and Juvenile Courts*. New York: New York University Press.

Kurlychek, Megan C., and Brian D. Johnson. (2010). "Juvenility and Punishment: Sentencing Juveniles in Adult Criminal Court." *Criminology* 48(3): 725–58.

Langan, Patrick A., and David J. Levin. (2002). *Recidivism of Prisoners Released in 1994*. Washington, DC: Bureau of Justice Statistics.

Lawrence, Richard A. (1984). "The Role of Legal Counsel in Juveniles' Understanding of Their Rights." *Juvenile and Family Court Journal* 34(4): 49–58.

Lawrence, Richard, and Craig Hemmens. (2008). *Juvenile Justice*. Thousand Oaks, CA: Sage Publications.

Leiber, Michael, Donna Bishop, and Mitchell B. Chamlin. (2011). "Juvenile Justice Decision-Making Before and After the Implementation of the Disproportionate Minority Contact (DMC) Mandate." *Justice Quarterly* 28(3): 460–92.

Leiber, Michael, and Nancy Rodriguez. (2011). "The Implementation of the Disproportionate Minority Confinement/Contact (DMC) Mandate: A Failure or Success?" *Race and Justice* 1(1): 103–24.

Leibowitz, Barry. (2011). *12-Year-Old Colo. Boy in Custody, Parents Shot Dead, Siblings Wounded*, Retrieved June 27, 2011, from http://www.cbsnews.com/8301-504083_162-20038517-504083.html.

Leigey, Margaret E., Jessica P. Hodge, and Christine A. Saum. (2009). "Kids in the Big House: Juveniles Incarcerated in Adult Facilities." In Rick Ruddell and Matthew O. Thomas (Eds.), *Juvenile Corrections*, pp. 113–35. Richmond, KY: Newgate Press.

Lenroot, Katharine F. (1923). "The Evolution of the Juvenile Court." *The Annals of the American Academy of Political and Social Science* 105(1): 213–22.

Lindsey, Edward. (1914). "The Juvenile Court Movement from a Lawyer's Standpoint." *Annals of the American Academy of Political and Social Science* 52(1): 140–48.

Lipsey, Mark W. (2009). "The Primary Factors That Characterize Effective Interventions with Juvenile Offenders: A Meta-analytic Overview." *Victims & Offenders* 4(2): 124–47.

Liptak, Adam, and Lisa Faye Petak. (2011, April 20). "Juvenile Killers in Jail for Life Seek a Reprieve." *The New York Times*, A13.

Livsey, Sarah. (2009). *Juvenile Delinquency Probation Caseload, 2005*. Washington, DC: Office of Juvenile Justice and Delinquency Prevention.

Loewy, Arnold H. (2010). "Taking Reasonable Doubt Seriously." *Chicago Kent Law Review* 85(1): 63–75.

Lynch, James P., and William Alex Pridemore. (2011). "Crime in International Perspective." In James Q. Wilson and Joan Petersilia (Eds.), *Crime and Public Policy*, pp. 5–52. New York: Oxford University Press.

Macallair, Daniel, Catherine McCracken, and Selena Teji. (2011). *The Impact of Realignment on County Juvenile Justice Practice: Will Closing State Youth Correctional Facilities Increase Adult Criminal Court Filings?* San Francisco: Center on Juvenile and Criminal Justice.

MacCormick, Austin H. (1949). "Children in Our Jails." *The Annals of the American Academy of Political and Social Science* 261(1): 150–57.

Mack, Julian W. (1909). "The Juvenile Court." *Harvard Law Review* 23(1): 104–22.

Mack, Julian W. (1911). "The State and the Child." *Proceedings of the Academy of Political Science in the City of New York* 1(4): 676–81.

Maguire, Kathleen. (2011). *Sourcebook of Criminal Justice Statistics.* Albany, NY: U.S. Department of Justice.

Maroney, Terry A. (2011). "Adolescent Brain Science after *Graham v. Florida*." *Notre Dame Law Review* 86(2): 765–93.

Marrus, Ellen. (2008). "*Gault*, 40 Years Later: Are We There Yet?" *Criminal Law Bulletin* 44(3): 1–17.

Mauer, Marc, and Meda Chesney-Lind. (2003). *Invisible Punishment: The Collateral Consequences of Mass Imprisonment.* New York: The New Press.

Mays, G. Larry. (2003). "Status Offenders." In Marilyn D. McShane and Frank P. Williams III (Eds.), *Encyclopedia of Juvenile Justice*, pp. 354–58. Thousand Oaks, CA: Sage Publications.

Mays, G. Larry, and L. Thomas Winfree, Jr. (2006). *Juvenile Justice* (2nd Ed.). Long Grove, IL: Waveland Press.

McNamara, Robert H. (2008). *The Lost Population: Status Offenders in America.* Durham, NC: Carolina Academic Press.

Mears, Daniel P. (2001) "Getting Tough with Juvenile Offenders: Explaining Support for Sanctioning Youths as Adults." *Criminal Justice and Behavior* 28(2): 206–26.

Mears, Daniel P. (2002). "Sentencing Guidelines and the Transformation of Juvenile Justice in the 21st Century." *Journal of Contemporary Criminal Justice* 18(1): 6–19.

Mears, Daniel P. (2003). "A Critique of Waiver Research: Critical Next Steps in Assessing the Impacts of Laws for Transferring Juveniles to the Criminal Justice System." *Youth Violence and Juvenile Justice* 1(2): 156–72.

Mears, Daniel P. (2008). "A Critique of Waiver Research." In Richard Lawrence and Craig Hemmens (Eds.), *Juvenile Justice*, pp. 287–301. Thousand Oaks, CA: Sage Publications.

Mears, Daniel P., Carter Hay, Marc Gertz, and Christina Mancini. (2007). "Public Opinion and the Foundation of the Juvenile Court." *Criminology* 45(1): 223–57.

Mears, Daniel P., Tracey L. Shollenberger, Janeen B. Willison, Colleen E. Owens, and Jeffrey A. Butts. (2010). "Practitioner Views of Priorities, Policies, and Practices in Juvenile Justice." *Crime & Delinquency* 56(4): 535–63.

Merlo, Alida V. (2003). "Juvenile Courts: History." In Marilyn D. McShane and Frank P. Williams III (Eds.), *Encyclopedia of Juvenile Justice*, pp. 77–83. Thousand Oaks, CA: Sage Publications.

Merlo, Alida V., and Peter J. Benekos. (2010). "Is Punitive Juvenile Justice Policy Declining in the United States? A Critique of Emergent Initiatives." *Youth Justice* 10(1): 3–24.

Minton, Todd D. (2011). *Jail Inmates at Midyear, 2010—Statistical Tables*. Washington, DC: Bureau of Justice Statistics.

Moon, Melissa M., Jody L. Sundt, Francis T. Cullen, and John P. Wright. (2000). "Is Child Saving Dead? Public Support for Juvenile Rehabilitation." *Crime & Delinquency* 46(1): 38–60.

Moore, David W. (1999). *Public Divided over Blaming Parents for Their Children's Crimes*. Retrieved Nov. 20, 2011, from http://www.gallup.com/poll/3418/Public-Divided-Over-Blaming-Parents-Their-Childrens-Crimes.aspx.

Moore, Eugene. (2000). *Sentencing Opinion*. Retrieved January 29, 2003, from www.courttv.com/trials/abraham/sentence_text_ctv.html.

Motivans, Mark, and Howard Snyder. (2011). *Summary: Tribal Youth in the Federal Justice System*. Washington, DC: Bureau of Justice Statistics.

Myers, David L. (2003). "Adult Crime, Adult Time: Punishing Violent Youth in the Adult Criminal Justice System." *Youth Violence and Juvenile Justice* 1(2): 173–97.

Nagin, Daniel S., Alex R. Piquero, Elizabeth S. Scott, and Laurence Steinberg. (2006). "Public Preferences for Rehabilitation versus Incarceration of Juvenile Offenders: Evidence from a Contingent Valuation Survey." *Criminology & Public Policy* 5(4): 627–651.

National Advisory Committee on Criminal Justice Standards and Goals. (1976). *Juvenile Justice and Delinquency Prevention*. Washington, DC: U.S. Government Printing Office.

National Council of Juvenile and Family Court Judges. (2005). *Juvenile Delinquency Guidelines*. Reno, NV: Author.

National Crime Victimization Survey. (2011). *Key Facts at a Glance*. Retrieved Nov. 21, 2011, from http://bjs.ojp.usdoj.gov/content/glance/offage.cfm.

National Institute of Justice. (1995). *State Laws on Prosecutors' and Judges' Use of Juvenile Records*. Washington, DC: U.S. Department of Justice.

Nellis, Ashley, and Ryan S. King. (2009). *No Exit: The Expanding Use of Life Sentences in America*. Washington, DC: The Sentencing Project.

Newport, Frank. (2010). *Economy Dominates as Nation's Most Important Problem*. Retrieved Nov. 21, 2011, from http://www.gallup.com/poll/141275/economy-dominates-nation-important-problem.aspx.

Nicholson, Kieran and Jordan Steffen. (2011). *12-Year-Old Boy Held in Deaths of Parents, Injuries to Siblings at Burlington Home*. Retrieved Nov. 20, 2011, from: http://www.denverpost.com/news/ci_17525725.

Nicholson-Crotty, Sean, and Kenneth J. Meier. (2003). "Crime and Punishment: The Politics of Federal Criminal Justice Sanctions." *Political Research Quarterly* 56(2): 119–26.

Nicholson-Crotty, Sean, David A. M. Peterson, and Mark D. Ramirez. (2009). "Dynamic Representation(s): Federal Criminal Justice Policy and an Alternative Dimension of Public Mood." *Political Behavior* 31(4): 629–55.

Noonan, Margaret E. (2010a). *Deaths in Custody: Local Jail Deaths, 2000–2007—Statistical Tables*. Retrieved Nov. 20, 2011, from: http://bjs.ojp.usdoj.gov/index.cfm?ty=pbdetail&iid=2092.

Noonan, Margaret E. (2010b). *Deaths in Custody: State Prison Deaths, 2001–2007—Statistical Tables*. Retrieved Nov. 20, 2011, from: http://bjs.ojp.usdoj.gov/index.cfm?ty=pbdetail&iid=2093.

Nunez, Narina, Mindy J. Dahl, Connie M. Tang, and Brittney L. Jensen. (2007). "Trial Venue Decisions in Juvenile Cases: Mitigating and Extralegal Factors Matter." *Legal and Criminological Psychology* 12(1): 21–39.

Office of Juvenile Justice and Delinquency Prevention. (2000). *Kids and Guns: 1999 National Report Series*. Retrieved November 20, 2011, from: https://www.ncjrs.gov/pdffiles1/ojjdp/178994.pdf.

Office of Juvenile Justice and Delinquency Prevention. (2011). *The Juvenile Justice and Delinquency Prevention Act of 1974: Prior Federal Juvenile Delinquency Activity*. Retrieved Nov. 20, 2011, from: http://www.ojjdp.gov/compliance/jjdpchronology.pdf.

Ohlin, Lloyd E. (1983). "The Future of Juvenile Justice Research and Policy." *Crime & Delinquency* 29(3): 463–72.

Parenti, Christian. (2000). *Lockdown America: Police and Prisons in the Age of Crisis*. New York: Verso Press.

Patenaude, Allan. (2003). "Diversion Programs." In Marilyn D. McShane and Frank P. Williams III (Eds.), *Encyclopedia of Juvenile Justice*, pp. 132–40. Thousand Oaks, CA: Sage Publications.

Paulsen, Monrad G. (1966). "*Kent v. United States*: The Constitutional Context of Juvenile Cases." *The Supreme Court Review* 1966: 167–92.

Paxman, Monroe J. (1959). "Evolution of the Standard Juvenile Court Act." *Crime & Delinquency* 5(4): 392–403.

Pearson, Geoffrey. (1983). *Hooligan: A History of Respectable Fears*. Basingstoke, UK: MacMillan.

Perrone, Paul A., and Meda Chesney-Lind. (1997). "Representations of Gangs and Delinquency: Wild in the Streets?" *Social Justice* 24(4): 96–116.

Philadelphia House of Refuge. (1835). *The Seventh Annual Report of the Philadelphia House of Refuge.* Philadelphia, PA: Author.

Piquero, Alex R., Francis T. Cullen, James D. Unnever, Nicole L. Piquero, and Jill A. Gordon. (2010). "Never Too Late: Public Optimism about Juvenile Rehabilitation." *Punishment & Society* 12(2): 187–207.

Piquero, Alex R., and Laurence Steinberg. (2010). "Public Preferences for Rehabilitation versus Incarceration of Juvenile Offenders." *Journal of Criminal Justice* 38(1): 1–6.

Pisciotta, Alexander W. (1982). "Saving the Children: The Promise and Practice of *Parens Patriae*, 1838-98." *Crime & Delinquency* 28(3): 410–25.

Platt, Anthony M. (1977). *The Child Savers: The Invention of Delinquency* (2nd Ed.). Chicago: University of Chicago Press.

President's Commission on Law Enforcement and the Administration of Justice. (1967). *The Challenge of Crime in a Free Society.* Washington, DC: U.S. Government Printing Office.

Puritz, Patricia, and Katayoon Majd. (2007). "Ensuring Authentic Youth Participation in Delinquency Cases: Creating a Paradigm for Specialized Juvenile Defense Practice." *Family Court Review* 45(3): 466–84.

Putnam, Robert D. (2000). *Bowling Alone: The Collapse and Revival of American Community.* New York: Simon and Schuster.

Puzzanchera, Charles. (2009). *Juvenile Arrests 2008.* Washington, DC: Office of Juvenile Justice and Delinquency Prevention.

Puzzanchera, Charles, Benjamin Adams, and Wei Kang. (2009). *Easy Access to FBI Arrest Statistics 1994–2007.* Retrieved Nov. 20, 2011, from: http://www.ojjdp.gov/ojstatbb/ezaucr/.

Puzzanchera, Charles, Benjamin Adams, and Melissa Sickmund. (2010). *Juvenile Court Statistics: 2006–2007.* Washington, DC: Office of Juvenile Justice and Delinquency Prevention.

Puzzanchera, Charles, T. J. Sladky, and Wei Kang. (2010). *Easy Access to Juvenile Populations: 1990 to 2009.* Retrieved Nov. 20, 2011, from http://ojjdp.ncjrs.gov/ojstatbb/ezajcs/.

Quigley, William P. (1996). "Five Hundred Years of English Poor Laws, 1349-1834: Regulating the Working and Nonworking Poor." *Akron Law Review* 30(1): 73–128.

Rand, Michael R., and Jayne E. Robinson. (2011). *Criminal Victimization in the United States, 2008—Statistical Tables.* Washington, DC: Bureau of Justice Statistics.

Redding, Richard E. (2003). "The Effects of Adjudicating and Sentencing Juveniles as Adults: Research and Policy Implications." *Youth Violence and Juvenile Justice* 1(2): 128–55.

Redding, Richard E. (2010). *Juvenile Transfer Laws: An Effective Deterrent to Delinquency?* Washington, DC: Office of Juvenile Justice and Delinquency Prevention.

Redding, Richard E., and Elizabeth J. Fuller. (2004). "What Do Juvenile Offenders Know about Being Tried as Adults? Implications for Deterrence." *Juvenile and Family Court Journal* 55(3): 35–44.

Reed, Ellery F. (1941). "Relation of Relief to Increase of Juvenile Court Cases." *Social Science Review* 15(1): 104–15.

Regnery, Alfred S. (1985). "Getting Away with Murder: Why the Juvenile Justice System Needs an Overhaul." *Policy Review* 34(1): 65–68.

Reiman, Jeffrey, and Paul Leighton. (2010). *The Rich Get Richer and the Poor Get Prison* (9th ed.). New York: Prentice Hall.

Risler, Edwin A., Tim Sweatman, and Larry Nackerud. (1998). "Evaluating the Georgia Legislative Waiver's Effectiveness in Deterring Juvenile Crime." *Research on Social Work Practice* 8(6): 657–67.

Roberts, Julian V. (2004). "Public Opinion and Youth Justice." *Crime and Justice* 31: 495–542.

Rogers, Joseph W., and G. Larry Mays. (1987). *Juvenile Delinquency and Juvenile Justice*. New York: Wiley.

Rosenberg Irene M. (2009). "The Rights of Delinquents in Juvenile Court: Why Not Equal Protection?" *Criminal Law Bulletin* 45(5): 723–43.

Rosenberg, Irene M., and Yale L. Rosenberg. (1976). "The Legacy of the Stubborn and Rebellious Son." *Michigan Law Review* 74(4): 1097–1165.

Rossum, Ralph A. (1995). "Holding Juveniles Accountable: Reforming America's 'Juvenile Injustice System.' " *Pepperdine Law Review* 22(3): 907–31.

Rottman, David B., and Shauna M. Strickland. (2006). *State Court Organization, 2004*. Washington, DC: Office of Justice Programs, U.S. Department of Justice.

Rubin, Sol. (1986). *Juvenile Offenders and the Juvenile Justice System*. Dobbs Ferry, NY: Oceana Publications Inc.

Ruddell, Rick. (2009). "Ensuring Accountability." In Rick Ruddell and Matthew O. Thomas (Eds.), *Juvenile Corrections*, pp. 315–32. Richmond, KY: Newgate Press.

Ruddell, Rick, and Scott H. Decker. (2006). "Kids and Assault Weapons: Social Problem or Social Construction?" *Criminal Justice Review* 30 (1): 45–63.

Ruddell, Rick, and G. Larry Mays. (2006). "Expand or Expire: Jails in Rural America." *Corrections Compendium* 31(6): 1–5, 20–21, 27.

Ruddell, Rick, and Matthew O. Thomas. (2009). *Juvenile Corrections*. Richmond, KY: Newgate Press.

Russo-Myers, Bernadette. (2003). "*Parens Patriae* Doctrine." In Marilyn D. McShane and Frank P. Williams III (Eds.), *Encyclopedia of Juvenile Justice*, pp. 279–81. Thousand Oaks, CA: Sage Publications.

Sabol, William J., Heather C. West, and Matthew Cooper. (2009). *Prisoners in 2008*. Washington, DC: Bureau of Justice Statistics.

Sanborn, Joseph B., Jr. (2003). "Hard Choices or Obvious Ones: Developing Policy for Excluding Youth from Juvenile Court." *Youth Violence and Juvenile Justice* 1(2): 198–214.

Scahill, Megan C. (2000). *Person Offense Cases in Juvenile Court, 1988–1997*. Washington, DC: Office of Juvenile Justice and Delinquency Prevention.

Schlossman, Steven L. (1977). *Love and the American Delinquent: The Theory and Practice of "Progressive" Juvenile Justice 1825–1920*. Chicago: University of Chicago Press.

Schiraldi, Vincent, and Mark Soler. (1998). "The Will of the People? The Public's Opinion of the Violent and Repeat Juvenile Offender Act of 1997." *Crime & Delinquency* 44(4): 590–601.

Schwartz, Ira M. (1989). *(In)Justice for Juveniles: Rethinking the Best Interests of the Child*. Lexington, MA: Lexington Books.

Schwartz, Ira M. (1992). "Juvenile Crime-Fighting Policies: What the Public Really Wants." In Ira M. Schwartz (Ed.), *Juvenile Justice and Public Policy: Toward a National Agenda*, pp. 214–48. Lexington, MA: Lexington Books.

Schwartz, Ira M., Shenyang Guo, and John J. Kerbs. (1993). "The Impact of Demographic Variables on Public Opinion Regarding Juvenile Justice: Implications for Public Policy." *Crime & Delinquency* 39 (1): 5–28.

Schwartz, Robert G., and Marsha Levick. (2010). "When a 'Right' Is Not Enough: Implementation of the Right to Counsel in an Age of Ambivalence." *Criminology & Public Policy* 9(2): 365–73.

Scott, Charles L. (2005). "*Roper v. Simmons*: Can Juvenile Offenders be Executed?" *The Journal of the American Academy of Psychiatry and the Law* 33(4): 547–52.

Scott, Elizabeth S., N. Dickon Reppucci, Jill Antonishak, and Jennifer T. De Gennaro. (2006). "Public Attitudes about the Culpability and Punishment of Young Offenders." *Behavioral Sciences & The Law* 24(6): 815–32.

Sedlak, Andrea J., and Carol Bruce. (2010). *Youth's Characteristics and Backgrounds: Findings from the Survey of Youth in Residential Placement*. Washington, DC: Office of Juvenile Justice and Delinquency Prevention.

Shallo, J. P. (1947). "The Rise of Juvenile Institutions in the United States." *The Prison Journal* 27(3): 293–98.

Shelden, Randall G. (2003). "Child-Saving Movement." In Marilyn D. McShane and Frank P. Williams III (Eds.), *Encyclopedia of Juvenile Justice*, pp. 56–59. Thousand Oaks, CA: Sage Publications.

Shepherd, Robert E., Jr. (2000). "Collateral Consequences of Juvenile Proceedings: Part 1." *Criminal Justice Magazine* 15(2). Retrieved July 5, 2011, from http://www.americanbar.org/.

Sickmund, Melissa. (2002). *Juvenile Residential Facility Census, 2000: Selected Findings*. Washington, DC: Office of Juvenile Justice and Delinquency Prevention.

Sickmund, Melissa. (2009). *Delinquency Cases in Juvenile Court, 2005*. Washington, DC: Office of Juvenile Justice and Delinquency Prevention.

Sickmund, Melissa. (2010). *Juveniles in Residential Placement, 1997–2008*. Washington, DC: Office of Juvenile Justice and Delinquency Prevention.

Sickmund, Melissa, T. J. Sladky, and Wei Kang. (2011). *Easy Access to Juvenile Court Statistics: 1985–2008*. Retrieved Nov. 20, 2011, from http://ojjdp.ncjrs.gov/ojstatbb/ezacjrp/.

Sickmund, Melissa, T. J. Sladky, Wei Kang, and Charles Puzzanchera. (2011a). *Census of Juveniles in Residential Placement Databook*. Retrieved Nov. 20, 2011, from http://www.ojjdp.ncjrs.gov/ojstatbb/cjrp/.

Sickmund, Melissa, T. J. Sladky, Wei Kang, and Charles Puzzanchera. (2011b). *Easy Access to the Census of Juveniles in Residential Placement*. Retrieved July 5, 2011, from http://www.ojjdp.gov/ojstatbb/ezacjrp/.

Singer, Simon I. (1996). *Recriminalizing Delinquency: Violent Juvenile Crimes and Juvenile Justice Reform*. New York: Cambridge University Press.

Singer, Simon I. (2003). "Incarcerating Juveniles into Adulthood: Organizational Fields of Knowledge and the Back End of Waiver." *Youth Violence and Juvenile Justice* 1(2): 115–27.

Singer, Simon I. (2011). "Sentencing Juveniles to Life in Prison: The Reproduction of Juvenile Justice for Young Adolescents Charged with Murder." *Crime & Delinquency* 57(6): 969–86. Singer, Simon I., and David McDowall. (1988). "Criminalizing Delinquency: The Deterrent Effects of the New York Juvenile Offender Law." *Law & Society Review* 22(3): 521–35.

Smith, Bradford. (1998). "Children in Custody: 20-Year Trends in Juvenile Detention, Correctional, and Shelter Facilities." *Crime & Delinquency* 44(4): 526–43.

Smith, Kevin B. (2004). "The Politics of Punishment: Evaluating Political Explanations of Incarceration Rates." *Journal of Politics* 66(3): 925–38.

Smith, Robert, and G. Ben Cohen. (2010). "Redemption Song: *Graham v. Florida* and the Evolving Eighth Amendment Jurisprudence." *Michigan Law Review* 108(1): 86–94.

Smith, Tom W. (2011). *Trends in National Spending Priorities, 1973–2010*. Chicago: National Opinion Research Center.

Snyder, Howard N. (2000). *Juvenile Arrests 1999*. Washington, DC: Office of Juvenile Justice and Delinquency Prevention.

Snyder, Howard N., and Melissa Sickmund. (2006). *Juvenile Offenders and Victims: 2006 National Report*. Pittsburgh, PA: National Center for Juvenile Justice.

Snyder, Howard N., and Melissa Sickmund. (2007). *Relative Rate of Death in Juvenile Facilities*. Pittsburgh, PA: National Center for Juvenile Justice.

Soler, Mark. (2001). *Public Opinion on Youth, Crime and Race: A Guide for Advocates*. Washington, DC: Youth Law Center.

Soler, Mark. (2010). "Missed Opportunity: Waiver, Race, Data, and Policy Reform." *Louisiana Law Review* 71(1): 17–33.

Spelman, William. (2009). "Crime, Cash, and Limited Options: Explaining the Prison Boom." *Criminology & Public Policy* 8(1): 29–77.

St. Vincent, Stephen. (2010). "Kids Are Different." *Michigan Law Review* 109(9): 9–15.

Steffen, Jordan. (2011a). *On Colorado's Plains, Burlington Residents Uncertain how Law Should Treat 12-Year-Old Accused of Killing Parents*. Retrieved Nov. 20, 2011, from: http://www.denverpost.com/news/ci_18208996.

Steffen, Jordan. (2011b) *Burlington boy gets 7 years in juvenile detention for fatal attack on family*. Retrieved Nov. 20, 2011, from: http://www.denverpost.com/news/ci_19000726.

Steinberg, Laurence, and Alex R. Piquero. (2010). "Manipulating Public Opinion about Trying Juveniles as Adults: An Experimental Study." *Crime & Delinquency* 56(4): 487–506.

Steiner, Benjamin, and Emily Wright. (2006). "Assessing the Relative Effects of State Direct File Waiver Laws on Violent Juvenile Crime: Deterrence of Irrelevance?" *The Journal of Criminal Law and Criminology* 96(4): 1451–77.

Steinhart, David. (1988). *California Opinion Poll: Public Attitudes on Youth Crime.* Oakland, CA: National Council on Crime and Delinquency.

Stevens, Holly R., Colleen E. Sheppard, Robert Spangenberg, Aimee Wickman, and Jon B. Gould. (2010). *State, County and Local Expenditures for Indigent Defense Services, Fiscal Year 2008.* Fairfax, VA: Spangenberg Project, George Mason University.

Streib, Victor L. (2005). *The Juvenile Death Penalty Today: Death Sentences and Executions for Juvenile Crimes, January 1, 1973–February 28, 2005.* Retrieved July 5, 2011, from http://www.law.onu.edu/faculty_staff/faculty_profiles/coursematerials/streib/juvdeath.pdf.

Streib, Victor L. (2010). "Intentional Wrongful Conviction of Children." *Chicago Kent Law Review* 85(1): 163–77.

Strom, Kevin J. (2000). *Profile of State Prisoners under Age 18, 1985–1997.* Washington, DC: Bureau of Justice Statistics.

Stucky, Thomas D., Karen Heimer, and Joseph B. Lang. (2007). "A Bigger Piece of the Pie? State Corrections Spending and the Politics of Social Order." *Journal of Research in Crime and Delinquency* 44 (1): 91–123.

Subcommittee to Investigate Juvenile Delinquency. (1954, April 14, 15). *Investigation of Juvenile Delinquency in the United States*, Washington, DC: Author.

Sullivan, Dermot. (1998). "Employee Violence, Negligent Hiring, and Criminal Record Checks: New York's Need to Reevaluate Its Priorities to Promote Public Safety." *St. John's Law Review* 72(2): 581–605.

Sullivan, Patrick M. (2009). "A Short History of Juvenile Corrections." In Rick Ruddell and Matthew O. Thomas (Eds.), *Juvenile Corrections*, pp. 23–39. Richmond, KY: Newgate.

Sutton, John R. (1993). *Stubborn Children: Controlling Delinquency in the United States, 1640–1981.* Berkeley, CA: University of California Press.

Szymanski, Linda A. (2008a). *Juvenile Delinquents' Right to a Jury Trial (2007 Update).* Pittsburgh, PA: National Center for Juvenile Justice.

Szymanski, Linda A. (2008b). *Oldest Age Juvenile Court May Retain Jurisdiction in Delinquency Matters (2008 Update).* Pittsburgh, PA: National Center for Juvenile Justice.

Szymanski, Linda A. (2009a). *DNA Registration of Juvenile Offenders (2008 Update)*. Pittsburgh, PA: National Center for Juvenile Justice.

Szymanski, Linda A. (2009b). *Megan's Law: Juvenile Sex Offender Registration (2009 Update)*. Pittsburgh, PA: National Center for Juvenile Justice.

Szymanski, Linda A. (2010a). *Can Juvenile Delinquents Be Fingerprinted?* Pittsburgh, PA: National Center for Juvenile Justice.

Szymanski, Linda A. (2010b). *Can Juveniles Transferred for Criminal Prosecution Be Held for Pre-Trial Detention in Adult Jails?* Pittsburgh, PA: National Center for Juvenile Justice.

Szymanski, Linda A. (2010c). *Can Sealed Juvenile Court Records Ever Be Unsealed or Inspected?* Pittsburgh, PA: National Center for Juvenile Justice.

Szymanski, Linda A. (2010d). *What States Allow for Open Juvenile Delinquency Hearings?* Pittsburgh, PA: National Center for Juvenile Justice.

Szymanski, Linda A. (2011). *Once a Juvenile is Transferred to Criminal Court Must They Be Tried as Adults for All Future Offenses?* Pittsburgh, PA: National Center for Juvenile Justice.

Tang, Connie M., and Narina Nunez. (2003) "Effects of Defendant Age and Juror Bias on Judgment of Culpability: What Happens When a Juvenile Is Tried as an Adult?" *American Journal of Criminal Justice* 28(1): 37–52.

Tappan, Paul W. (1946). "Treatment without Trial." *Social Forces* 24(3): 306–11.

Task Force on Juvenile Delinquency. (1967). *Juvenile Delinquency and Youth Crime*. Washington, DC: U.S. Government Printing Office.

Titus, Jordan J. (2005). "Juvenile Transfers as Ritual Sacrifice: Legally Constructing the Child Scapegoat." *Youth Violence and Juvenile Justice* 3(2): 116–32.

Tonry, Michael. (2009). "Explanations of American Punishment Policies: A National History." *Punishment & Society* 11(3): 377–94.

Torcal, Mariano. (2003). *Political Disaffection and Democratization History in New Democracies*. Retrieved Nov. 20, 2011, from http://www.nd.edu/~kellogg/publications/workingpapers/WPS/308.pdf.

Truman, Jennifer L., and Michael R. Rand. (2010). *Criminal Victimization, 2009*. Washington, DC: Bureau of Justice Statistics.

Trulson, Chad R., Jonathan W. Caudill, Scott H. Belshaw, and Matt DeLisi. (2011). "A Problem of Fit: Extreme Delinquents, Blended

Sentencing, and the Determinants of Continued Adult Sanctions." *Criminal Justice Policy Review* 22(3): 263–84.

Tyler, Tom R. (2006). *Why People Obey The Law*. Princeton, NJ: Princeton University Press.

Tyler, Tom R., and Yuen J. Huo. (2002). *Trust in the Law: Encouraging Public Cooperation With the Police and Courts*. New York: Russell Sage.

Urbina, Martin G. (2005). "Transferring Juveniles to Adult Court in Wisconsin: Practitioners Voice Their Views." *Criminal Justice Studies: A Critical Journal of Crime, Law and Society* 18(2): 147–72.

U.S. Department of Justice. (2011a). *Juvenile Correctional Facilities*. Retrieved June 24, 2011, from http://www.justice.gov/crt/about/spl/juveniles.php.

U.S. Department of Justice. (2011b). *Summary of Civil Rights of Institutionalized Persons*. Retrieved Nov. 20, 2011, from http://www.justice.gov/crt/about/spl/cripa.php.

U.S. Government Accountability Office. (2007). *Residential Treatment Programs: Concerns Regarding Abuse and Death in Certain Programs for Troubled Youth*. Washington, DC: Author.

van den Haag, Ernest. (1986). "The Neoclassical Theory of Crime Control." *Criminal Justice Policy Review* 1(1): 91–109.

Van Waters, Miriam. (1922). "The Socialization of Juvenile Court Procedure." *Journal of the American Institute of Criminal Law and Criminology* 13(1): 61–69.

Verrecchia, Philip J. (2011). "The Effect of Transfer Mechanism from Juvenile Court on Conviction on a Target Offense in Criminal Court." *Contemporary Justice Review* 14(2): 189–201.

Waite, Edward F. (1923). "The Outlook for the Juvenile Court." *The Annals of the American Academy of Political and Social Science* 105(1): 229–42.

Walker, Charity M., and William D. Woody. (2011). "Juror Decision Making for Juveniles Tried as Adults: The Effects of Defendant Age, Crime Type, and Crime Outcome." *Psychology, Crime and Law* 17(8): 659–75.

Walsh, Charlotte. (2011). "Youth Justice and Neuroscience: A Dual-Use Dilemma." *British Journal of Criminology* 51(1): 21–39.

Warling, Diane, and Michele Peterson-Badali. (2003). "The Verdict on Jury Trials for Juveniles: The Effects of Defendant's Age on Trial Outcomes." *Behavioral Sciences & The Law* 21(1): 63–82.

Weinstein, Noah, and Corinne R. Goodman. (1967). "A Constructive Response for Juvenile Courts." *American Bar Association Journal* 53(March): 257–60.

Weisheit, Ralph A., and Diane M. Alexander. (1988). "Juvenile Justice Philosophy and the Demise of *Parens Patriae*." *Federal Probation* 52(4): 56–63.

West, Heather C. (2010). *Prison Inmates at Midyear 2009—Statistical Tables*. Washington, DC: Bureau of Justice Statistics.

West, Heather C., William J. Sabol, and Sarah J. Greenman. (2010). *Prisoners in 2009*. Washington, DC: Bureau of Justice Statistics.

Western, Bruce, and Christopher Wildeman. (2009). "The Black Family and Mass Incarceration." *The Annals of the American Academy of Political and Social Science* 621(1): 221–42.

Wizner, Stephen. (1972). "The Child and the State: Adversaries in the Juvenile Justice System." *Columbia Human Rights Law Review* 4 (4): 389–99.

Wood, Keith. (2009). "Starting the At-Bat Behind in the Count: California's Improper Use of Juvenile Adjudications as a Strike in California's Three Strikes Program." *Western State University Law Review* 36(2): 223–34.

Wu, Bohsiu. (2000). "Determinants of Public Opinion toward Juvenile Wavier Decisions." *Juvenile and Family Court Journal* 51(1): 9–20.

Yoon, Seokhee, and Nanci Wilson. (2008). *Crime, Perception and Politics: Follow-up Report 4*. New York: John Jay College of Criminal Justice Center on Media, Crime & Justice.

Zimring, Franklin E. (1981). "Notes toward a Jurisprudence of Waiver." In John C. Hall, Donna M. Hamparian, John M. Pettibone, and Joseph L. White (Eds.), *Major Issues in Juvenile Justice Information and Training: Readings in Public Policy*, pp. 193–205. Columbus, OH: Academy for Contemporary Problems.

Zimring, Franklin E. (2010). "The Power Politics of Juvenile Court Transfer: A Mildly Revisionist History of the 1990s." *Louisiana Law Review* 71(1): 1–15.

Index

About the Authors

G. Larry Mays is Regents professor emeritus of criminal justice at New Mexico State University. He was a police officer in Knoxville, Tennessee, in the early 1970s and taught at East Tennessee State University (1975–1979), Appalachian State University (1979–1981), and New Mexico State University (1981–2010). Dr. Mays is author or editor of 18 books and nearly 100 scholarly articles, book chapters, encyclopedia entries, and practitioner publications. He has a Ph.D. in political science from the University of Tennessee.

Rick Ruddell, the Law Foundation of Saskatchewan chair in police studies, joined the Department of Justice Studies at the University of Regina in September 2010. Prior to this appointment he served as director of operational research with the Correctional Service of Canada and held faculty positions at Eastern Kentucky University and California State University–Chico. A graduate of the Ph.D. program in criminology and criminal justice at the University of Missouri–St. Louis, Rick Ruddell's research has focused upon policing, criminal justice policy, and juvenile justice.